PRAISE FOR *FAMILY DON'T E...*

"No one knows the world of *Supernatural* better than Lynn Zubernis—and this collection is a compelling exploration of the powerful binding spell woven by the Winchester brothers' saga, and a terrific road map of the heavenly rewards that come from being part of the show or its one-of-a-kind fandom. In short, this book rocks."

—MAUREEN RYAN, *Variety*

"The intricate, delicate, and symbiotic relationship between actor and fan that has developed between the *Supernatural* cast and its impassioned following is the stuff of TV history. This book explores the nuances of that unique connection through the eyes of those who have experienced it firsthand, providing lessons in humanity, humility, and perseverance of the human spirit. The *Supernatural* family truly is lightning in a bottle. It's been amazing to be right there to watch it strike."

—RICHARD SPEIGHT, JR., actor and director

"The time I spent as a member of the *Supernatural* family remains a powerful professional and personal memory for me. Now, from a distance, I watch them all still; my former colleagues and the people who love them, on stage and screen, practically coining joy and inclusiveness, endlessly entertaining and always a part of something bigger. The thrilling levels of love and family play out forever, it seems, and I was fortunate to be a part of it, even for a short time. Of course, I don't need to encourage the fans to read it. But for those who don't know, or don't get it, for those who think that *Supernatural* is just another show, or who think its Fandom is just like any other fandom, *Family Don't End with Blood* is a sweet introduction to everything that makes the *Supernatural* experience unique. I can offer it no higher praise than this: It already occupies an honored place on Metatron's bookshelf!"

—CURTIS ARMSTRONG, author of *Revenge of the Nerd*
and actor on *Supernatural, Revenge of the Nerds, Risky Business, Better Off Dead,* and *Moonlighting*

FAMILY
DON'T END WITH
BLOOD

CAST AND FANS ON HOW *SUPERNATURAL* HAS CHANGED LIVES

Edited by LYNN S. ZUBERNIS

An Imprint of BenBella Books, Inc.
Dallas, TX

Smart Pop is an imprint of BenBella Books, Inc.
10440 N. Central Expressway
Suite 800
Dallas, TX 75231
www.benbellabooks.com
Send feedback to feedback@benbellabooks.com

Printed in the United States of America
10 9 8 7 6 5 4 3

Library of Congress Cataloging-in-Publication Data is available upon request.
ISBN 978-1-944648-35-0
e-ISBN 978-1-944648-36-7

Editing by Leah Wilson
Copyediting by Karen Levy
Production editing by Monica Lowry
Proofreading by Michael Fedison and Sarah Vostok
Text design and composition by Aaron Edmiston
Cover design by Sarah Avinger
Cover illustration by Christine Griffin, quickreaver.com

Distributed by Perseus Distribution
www.perseusdistribution.com
To place orders through Perseus Distribution:
Tel: (800) 343-4499
Fax: (800) 351-5073
E-mail: orderentry@perseusbooks.com

**Special discounts for bulk sales (minimum of 25 copies) are available.
Please contact Aida Herrera at aida@benbellabooks.com.**

To my dad, Kevlin Walter Smith, who encouraged me all my life in every single thing I wanted to do—this book included. Miss you, Dad.

CONTENTS

INTRODUCTION

LYNN ZUBERNIS

When we think of the sorts of things that help people change for the better, we might imagine that perfect self-help book that contains the heretofore well-kept secret to happiness. Snap! You're a changed person, just like the title claimed. Or maybe changing for the better means hitting bottom and turning your life around, like so many Hollywood films contend. Maybe it's finding Prince (or Princess) Charming—or maybe it's finding a good therapist. Most of us don't think of a television show as something that helps people change for the better. I certainly didn't.

I make my living helping people. As a psychologist, I have to understand what makes people happy and what makes them want to hide under their bedcovers and never come out again. I've been privileged to learn from countless inspiring individuals who had a lot of crap fall in their paths and yet were able to eventually kick it out of their way or slog through it and keep going. In the process, I've learned quite a bit about human nature and what we yearn for in that constant search for things that make us feel okay about ourselves and everyone else: Belonging and acceptance. Self-expression and creativity. A sense of excitement. Something to ignite our passion, inspire our intellect, and validate our emotions. These are the things humans long for; they are the things that make us happy.

For most of my career, I never thought of a television show, or a film or a book or a band, as something capable of offering all those things. That was before I fell in love with a television show and learned about the incredible community known as fandom.

Falling in love with a TV show was unexpected. It wasn't even one of those programs that "everyone is watching" (which could be anything from *Game of Thrones* to *The Bachelor*, depending on your experience of "everyone"). No, this was a sci-fi fantasy genre show on a second-tier network that didn't know quite what to do with it—*Supernatural.*

As most readers of this book no doubt already know, *Supernatural* follows demon-hunting brothers Sam and Dean Winchester as they travel the United States in a beautiful black '67 Chevy Impala, carrying on "the family business": saving people, hunting things. The show has been around so long that it premiered on the long-defunct WB Network back in 2005, and has been on its successor network, the CW, ever since. It's a scary show about monsters and the apocalypse, and it's also a surprisingly emotional show about love and family and the need to always keep fighting no matter the odds. The combination has brought *Supernatural* unexpected and enduring popularity. Doesn't hurt that it stars actors who are gorgeous (and talented) enough to make you wonder whether they're real.

I fell in love the way you do when you're thirteen and falling for the first time: head over heels, all at once, so fast I was dizzy with it. When I came up for air, I was mystified. What was happening to me? At first, I felt silly. Was it really okay for me—a grown woman, a mom, a professor—to put aside my briefcase and research papers and oh-so-serious responsibilities to binge-watch an entire season of a science fiction TV show? To scour the web for pictures of its stars? To read lots and lots of fan fiction, and then to spend less time writing textbooks and more time writing fan fiction myself?

I wasn't the only one asking those questions. My partner was asking, my children were asking, my colleagues were asking. Especially when I threw caution to the wind and started flying across the country to go to fan conventions.

"You're going *where*?" was a constant refrain. But meeting other fans, both in person and in the (at the time cloistered and secret) world of online fandom, turned out to be as life-changing as discovering *Supernatural* in the first place. The show and the fandom were a gateway to a sort of self-discovery that I thought I had put aside decades earlier.

Like many works of fantasy, the world of *Supernatural* is a place fans can escape to. Escape itself has benefits, as long as you manage to poke your head out from the fantasy long enough to hold down your job or take care of your family or hang out with your best friend. But *Supernatural* offers more. Some fans have grown up with this show, their teenage infatuations evolving into adult love affairs. Some fans have navigated midlife crises with Sam and Dean. In the Winchesters and their rebel angel friend Castiel, many fans have found the inspiration and courage to fight the monsters and demons that exist in real life.

In a television show.

While television is now considered a respectable medium, not all television programs are viewed equally. Perhaps PBS can offer some educational value, but "popular culture" still carries an implication of being unimportant and frivolous, meant for mindless consumption. Critically acclaimed series like *Orange Is the New Black* or *Breaking Bad* are accorded some respect, but genre shows like *Supernatural* are less likely to warrant serious consideration. Being a fan also raises eyebrows; the stereotypes of the loser fanboy living in his parents' basement and the hysterical fangirl fainting in the presence of her idol have been less prevalent in the last decade, but still persist in mainstream media. Many people, when they think of fans, still think of the negatives: bad decisions, out-of-control emotions, overspending. The media snicker at fans cosplaying at Comic-Con, or lining up for three days to get tickets to the new *Star Wars* movie, or screaming when One Direction comes onstage. Being a fan is often seen as frivolous at best, and immature—or even dangerous—at worst.

After more than a decade of being a fan and researching fans, I know that's not the real story. Can fans fall prey to bad choices? Sure. So can accountants and stockbrokers and physicians and hairdressers. And everyone else. Are there risks to being passionate about something? Sure. But there are also benefits. It's healthy for us to pursue the things that bring us joy, and to allow ourselves to experience those positive feelings. It's good for us to *care*—about the things we love, about ourselves, about others. Being a fan brings with it access to fandom, the community of fellow fans who care about one another. Within that uniquely supportive community, a surprising amount of change is possible.

Within the safe space of the fan community, I discovered that fans were shockingly real with one another. As a woman, I found this remarkable. There are still few places in which women are comfortable expressing their genuine hopes and fears and angers and sadness, let alone talking about something like sex. Within the fan community, we forged relationships, explored our sexualities, shared and understood and ultimately normalized past traumas and losses. Contrary to the popular opinion that fans were lonely losers, I found an intelligent, diverse community of people—who just also happened to be fans. Within that community, I found many of the things that being a psychologist has taught me all of us are looking for: validation, acceptance, self-expression, belonging.

I also found a community rich with creativity, and about as far from mindless consumption as you can get. Instead, there were amazing works of fan fiction, fanvids, mashups, fanart, photography, and essays that rivaled what academics were publishing. The passion that gets judged so harshly from the outside was being channeled into creative expression, and then shared with the rest of the community. For free! Far from being pathological, all that passion and imagination and self-expression seemed healthier than the current state of many of the clients I saw on a daily basis. Indulgence in imagination and fantasy can be a healthy and positive part of life, and passion is what makes life worth living. Show me someone without passion and I'll show you someone I'm worried about.

I also worry when people feel isolated and alone. We all need to feel we belong somewhere; it's left over from the early days of humanity when being kicked out of the group literally meant you were going to die. When we feel alone, that evolutionarily ingrained panic sets in, along with a whopping dose of depression. Fandom, I found, was an antidote. Within the diverse global community of people who share a passion, fans establish relationships and find acceptance. The norms for self-expression are vastly different in fandom; there is more encouragement to be genuine, even if who you are isn't exactly who Mom and Pop said you should be. Once you've taken the plunge and spoken out as your real self, the validation that comes back can be life-changing.

Identity development, belonging, validation. A support system, intellectual stimulation, creativity. It turns out that being a fan of a television show can be the source of all those positive, healthy things psychology tells us we need. Watching your favorite television show, with its familiar and beloved characters, can produce the same good-feeling brain chemicals as being at a family dinner. When whatever or whomever we fan succeeds, fans experience an endorphin rush as powerful as the actual players on a winning sports team. Far from being unimportant and frivolous, the shows (and sports teams and films and books and bands and actors) we fan are an integral part of our identity, contributing to self-concept and self-esteem.

The personal stories fans share in this book are examples of the self-expression and good feelings that being part of fandom—whether for a television show or a film or a book or a band—makes possible. They are courageous, inspiring, and powerful. For many television shows, that would be the whole story . . . but not for *Supernatural.*

Early research on fandom described (and pathologized) the so-called "parasocial relationship" between stars and fans, a reference to the one-way nature of that relationship. The fan might feel like they know the celebrity, but the celebrity doesn't know the fan exists. Not so for *Supernatural.* Over the past decade-plus, the cast—and the writers, producers, directors, and crew—have come to know the fans. Not just through Twitter and Facebook exchanges, which happen with many shows, but in person. *Supernatural* has the most extensive convention calendar of any television show in history. Last year, there were more than twenty *Supernatural* conventions all over the world. That's more than even *Star Trek* had in the show's convention heyday!

The reciprocal relationship that has developed as a result is unusual. There is rarely such a significant amount of face-to-face contact between fans and "the talent," and nothing breaks down barriers and eliminates stereotypes like interacting with another human being. Despite the conventions maintaining boundaries and a celebrity/fan hierarchy, the fans and actors involved have gotten to know one another. With that familiarity comes trust and respect. The same thing has happened online, as fans and actors have interacted on Twitter and Facebook and Tumblr and Snapchat. The *Supernatural* cast members are unusual for the extent of their willingness to engage with fans online, both in serious conversations and in a shared sense of humor. This greater than average amount of contact at conventions and on social media has brought fans and actors closer. When both cast and fans call themselves the SPNFamily, they all mean it.

This unusual level of reciprocity has increased the show's ability to influence its fans. Some of that influence is found in the show's canon, through which writers and producers regularly "speak to" fans. *Supernatural* doesn't take itself too seriously, but it does take its fans' passion seriously; in tongue-in-cheek "meta" episodes, *Supernatural* has shown its gratitude even as it affectionately poked fun at fandom and at itself. Sometimes that influence is found in the actors' direct communications on social media. Lead actors Jared Padalecki, Jensen Ackles, and Misha Collins have a hugely successful mental-health awareness campaign that uses their characters' mantras to encourage fans to remain hopeful and stay alive: "Always Keep Fighting." "You Are Not Alone." A reminder that "I Am Enough." Collins's Random Acts charity has brought fans together as a force for good in the world (and a celebration of being weird, in keeping with fandom's challenge of "normalcy," in the annual GISHWHES scavenger hunt). Cast members Kim Rhodes and Briana Buckmaster spread the message that it's okay to be "Wayward AF" with their charity campaign.

The show inspires the fans. The actors inspire the fans. The fan community supports one another. But even that is not the whole story.

During the past decade of researching fandom and *Supernatural*, I met tens of thousands of fans. I was witness to many powerful stories of fans whose lives have been changed by their love of this show and the support of the fandom. I heard story after story of how *Supernatural* changed— and, in some cases, saved—lives. Fans talked about finding themselves in the fan community; rediscovering a spark of creativity; finding the courage to change jobs or partners or cities, or to leave the house for the first time in years. To get and stay sober when nothing else had helped. To leave a cult behind and start to live in the world again. To stay alive when they had decided there was no reason for living. They talked about their passion for Sam and Dean and Castiel, and how their favorite characters inspired them to do all these things. I nodded, because I understood. After all, I had been changed, too.

But—call it celebrity tunnel vision, or reading too many academic articles on that silly parasocial relationship thing—I had never stopped to consider that the impact could be equally life-changing on both sides of the fence. A year or so ago, Jared Padalecki asked if I was planning to write another book about the show. I said maybe, because I wanted to share all those powerful fan stories I'd heard. I wanted the world to know that a television show could be a positive, healthy, life-changing force in people's lives. To my surprise, Jared said that his life had been changed, too—and he wanted to share his story as much as the fans wanted to share theirs. I contacted the other *Supernatural* actors I'd gotten to know over the years. Had their lives also been changed by their experiences on the show and with the fandom? The answer was a resounding yes. Suddenly, this was a very different book.

Not every television show is life-changing for the actors who work on it. No other television show's years on the air have been accompanied by a parallel venture that has put the cast and the fans in contact so intimately and so often. In a decade of frequent conventions and constant online conversation, the show's cast has been as affected by the fans as the fans have been by them. The fan essays in this book make clear the many ways in which the show has been life-changing; the essays written by the actors who bring the show to life do the same.

That might be surprising on the surface. Sometimes we forget that "celebrities" are people, too, with the same hopes and fears and insecurities we all have. We're all looking for the same things from life: a safe space in which to find ourselves, a support system when we're afraid to fail. The freedom to discover our own identity and celebrate our own creativity. A sense of belonging and some good friends beside us on life's journey. The opportunity to heal ourselves by helping others. The actors redefined themselves within the reciprocal relationships of the fan community just as the fans did—and on two notable occasions, an actor is alive today because of the connections made through the show and the fandom.

One of the take-home messages of this book is that maybe we're not so different after all. Both fans and actors, each writing on their own and without any knowledge of what others were writing, said the exact same things. Like so many of us, fans and actors alike struggled with the nagging suspicion that they weren't good enough, that they were different. That sense of difference had kept them quiet their whole lives, until *Supernatural* and the acceptance of the SPNFamily gave them the courage to confront that insecurity. Fans Karen Cooke and Laurena Aker and actors Osric Chau, Kim Rhodes, Briana Buckmaster, and Ruth Connell all found their voices and dared to speak up and try new things, even if they weren't perfect. As Kim Rhodes writes, "The truth is, I showed a bunch of strangers the broken, fragile, cussing, awkward, overly energetic creature that is my heart, and they said 'Yes!' and quit being strangers. I found the identity I had been searching for."

Supernatural's message that it's okay to be different, reinforced within the fan community, has helped many fans figure out who they are—or who they want to be. Kim Prior and Sabrina Greenwood-Briggs confronted their identity crises head-on within the safe space of fandom, and with the inspiration of *Supernatural*'s characters, they found the courage to reinvent themselves and rediscover their passions. Actors Matt Cohen and Gil McKinney also found encouragement within the fandom to be themselves. As Matt writes to the fandom, "I am so grateful you have allowed me to find me."

Fan Lucy Schneider and *Supernatural* special effects supervisor Adam Williams also discovered who they really were—and discovered each other. The two found love across two continents through their shared association with *Supernatural,* and dared to pursue it despite the odds.

The international support system that is the SPNFamily has been, for both fans and cast, a source of strength. A photo op at a con helped fan Stacey Anderson come to terms with her grief after losing her mother. Fan Sheri Chen's life was turned upside down with a cancer diagnosis; she found healing within the *Supernatural* fandom and inspiration to keep going in the show's story. After actor Rachel Miner's multiple sclerosis diagnosis, the *Supernatural* fandom helped her rediscover a sense of purpose.

One of the best ways to heal ourselves is to help others, and *Supernatural* has frequently been an inspiration to do just that. Fan Karla Truxall, devastated by her nephew's suicide, was inspired by *Supernatural*'s message of never giving up to start SPN Survivors, which helps others who are overwhelmed by anxiety and depression. Actor Jim Beaver calls the opportunity to give back "the *Supernatural* effect," and considers it the greatest gift of his public life.

The richly drawn characters on *Supernatural*, who have fought demons both literal and figurative, are an inspiration to fans to fight their own demons. Fan Lydia Cyrus was inspired by the character Bobby Singer (played by Jim Beaver), a fellow survivor of abuse, whose refusal to stay silent convinced Lydia to confront her own demons—just as powerful a "*Supernatural* effect" as Jim Beaver himself experienced. Claudine Hummel was inspired by the character Castiel, an angel who is a misfit both in heaven and on earth, and by the actor who plays Castiel, Misha Collins. Following his lead in celebrating "death to normal" and the importance of random acts of kindness, Claudine discovered the power of making a difference through giving to others.

Many fans have found inspiration in the character of Sam Winchester, played by Jared Padalecki. Sam never felt like he fit in, with his family or with friends, as the Winchesters constantly moved from town to town. His identity struggles and subsequent fall into addiction, rage, and depression are things many fans grapple with as well. Fan Hallie Bingaman was so inspired that she became "sober for Sam." As she struggled to hang onto sobriety, Hallie reminded herself that Sam had also been an addict. If he could get through detox and stay clean, she told herself, she could, too. Fan Kristin Ludwig also related to Sam. Like him, she struggled with self-doubt, along with crippling anxiety. Her world had narrowed down to four walls she found difficult to leave . . . until a *Supernatural* convention came to town. The desire to meet Jared trumped the panic, and Kristin ventured out despite her fear.

Not only can a television show change lives, but it can also save them. Both fans and actors credit the show and the fandom for literally helping them stay alive. After a traumatic childhood in a repressive cult, Breda Waite found the Winchesters' story gave her the courage to think of herself as an individual. Breda and her sister credit *Supernatural* and the SPNFamily with saving their lives. Actor Rob Benedict suffered a stroke while at a convention, surviving only because of his relationships with his fellow cast members. And, like many fans, Rob turned to the SPNFamily for support on his road to recovery. Fan Burner Cade credits *Supernatural* and Sam Winchester with bringing her back from the brink of hopelessness and convincing her to keep going. Planning to end her life, she went to a *Supernatural* convention as a last hurrah. There, Jared Padalecki saw something in her face that others had missed, asking her the question no one else had: "Are you okay?" She answered honestly, and with his encouragement, began to fight for herself.

Fan Laurena Aker also found inspiration in Jared's portrayal of Sam, and had written to tell him so. Months later, when Jared himself was having a hard time, reading Laurena's letter helped him rediscover a sense of purpose. Padalecki, whom so many fans credit for changing—or saving—*their* lives, has been just as affected by the show and the fandom. He shares his battles with depression and his fight for self-acceptance. And when Jared was at his lowest point, it was his friends and the support of the fandom that saved him.

So much for that one-way parasocial relationship. So much for the idea that television can offer nothing to viewers and fans but a fleeting escape from reality. So much for the idea that being a fan is something negative and dangerous. The personal stories shared in this book, by both fans and actors, make clear television and fandom's potential for positive change through inspiration, support, hope, and belonging.

Improbable as it sounds, a television show really can change lives.

SITTING SHOTGUN WITH
JENSEN ACKLES

How much has my experience on *Supernatural* and with the *Supernatural* fandom changed me? A lot.

I'll give you just one example. Before *Supernatural*, the idea of doing a "meet and greet"—something I do all the time at conventions, where a small group of twenty or so fans ask me questions—would have freaked me out. Before this experience, even at family events, I was anxious. I remember at my brother's wedding, when I had to give a toast, I was so nervous it was like I had cottonmouth. I couldn't even speak! I remember thinking, *What's wrong with me?* I was already a professional actor by that time, so I couldn't understand why I couldn't just get up and give a toast. It was like Bizarro Jensen!

The thing is, on television you have a script. You don't have to be your real self when you're acting. Unlike at that wedding. So that was bad enough. And then came the first awards ceremony that I had to do. I was so nervous I felt like I was just going to pass out right on the stage. Even though I knew the lines—and they were on a teleprompter! It didn't matter. I felt like I was about to faint just trying to do that.

Fast-forward to ten years later. *Supernatural*, and my experience with fans and doing conventions, has changed that for me. And it's because of the interaction between us. I think Jared—and everyone else—would say the same thing. It's because of the flow of love between us. We get so much energy from you. It's fuel. That back and forth of emotion between us is fuel for me. And that emotion is genuine; it's real. That makes all the difference.

Recently Jared and I presented at the Saturn Awards, and it was a completely different experience than my first awards ceremony. It was comfortable, like we were at a convention with all of you. We were so comfortable that we went off script and started joking around—even with William Shatner himself right there! What we have with you, the fandom, has transferred over to the rest of my life. That comfort has carried over. You see, you're not strangers anymore. You're not strange to me. Of course, we're all a *little* strange—and we take the little bit of strange in each of us and mix those little bits all up together, all of us, and that's why we love the relationship we have.

You're family. And you've changed me.

I FOUND MY TRIBE

KAREN COOKE

O ne of my all-time favorite quotes is from *Charlie and the Chocolate Factory*, by Roald Dahl: "A little nonsense now and then, is relished by the wisest men." Prior to discovering this little show called *Supernatural*, the Joker's question, "Why so serious?" would have been a more apt description of me.

I credit the people behind and in *Supernatural* with inspiring me to reinvent my whole perspective on work and on play and on friendships. I struggle to explain to my family and non-*Supernatural* friends just what this show means to me. My current coworkers kind of get it. Some of them watch the show and really enjoy it. None of them is into it to the extent I am, but they *get* it. And that is another gift this show gave me: a workplace and coworkers who celebrate and encourage idiosyncrasies and passion.

My story is not extraordinary. I know many others have had more intense experiences. However, it was through this show that I discovered my community and I rediscovered my passions. I found a way to turn a miserable work life into a supporting and life-affirming environment. I

13

learned what true leadership was like. I learned that having fun was not just for children and was an essential part of life. I learned that it was okay to be silly. My involvement with this show helped me save my sanity and find my happiness.

I have been working in IT for most of my professional life. I found my way into IT because I was a geek. I grew up with computers in our home, in the years before home computers were commonplace. I was a girl during a time when girls weren't supposed to like technology or science fiction, but I loved both. I also loved to draw and to take photographs. While most of that fit in with my parents and two brothers, I was the only girl in that family and all of the girls I knew were more interested in playing with Barbies than Star Trek. And when older, they were more interested in makeup, school dances, and boys than in computers and theater/movies/ TV and art. I adjusted and didn't share my inner passions with very many people. After school, I found my professional niche in IT and thrived. I married and had kids. Gradually I moved into management positions and adopted a stereotypical professional business persona.

Over twenty years, I had slowly convinced myself that I was some-one I was not. I had fooled myself into thinking that my childhood and young-adult love of sci-fi, and my other interests in live theater, movies, TV, photography, and art, were a phase I had outgrown. Art and photog-raphy were fun ways to spend an hour here or there, but life was serious and I had responsibilities to my workplace and to my family. Notice the order there? That was the life I had formed for myself. Work then fam-ily—and nothing else.

Like a frog in a pot of slowly heating water, I didn't notice how unhealthy my life had become until the years 2006 to 2008. My work-place, in which I had overinvested time and my own self-worth, had become toxic. I had been with the company for more than twenty years and it had been a marvelous, people-oriented place to work. However, due to changes in executive leadership, changes in the industry, and the looming recession, the work environment had become focused more on the bottom line than on people. We were expected to work extreme hours, for no extra money (we were salaried), and through illness. The environ-ment became punitive. Mistakes were not tolerated and successes were under-recognized. It seemed people were operating out of fear or out of competitiveness. We learned not to trust our coworkers. We learned not to trust our leaders. I think we even learned not to trust ourselves. The toxicity was pervasive and infected even the best of us in a way that we all perpetuated. I learned to put on an even more fake face in order to survive. I started each morning battling inner thoughts of hating myself and dreading going in to work.

I am an introvert. I prefer to have a few very close friends rather than a large group of acquaintances. As I invested more time and more of myself in work, I lost touch with those friends. My husband and kids, and my small extended family, were my only support back then. They are wonderful. My husband is my rock and my foundation. But my perceived responsibilities to this toxic workplace were draining my life force as I continued to buy in to the workplace being serious and not a place for friendships. I was having trouble trusting anyone in the workplace, getting closer and closer to a breaking point. I was not being authentic to myself or to others, and I didn't even realize it at the time. The toxicity was threatening my belief in myself, and I no longer had any idea who I was.

Each morning when I woke up, I would envision the Joe Gideon character from *All That Jazz*, who would get ready for the day by standing in front of his mirror and exclaiming in an ironic voice with undertones of sadness, "It's showtime!" I literally said that out loud to myself each morning. Every day I felt more and more trapped in a job that was becoming a nightmare. I had followed all the business rulebooks, but it felt more and more alien to me. The dissonance in my soul was killing me. I was constantly sick. I lost count of the number of times I had monthlong bouts of chronic bronchitis. I put on weight. I developed arthritis.

Then, during this dark time at work, I stumbled into the *Supernatural* fandom. One day in 2006, I came across this statement on someone's blog: "I watched Jensen Ackles's lips last night. There appears to be some sort of show built around them. Huh."

I laughed out loud. I had no idea who Jensen Ackles was, or which TV show this was, but that short post tickled me so much that I had to go find out. I had stopped watching a lot of TV shows. I saw maybe one movie a year. I was busy. Too much to do in my serious world. But that online quip had made me laugh out loud, and I rarely laughed out loud in those days. I Googled "Jensen Ackles" and discovered he was on a show called *Supernatural*. I ended up getting DVDs of season 1, and my husband and I went through the season in a matter of days. I was still in my miserable, workaholic mode and pulling sixty-hour workweeks, while also going to school to get my long-delayed college diploma. I accepted all this as being a responsible grown-up. But I enjoyed spending evenings with my husband watching this sometimes campy, but very engaging show. My husband loved the classic rock, classic cars, and Dean's attitude. I loved the brothers' devotion and their messed-up relationship. And the chemistry between the two actors was mesmerizing.

I can still vividly remember the night we watched the episode "Faith." Blue Oyster Cult's "Don't Fear the Reaper" fantastically woven into the reaper story line. Sam doing everything to save his brother. Dean angsting about someone losing his life so Dean could live. I went online directly after watching to download "Don't Fear the Reaper," and played it repeatedly over the next several days—always reliving (and often rewatching) that scene from "Faith." By the time we watched the season 1 finale, I was hooked.

I went looking for more information about the show online. At the time I wasn't looking for community; I had no inkling that I had a huge hole in my life. What I found was fandom. I found and read fanfic. There were fantastic fan-made videos that I saved like gold nuggets. The artwork was astounding. I spent hours deciphering and learning the special language and phrases used within the fandom. I read about the history of fandom. In those days, online fandom was still a sheltered environment. Most *normal* people didn't know it existed. Fanfic, which had been around for decades, was still very much on the fringe and was not talked about outside of fandom. *Fandom* was not talked about outside of fandom. People used pseudonyms. "Outing" someone as a fan was a crime that brought the fandom down on anyone who crossed that line.

I turned a close friend on to the show, and together we obsessed over episodes and read fan reactions online. Mostly we didn't talk about fandom with our families or real-life friends. But we started to interact with other fans in this sheltered and safe environment.

We learned there were others just like us. People who had always felt on the fringe. Like they didn't belong. Like they were *other*. Like us, some of them had adopted normal real-life personas. Some flew their *other* flag loud and proud. Still others suffered in silence, being neither able to adapt to the real world nor to flaunt their otherness. My friend and I began to feel safe expressing a part of ourselves we had hidden down deep—in my case, so deeply that I truly thought it was a childish phase I had long ago outgrown. After an episode aired, we would laugh and/or angst online with fandom. We spent hours on the phone together, at lunches, at family gatherings, talking about the show and the fandom. Slowly we began to let our families in on our secret.

As I peeled back the layers on this show and its fandom, I began to sense something special about it. I've been a lifelong fan of storytelling, but there was something about the convergence of the story of Sam and Dean; of Jared and Jensen (individually and, even more special, together); of Eric Kripke, Kim Manners, and Bob Singer; of the away-from-Hollywood shooting location; of the crew, the writers, and the rest of the cast; and of the fandom. All of it melded together in the fertile Internet environment, to create this perfect storm of a show.

My friend and I considered flying to Dallas in the summer of 2007 to see Jensen appear in *A Few Good Men*. But, we sighed, there was no way we could justify the time and money to go to Dallas to see a community-theater play just because an actor we enjoyed was performing in it. Imagine telling our families that we were "going to Dallas to see Jensen Ackles in a play." Their response would no doubt be a confused "Who? What? . . . Why?!" So not going to happen.

Then we read fan reports of the first Chicago *Supernatural* convention in late 2007. We watched the few smuggled-out videos. Oh, what fun that looked to be! But not for us. We were mature grown-ups with responsibilities. Then a convention was announced for LA, to occur in the spring of 2008. We excitedly talked over the phone. Should we? Dare we? It's so close. Hell, why not? We'll do this just once and get it out of our system.

Going to that first *Supernatural* convention was like a shot of pure happiness.

I generally dislike crowds. In my profession I have to network and speak in front of groups and lead complex meetings with many participants. And I am good at it. But as an introvert, it's draining. My first *Supernatural* con, instead of draining me, left me so energized and giddy that when my daughter picked my friend and me up at the airport after that first convention, she was dumbfounded. We sat in the back seat laughing and giggling like we were high. I doubt my daughter had ever seen me like that. And when I returned to my workplace, my coworkers wanted to know what drug I was on.

At that first convention we could turn to anyone there and feel connected. We came from different countries, different backgrounds, different age groups, different personal situations, but we connected. With everyone. I had never experienced anything like it. The positive energy was through the roof. A group of fellow fans whom we'd just met got together in a hotel room and talked about the show. We laughed. We angsted. We shared information about the show and about ourselves. During the convention panels, photo ops, autographs, and other events, we met some of the cast. In the early years of the conventions, sometimes the cast and fan interactions were awkward. We still didn't know how to cross that *line* that we all had been operating within. The line that says fandom is separate. Fandom and the source do not mix. But we *did* mix. And slowly we got to know, trust, and enjoy one another.

My friend and I knew we were going to another convention. Perhaps just one more. After all, how much longer could the show go on? It probably wouldn't last more than two or three years. That was in 2008. Now eight years and many conventions later, the show and the fandom are going stronger than ever. And I've been to so many conventions that I've lost track of the number.

As my fandom involvement increased, I learned more about the work environment that *Supernatural* executive producer and director Kim Manners fostered. I learned that Kim would say, "We spend too much time together to not enjoy each other's company." I read about the easy camaraderie on set. How they worked long, hard hours and did quality work, while still supporting one another and having fun. That was everything I didn't have at work. Well, I had the long hours, but not the connection, fun, or support.

I left my toxic workplace at the end of 2008. We parted with the unstated agreement that we were incompatible. I was fortunate then in that I was able to take a year off from working to focus on healing my body and my spirit. I also started to build a vision of what I wanted in my next workplace. I had become convinced that work environments that cared about the people who worked there no longer existed. But as I learned more about the people who made *Supernatural*, I began to understand that healthy and happy work environments could and did exist. I started to think about what I wanted in a work environment. I wanted what the people who worked on *Supernatural* had: a supportive, connected, and fun work environment. I learned what true leadership was from the people who make this show. I wanted to be a leader like Kim Manners. And like Jensen and Jared, who, as I was learning, were clearly key players in setting the tone for their workplace.

When I found my new workplace in late 2009, I made a card showing Kim Manners and members of the cast and crew with the captions, "What would Kim do?" and "Kick it in the ass."

That card is still on the wall in my office. I look at it whenever I struggle with how to foster a positive work environment, when I want to remember how to lead people to work hard while supporting them and enjoying ourselves. I cannot express how grateful I am to this show and all the people who make it, for teaching me it was possible to have and create a supportive work environment.

Changing my ideas of leadership and what a work environment could be wasn't the only thing *Supernatural* did for me. It also changed my ideas of what I was capable of professionally. As I continued to attend conventions, I saw the photos taken by fans. I had loved photography my entire life. But photography was expensive and frivolous. When my kids were young, I had the excuse of taking photos of them as they grew. But my camera days were more or less over by the time I attended my first convention. As I experienced that convention, I was *itching* to capture on film what I was experiencing. It was like a physical thing. I *needed* to photograph it. I had taken a small camera with me and took some truly crappy photos. It frustrated the hell out of me.

I started studying other fans' photos. I started researching digital cameras. My friend and I signed up for our next convention, which led to more conventions. I caved and purchased a used DSLR. At each convention, I took hundreds of photos. Studied other fans' photos. Took online courses. Took in-person courses. Took a *lot* more photos. My photography passion was reignited. I wanted to photograph everything. Each panel at each convention gave me hundreds of chances to make mistakes and learn from them. And with each convention I got better. It was one of the most challenging situations in which to shoot photos, and it was fantastic for honing photography skills. As my skill increased, I began to think about doing this as more than a pastime. I started to shoot weddings and portraits. In 2012, I made it an official business. I was and am still doing my day job, but I live for photography. And I wouldn't have that if not for this show. Again with the inexpressible gratitude.

I love the fandom practice of freely sharing content. I made all my photos available online for anyone to see or use for fanart. Through my photos, my fandom friendships increased. I now have friends all over the world. And not just friends I talk with online. People I've met in real

Jared wearing moose antlers from a first-time con-goer fan, BurCon 2013.

Left: Rockstar Jensen, VanCon 2015.
Right: Jensen and Bob Singer, Jus in Bello 2015.

Jensen's first tweet, VanCon 2014.

life, spent days and nights with. Friends who have traveled from other countries and met my family and stayed with us. We no longer use pseudonyms. We know each other. Fangirls I used to fangirl are now my friends.

Then, after a few years, someone approached me at a convention and fangirled me. Fangirled *me*. I was flabbergasted. Truly. Then it happened again. And again. The number of hits on my online photos was approaching ten million. Ten. Million. Seriously? I was asked if I would allow some of my photos to be included in the *Fangasm* book. I was thrilled. I was able to sit in on an interview with a cast member and take photos. No words.

I no longer watch this show. I am *involved* with this show. Intrinsically involved. I've been involved now for over ten years. The other day my mother observed that it seemed like it wasn't the story I was involved with anymore. I was more involved with the people who made the story. "Definitely," I told her. This show now represents so much of what I want in life. Obviously, not the lives of Sam and Dean, but what I learned about the cast and crew. Learning about how they worked inspired me in many ways. Learning how they supported one another and enjoyed one another's company. It was Jared who sometime later coined the term "SPNFamily," and it was the as-yet-unnamed SPNFamily with which I was involved.

And I found myself again.

I was shocked to learn that what I viewed as a "childhood phase" of being a sci-fi geek and an artist that I thought I had outgrown was, in fact, *me*. I had lost me. I was not merely a project or a program manager or a wife or a mother. I was an artist. I was a photographer. I was a lover of storytelling and history. I loved technology and, yes, I loved being an IT program manager, but I loved it because through that role I could support and encourage people to thrive. I was a leader. It was through this show that I found *me* again and I found community.

I found my tribe.

THE SUPERNATURAL EFFECT

JIM BEAVER

By the time I first came to know anything substantive about the TV series *Supernatural*, it had been on the air for several months. Because I pay some attention to what my industry is producing, I knew the name of the show and had some vague sense that it was about a couple of young hunks engaged in fighting fantastical beings. That was all. Such a concept interested me not one bit. I've never been particularly interested in horror or fantasy films and shows. I grew up on the TV show *Adventures of Superman*, but even superhero stuff had long since faded from my radar. I did (and do) prefer straight drama, without ghosts or demons or bat-people or wormholes.

None of that changed when I was hired to do an episode of *Supernatural*, playing a demon hunter named Bobby (he didn't get the Singer until later). The part was great fun, the sort of guy I love playing: hard-bitten but sensitive, tough but thoughtful, gruff but lovable. I didn't get or care much about the whole demon exorcism stuff we did in that first episode, and, while actors are always hopeful that their role will repeat once or twice or sixty times during the course of a series, I had no expectation that this one would and no special desire to revisit this particular show. I had just come off of the greatest experience of my professional life, as one of the main characters on what I still think is the greatest TV show in history, HBO's *Deadwood*. My sights were aimed very high. No way was this *Route 66*-meets-Dracula show aimed at teenaged girls what I hoped would follow *Deadwood*.

The one element of the show that instantly appealed to me, however, even before seeing the episode we shot ("Devil's Trap"), was the people who made the show. The two young men at the center of the story were played not just by hunks, but by warm, decent, gregarious, and vastly welcoming actors (who also happened to be very good). It happens often enough to be a cliché that the handsome young studs who populate a certain kind of audience's favorite shows are thoughtless pricks. I'm extremely defensive of actors and know the vast majority of them to be amazing and generous human beings, but even I had sufficient experience to know that many of the beautiful boys on *Melrose Place*–type shows were people I would prefer to avoid. The exact opposite was true on *Supernatural*.

I had met Jensen Ackles years before when we were both on *Days of Our Lives* (he as a regular and I as a priest who only showed up when somebody croaked or got married—or both). In all probability, I'd never had a conversation with him in those days and I don't think he remembered me. But I didn't need an icebreaker with Jensen. He was the soul of hospitality, as was Jared Padalecki, who was totally unknown to me. It's another cliché of television that the atmosphere on set trickles down from the top, meaning that if the lead actors are jerks, nobody down the food chain is going to be happy. *Supernatural* is the happiest set I've ever worked on. You do the math.

That same happiness infused the crew, who were equally hospitable and generous of spirit. Being a guest actor on a show is often like wandering into a party where you don't know anyone, but everyone else knows one another well. I've been on shows where no one ever spoke to me except in terms of the business we were engaged in. I've had recurring roles on shows where, even after several episodes, I still felt like a stranger. More than any show I've ever been on, *Supernatural* was like going to camp with all my best friends—even on that first episode. I was blindsided by the kindness and friendliness of everyone I met.

That's no small thing. An actor's job is, more often than not, to be incredibly vulnerable, to look silly or pitiful or egotistical or awful in front of a bunch of people you may not know. Rosalind Russell reportedly said, "Acting is standing up naked and turning around very slowly." So if the crew or the other people in the cast are aloof or inhospitable or even hostile, it makes the work of revealing a character's true humanity and foibles that much more difficult. *Supernatural* is probably the easiest place to work I've ever encountered. Everyone there is utterly supportive.

Kim Manners directed my first episode. I'd met Kim several years earlier on an episode of *The X-Files*, and I'd richly enjoyed that experience. He was, through all the too-few years I knew him, the consummate combination of directorial excellence: friendly, firm, extraordinarily talented, and infinitely patient, even in his impatience. The show's creator, Eric Kripke, happened also to be on set during my first episode, and while I didn't get to know him well until later when I became a more frequent participant in the show, I found him to be another example of the top-down amiable hospitality that permeated the set. And the executive producer, Bob Singer—after whom, to his chagrin, my character was named—was an old friend from *Reasonable Doubts*, a show we'd done together a decade earlier.

I had no idea I would ever return to play Bobby again, but I'd have been happy to, and the crew was encouraging: "We didn't kill you. That's a good sign!" When I returned for the first episode of season 2, nothing had changed. It was still a warm, welcoming place to be. In nearly sixty episodes and eleven seasons (so far) since then, it still is.

Supernatural has had an enormous effect on me, even if one only counts the friendships I have gained working on the show. The number of people from the show whom I consider close personal friends is remarkable. Actors often congregate with actors, which is, no doubt, natural, given how closely we work and how singular is our focus. But on *Supernatural* I found myself with bosom friends throughout the crew and staff. I don't mean to suggest that such things never happened on other shows.

But the sheer number of friendships I gained on the *Supernatural* set is, to me, remarkable.

After my second episode ("In My Time of Dying"), I didn't hear anything from the *Supernatural* producers for a long time, and the show slipped from my consciousness. Actors are well advised to concentrate on what's happening at the moment and not to conjure much with what might happen someday. But shortly after the middle of season 2, I was called back to do four more episodes. It was a complicated time, because over the course of that year I was recurring on four other shows, and I barely knew which character I was playing on any given day. While it became clear that I was becoming a little more important to the epic tale of *Supernatural*, I had no sense that anyone *watching* the show knew or cared who I was, or had any interest in seeing more of the character. The audience's response to the character only slowly revealed itself as the shows we'd shot for the second half of season 2 began to be broadcast.

Around the time I first worked on *Supernatural*, I began to understand the phenomenon known as social media. The more I looked at this new way of communicating, the more I realized I had to make a decision: whether to engage fully and openly or, like most actors who have any public profile, to hunker down in the bunker and erect a wall around myself to keep out eyes intent on prying into my life. Only a couple of years earlier, during a period of personal tragedy, I had discovered the enormous gift of being as open as I could be, and I decided that anyone who thought I was interesting enough to interact with should be able to. I decided not to hide, and to talk to anyone who reached out. Now, at the time I was coming to this decision, I had some small following from *Deadwood*, but was pretty much unknown otherwise, and it didn't seem like an act of much bravery to throw open my cyber-gates. Within another year, though, all that would change.

By the time I started shooting the first episode of season 3 ("The Magnificent Seven"), I was beginning to realize that this *Supernatural* thing had a real reach. People were watching this show! Real people, people who stumbled onto me on Facebook or Twitter and wanted to tell me what they thought of the show and me and my character. This was new to me, and not just to me. Before the social media revolution, actors almost never had mass contact with the people who watched their work. Sure, people might hang out at a stage door after a play, or bump into Ted Danson at the supermarket. And there was fan mail, some of which was actually received and read by the actor in question. But the notion of hearing, in real time, from hundreds or thousands of people who could quote your own lines back to you better than you could, who wanted to know why you wore one cap in one episode and not in another, who wanted to know your favorite book or food or sexual position, or who just wanted to say "Hi" and hope for a "Hi" back—this was all new, and it was both exhilarating and frightening.

I decided fairly early to be myself to the extent I could: to talk about the things that were important to me, to share things that interested me, and not to shy away from things that might cost me fans (as fans who disagreed with me often warned me would happen). It took me a long life to realize the importance of authenticity, and I still struggle with it at times, but the large audience that opened itself up to *me* proved to me that I'd been right to so choose. But despite the extraordinary effect engaging with *Supernatural*'s fandom online had on me, nothing prepared me for meeting them all (or so it seemed) *in person*.

I'd heard about the fan convention appearances Jared and Jensen were making. I knew a little about fan conventions because I'd occasionally accompanied my late wife, Cecily Adams (who'd played Quark's mother, Ishka ["Moogie"], on *Star Trek: Deep Space Nine*), to her appearances at *Star Trek* conventions. As we finished shooting season 3, I got my first invitation to a *Supernatural* convention. It was held in April 2008, in Orlando, Florida. The last fan convention I'd attended with my wife was in a small comic-book store in Bologna, Italy, and about twenty fans showed up. So I was utterly flabbergasted by the turnout in Orlando. For a guy who'd spent thirty-six years acting without anyone paying any particular attention, walking into the EyeCon ballroom felt like I'd been reincarnated as Elvis. It was extraordinary and very touching and gratifying.

In some ways, that first convention was also the most important I've attended, because it was there that I really learned who our audience was. First off, since the *Star Trek* events I'd gone to with Cecily were dominated by male fans, I was floored in Florida by the near-total absence of testosterone. I think I counted four or five men in attendance. For a long time, this gave me the impression that only women watched *Supernatural*. It took me a long time to figure out that, no, lots of men watch *Supernatural*. But mainly women attend the conventions. At least the numbers are overwhelmingly in their favor. (I don't mind. I don't mind at all.)

The warmth with which I was treated at that first convention, and at every subsequent one, startled me. I don't think I'd realized what a chord the character of Bobby had struck in the audience, nor was I prepared for the affection they showed the fellow who played him. The convention was small enough that I was able to mingle with the fans between events and to hang out for hours together in the evenings. That weekend I made friends who are still vital parts of my life—dear, treasured friends.

I also learned a lot about how the fans felt about the show. The most startling revelation was when someone told me that she watched the show mostly for the relationships, *that she would watch* Supernatural *even if there weren't any monsters*. It was said to me in a crowd and I asked, "Really?" Almost in unison, the crowd yelled, "Yes! Absolutely!" The effect of this information on me was remarkable. It made me understand that the aspects of the show that would not have interested me as a viewer (the supernatural parts) were only the icing on the cake for these fans. It made me realize that I *was* doing a straight drama of the kind I preferred, that we were telling human tales that resonated in viewers' hearts and not just in their thrill zones. I had always taken my character seriously—there's no other way to act well than to believe in the guy you're playing—but for the first time I felt like I was doing something with true worth and not just a time passer. I've been to dozens of fan conventions since 2008, and this impression has been reinforced at every such event.

The final real and lasting effect of *Supernatural* on my life, beyond the friendships and insights, has been the realization that through the vast community of fans of this show, I can have an enormous effect for good. Social media has been invaluable for this. A few years ago, one of the crew on *Supernatural* asked me to tweet something about the cancer charity he was supporting. Because I'd lost both my wife and my dear friend Kim Manners to the disease in recent years, I was more than willing to do whatever I could, and God knows a simple tweet was not hard to do.

What shocked me was that within an hour or two of that tweet, the charity's tote board shot up thousands of dollars. I began to realize that I might not have been placed in this remarkable and wonderful position simply to do what I love (acting) and to meet adoring fans. Maybe I was here to make a difference, and to make that difference by helping the gigantic *Supernatural* fan base make a difference.

Since then, I've tried (judiciously) to bring the *Supernatural* Family (and that's what it is, a family) together to support things that seem worthy and helpful to the world. Recently, a T-shirt with one of my lines from the show on it raised nearly $30,000 to bring much-needed food and clothing to the destitute of the Cherokee nation. I don't think anyone can imagine how much this sort of thing means, not just to the people who benefit directly, but also to my sense of worth in the world. It's a large world, peopled by billions. To have any positive effect outside our own personal circles is a blessing few of us are allowed to achieve. I have done so only through the worldwide family of *Supernatural*.

It is difficult for me to overstate the effect being Bobby Singer has had on me. It has given me more visibility than I ever dreamed likely. It has given me a raft of friends (and even a romance or two) among my colleagues and fans of the show. It has allowed me to travel around the world (literally!) meeting people I'd never otherwise have learned about. It has made a rather shy and private person into someone who revels in the company of people he has never before met. It has made me feel appreciated and loved, not only for my work but also for myself, which is a pretty amazing accomplishment for even a few million people to pull off. And it has shown me that the vast weight of love and kindness and humanity in the world can and does overwhelm the forces of spite, hate, and ingratitude. The *Supernatural* effect on me has been the greatest gift of my public life. And anyone who doesn't think so is an idjit.

WE LOVE YOU ANYWAY

LYDIA A. CYRUS

The last semester of my senior year of high school, my mother left my dad. Suddenly, everything I had ever known changed. We were never a white-picket-fence family, and my dad could give John Winchester a run for his money (like John, my father was critical of everything I did and seemed to always be behind me, dictating my every move; like Dean, I also played the role of a pseudo-parent for my younger brother), but we'd still lived together. Then, my senior year of high school, my mom moved into a house that was about an hour away from where I grew up. It was this huge four-bedroom house in the middle of nowhere: no neighbors, no cable, no Internet, and worst of all, it didn't feel like home.

The bedroom that had been picked out for me was small and there was no furniture. I had a small mattress on the floor and an old television across from it. The real kicker was how disconnected I was when I stayed there. I had no way of talking to anyone unless I used the landline to make long-distance calls. It was a really hard time in my life, to be going through such an important time of growing up and having everything turned upside down. I would be graduating from school in just four months and my life would be transitioning. I couldn't talk to my mom or my dad about it, and my younger brother didn't understand. It wasn't until I ran across a forgotten Christmas gift that I found the support and love I'd been missing.

My mom had purchased season 1 of this television show she thought I liked. In truth, I had never seen it or heard much about it. It ended up going on the shelf and I never thought twice about it after I opened it. But when Mom broke the news that I had a three-day weekend ahead of me, but no friends around to do anything with, I grabbed the DVD set along with some other movies to watch while I lay on the floor at the house I hated. I had no idea that decision would change my life.

I popped the DVD in the player and kicked back and watched these two brothers kick ass. At first it just seemed like a nice way to kill time. But then it hit me. Dean and Sam had a father who expected way too much of them and was terrible at being a dad. Isn't that the way I described my dad? Sam and Dean both had these conflicting ideas of who they were and what they wanted. Didn't I have the same thing going on in my own heart? I started to realize that these brothers were my brothers. I'm not anywhere as good-looking as they are, but on the inside we were the same.

I don't know how to explain it, but within two months I had blown through five seasons of *Supernatural*, and it became my center. When I had nothing else, I knew I could go home after a long day and fight the good fight with Sam and Dean. I never stopped to think about it in an in-depth way. I never tried to figure out *why* this show meant so much. It wasn't until season 7, when a certain character died, that I realized what was going on.

Ever since Bobby Singer first appeared on the show, I loved him. I think almost every fan does, but I didn't know why I did. Sure, he's a hard-ass and he's funny. He always knows what to say to Sam and Dean and he knows how to fix the broken things. Over the course of several seasons, I had become attached to Bobby. As we all know now, in season 7, Bobby catches a slug in the brain and later dies because of it. That episode probably lasted forty-five minutes, but for me it will last forever.

In Bobby's final moments he travels through memories and has to face his fears. The audience finds out things about Bobby that explain everything about him. Bobby grew up in an abusive home and killed his dad after his dad stepped across the line. The second young Bobby shot his dad, I had to pause the episode and walk away. Growing up, I had always been afraid of my dad. I never once stepped out of line or said anything I shouldn't have. I always did my best in school, because I knew I had to go home and face him. The things Bobby's dad said to him rang through my ears and my chest and I couldn't stop crying; I know what that's like, and even though I was young when those things happened, it shaped the woman I am. I understood at once why Bobby said and did the things he did for seven seasons. It all made sense. That's when I realized that I had more in common with Bobby Singer than I did with the Winchesters. Sitting alone in an almost empty room, I understood the complex character development I had been brushing past all that time before.

I've always said I don't think I'll ever have kids. Everyone says, "You're so young! You'll change your mind!" It has nothing to do with being selfish or wanting to be a rebel. Instead, I'm afraid I'll be just like my dad was to me. Forget vampires, werewolves, and ghosts, because that would be the scariest thing I can imagine: to turn into him. Bobby and I have that in common. We have a lot in common.

It's not just the sentimental things that make me love this show so much. I'm at the stage in my life where everything is changing. I'm putting myself through college, and with that comes many other journeys. I'm finding out who I am as a person and who other people are as well. As it turns out, I'm a lot like Charlie Bradbury: a smart, nerdy girl with ambition and compassion. Because I love this show, I've been able to log on to social media and meet other people who do, too. Through this show, I gained a family. A family that, instead of saying who I am is "nothing," embraces who I am and says, "Come on in. We love you anyway."

I think people have to be reminded sometimes how beautiful and wonderful they really are. As fans, we always talk about how we wish Dean knew how much he meant to us or how much Sam is capable of. I think the same goes for us as fans. I can only speak for myself, but I avoided anything and everything that had to do with my personal life. Until Bobby's death confronted me head-on, I kept that stuff locked away. Even though all the bad experiences in life have made me a better person, sometimes

I'm still ashamed to talk about them. I think we all are, but here is this show about two brothers who are more like us than we realize and they're confronting all of it. So why can't we?

Sometimes, when I'm having a bad day, I look on my bookshelf and I see my copy of *The Hobbit*, and I remember Charlie Bradbury and her struggles. Or I'll catch myself saying, "So get this," or having a certain Kansas song stuck in my head, and I remember. I remember how Dean sold his soul so Sam could live, and I remember how far I have come as a person, too. I've grown so much since I first started watching the show. I found it because I needed it. I don't think it was an accident that my mom picked up season 1, and I don't think it was an accident that I picked it up again two months later. Everything happens for a reason, and I'm forever grateful I have this show.

It's silly—I know that. People like to tell me all the time how geeky I am and I've been made to feel like a loser more than once. But that doesn't matter anymore, because I know who I am and what I am capable of.

I'll probably never run into a wendigo, but I know how to handle it if I do. It's more likely that I'll run into other monsters, monsters of the human variety. I know how to handle those, too. Just like Charlie and Jo and my main man Bobby, I'll save myself when I need to and I'll fight for the ones I love when they need me.

I've never been to a convention, but, as I write this, I'm planning on going to one next July. I'll probably be a mess and I know I'll cry a lot. But I know I'll be in good hands, with people who won't care that I showed up wearing anti-possession symbols or that I came with tears in my eyes. I know I'll meet people who I will become friends with and who will love me for who I am. I also know I'll get to meet the actors who bring this show to life. I don't know what grade I'm going to get in Latin 101 next semester or how much student-loan debt I'll have this time next year, but I know that going to that convention will be the best thing I've ever done.

Before I started watching this show I had very little reason to smile. I was shy and didn't stand up for myself and I was ashamed of who I was. Ten seasons later? I'm very different. If you ask me anything about my hobbies or my life in general, I'll talk about it. I smile more often, and even when it seems like everything is lost, I remind myself to keep going because more than once the Winchesters have saved humanity, because Dean and Sam can do anything, because there's this adorable angel who loves humankind despite everything we've done, *because I can.* I know now that I'm a huge nerd with a heart of gold and I have the power to change things if I choose to do so.

I know I'm not the only one with a story like this. Maybe someone will read this and see me at that convention and ask if I care to chat. I'll probably say yes, and maybe that person will tell me their story. I'm no Metatron, but I'll listen and I'll pat them on the back and hug them. (Well, only if they're okay with it, because I don't like strangers touching me, so I know how that goes.) Maybe if I can be brave enough to say what is in my heart, others will be, too.

This show will always mean more to me than just some show about two dudes chasing monsters. Even though it is about those two brothers . . . it's bigger than that. It's far bigger than I think anyone expected it to be. I'm proud of this show and the actors and the people behind the scenes. And to anyone who reads this and feels a deeper connection to the show: I'm proud of us.

COMPLETELY NATURAL

RACHEL MINER

You don't need me to tell you how amazing you are, or how wonderful it is when such kind, supportive, funny, strong, smart, geeky, silly, loving people come together.

You don't need me to tell you how much brighter life is when we share it with others, when we don't hide, when we are true to ourselves, when we can always find a reason to laugh and a friend to laugh with, when we live and love for one another, for something greater then ourselves.

You don't me to tell you these things because that is just who and what you are.

And beyond what words can ever capture, I truly and deeply love you, and all of *Supernatural* fandom, for it.

It seems redundant to tell you tales of how the incredible and loving people drawn together by this show—this phenomenon, this alchemical force for good—have brought me back to life a thousand times in a thousand ways. When we are lucky enough to find our tribe, we often end up expressing precisely the same thing as others in it. I lose count of the number of times when I say something, and then am shown a clip of one of my fellow SPNers saying *exactly* the same thing. So rather than repeating what has already been said, I will simply say I would fight for, and defend with all my power, the members of this tribe.

The funny thing is that one of the attributes of the members of this group is your beautifully unassuming lack of ego about it all, so I am guessing that none of you really gets how much you mean to me, or to countless others.

It is true that I'm weird beyond measure. It doesn't take careful study to see that I don't quite fit in. I have spent my whole life being told things like, "No one *actually* talks that way," and being laughed at (sometimes lovingly) for the odd way in which I process the world. Perhaps that is one of the many reasons why I so enjoy acting, because I can take the time to study and understand the whole "being human" thing. I know that characters like Meg and Castiel (also Sherlock Holmes, Spock, Data, and Doctor Who, to name some of my favorites) make so much sense to me because, like me, they tend to process the macro data easily and miss the nuance of (or, from my view, the completely illogical rationale for) human behaviors.

So it is somewhere between rarely and never that I feel like I actually make sense within the context of a group. I read and study a lot, which leaves me feeling very connected to humanity, and my "friends" are often the philosophers, historians, scientists, and great thinkers whose thoughts make me feel understood and less alone in my way of seeing the world.

This group, this SPNFamily, is a different story. I am always moved by how loving, loyal, inclusive, and embracing it is (within the larger circle at conventions, on social media, and in the group of actors/crew I have spent time with). It's a subtle thing—it doesn't happen because people are advertising how "lovely and inclusive" they are, but because I leave their presence feeling happier, more fulfilled, and freer to express my true self.

There is another thing about this tribe. We love to help one another.

I think we have discovered the wonderful gift that comes in having someone you would give your all to help. It is when we can achieve this that we ourselves are helped the most. This is the gift I am without a doubt most grateful for—to feel there is some purpose for my existence, that perhaps I can make someone else's life a bit better. This family is so good, not only at helping one another, but also at accepting and acknowledging others for helping them.

My primary motivation has always been to be, in some way, of service to others (I think perhaps that is true of us all), and when I got sick with MS, the thing that challenged me most was that I didn't know if I could still be helpful or useful in any way. I can never say *thank you* enough, or express enough gratitude, to show what it means to me to find some sense of meaning and purpose. And when, as we all do, I come up against obstacles in life that take all my effort to overcome, the thing that pushes me over the hurdle is the idea that I am not doing it for myself alone, but for this group of other people whom I love.

I know I am not alone in any of this, because I have you around to remind me every day, and I feel a wonderful sense of purpose because I want to be here to remind you of the same thing.

At Ladies of SPN Con, May 2016.

A SUPERNATURAL LOVE STORY

ADAM WILLIAMS AND LUCY SCHNEIDER

ADAM:

To say that *Supernatural* has had an impact on my life is a definite understatement. It's been a journey beyond anything work related at this point, and a story I would love to share in its entirety, but parts are far too personal for public exposure at this time in my life. That considered, there is still much to say.

Before I started at *Supernatural* I was, from the outside, a much different beast. I was isolated from most people, in a dead-end job, and making the most of a roughneck environment in a small rural suburb of Vancouver. To relieve the boredom and monotony of my existence, I was a regular contributor for a print magazine and made YouTube video tutorials. Not the most exciting things to do, but making the videos gave me some skill and experience in editorial software, codecs, and remedial visual effects . . . and those skills were, when the opportunity arose, transferable to the job haven I was about to find.

Life is as often who you know as what you know, and in my case that rang true. The "who" for me was a friend I had known since high school who had, himself, branched into film a couple of years prior and had managed to work his way into the visual effects department of a little show we all know and love: *Supernatural*. An editorial position became available in the visual effects department and, knowing I had familiarity with editorial software, he recommended that I apply.

Suffice to say, I got the job as the visual effects I/O coordinator. That meant I was less isolated, enjoying a relaxed work environment. Yet life still had some serious changes in store for me, and not all of them were pleasant. Not much more than a year after I started at *Supernatural* my world was turned upside down when my wife and I separated, and before I knew it I was leaving my little town to move closer to work.

During that stressful time, the interactions I had with fans of *Supernatural* were a bright spot. One of the most significant impacts working on the show had on me was through social media. I had been on Twitter for probably five years prior and had very little interaction, since my following/followers network was limited. I made a new account as @adamwvfx to interact with people as the I/O coordinator, and within a few hours I had more followers than I could have imagined. I followed back, chatted with people, and befriended several fans of the show. Within three months of working at *Supernatural* I had been sent three different gift baskets of treats, chocolates, and gifts. Talk about unexpected! My level of appreciation is beyond words, not only for the gifts but also for the acceptance I got from the fandom community.

What I didn't expect was that interacting with people on Twitter would ever lead to love. I am not really that guy, for one, and being recently separated, the last thing I wanted to do was fall for someone. In fact, had I been asked, I would have said that my limited emotional resources were already designated. I am also not what anyone would call a great catch— few can tolerate my idiosyncrasies, overbearing personality, and unfettered hedonism. But lo and behold, I would soon discover someone who could. And would—happily.

The Twitterverse had introduced me to something called "VanCon" during my first year at *Supernatural*, but I was a n00b and thought it was just a hashtag. Like, *Come to the hashtag #vancon* (however that would work) *and talk to fans from the city*. Or something. It wasn't until after it ended that I discovered it was a literal convention of humans. Humans who love *Supernatural*! Being a person who loves attention (think retired front man musician), I was not going to miss the convention the following year. As VanCon 2013 approached, I chatted with a few people about meeting up and having a drink or a meal, and looked forward to socializing with this strange breed of human we call *Supernatural* fans. One of those people was Lucy Schneider, @SpnUK, whom I had chatted with on Twitter.

We met at the convention on Friday and, as I recall, spent most of our free time together during the weekend. Which was not a lot. Lucy had loads of photos and autographs planned as well as panels to see, and I had a lot of socializing to do (so many autographs given that year). So the weekend blew by before we knew it. When it came time for Lucy to leave for Britain we were torn. We barely knew each other, but really wanted to. Both of us could feel the draw to each other, but it was a draw that would soon be cleaved by 5,000 miles. She had a house, a good job, and family in the UK; it didn't seem reasonable or responsible to consider "us" as a thing . . . but we did. It was impossible not to.

So we decided to make a go of it. Sitting on a hotel bed at the Sheraton, wrapped in each other's arms like bacon on a prime rib (sorry for the analogy, but it's about lunchtime for me), we decided to toss caution to the wind and follow our inner fools. At the time it seemed like a difficult challenge, but we had no idea how long and arduous the journey would be. We floated like driftwood on a river of uncertainty as weeks became months. Lucy tried to find work in B.C., jumping through hoop after hoop to appease the seemingly infinite bureaucratic red tape that prevents gorgeous British women from finding their dreams in Canada.

In the end we succeeded, and the *Supernatural* fandom community added one more story to its legacy of bringing people together—people who had no idea they were looking for each other or needed someone. All over the world people join the fandom and are drawn to social media to discuss the show, discover others who share their celebrity crush, or read reviews by other fans. What they find is something much more vast and complex than any simple review blog or Facebook group for Jensen fangirls. They find an enormous and active community of fans spanning all the social media platforms: folks who ship characters, people who create fanart or fan fiction, musicians who write songs or adapt cover tunes around the show, and literally tens of thousands of fan accounts on Twitter and Tumblr that buzz day in and day out with fandom fervor.

When I came to work at *Supernatural*, I had no idea that it could have such an impact on my life—let alone me as a person. Jobs don't usually involve forming new social networks beyond the odd beer with coworkers. Jobs aren't expected to come with life-changing experiences, personal growth, or romance. That's not part of the program. But this one time, to this one guy named Adam, it came with that and more. And I have no idea what to expect for the future, because nobody could have predicted the past.

But I will keep calm and carry on.

LUCY:

I couldn't proudly call myself a fangirl until about six years ago when I stumbled across an interview about *Supernatural* in a magazine, which led to me purchasing season 1 on DVD with literally no idea what effect it would have on me. I was at a stage in my life, after ending a fifteen-year relationship, where I was gaining my independence and exploring what it meant to actually be me. I was also quite lonely at the time and felt like I needed something, a distraction, in my life. My first foray into fandom came through Twitter when I set up my Twitter account, @SpnUK, and did a search for *Supernatural*.

Very quickly I followed and started interacting with every single person that I could find who worked on the show or who was a part of the fandom. The responses that I got were encouraging and the posts that others made were inspiring. I hadn't really considered being a part of a "fandom" before my exposure to the SPNFamily. Being a "fan" was always quite taboo among my peers, as it is in a lot of circles, and before experiencing the *Supernatural* fandom firsthand I didn't even really know what a fandom was or did.

Once I discovered how wonderful the community that called themselves the SPNFamily was, I began to immerse myself as much as possible. I tried to get involved in as many online fandom projects as I could, and at this point it was as much about the fun and friendships I was forming as it was about my own need for distraction. By the end of 2012 I had not only launched my own site, www.spnuk.com, but also joined the SuperWiki and started helping with editing as well as carrying out interviews with cast members via email or Skype.

One of the projects that I am most proud of being a part of is the one set up when *Supernatural* was canceled in the UK. I joined a fantastic group of UK fans who were attempting to get "Carry on Wayward Son" by Kansas to number 1 on the UK charts, to raise awareness and show just how many people in the UK loved *Supernatural* and wanted it to continue to be broadcast. We made T-shirts and flyers, which were handed out at a Kansas concert in London with permission from the band. After a short time the song made it to number 1 in the UK rock download chart, and the efforts of numerous fans all working together was noticed by Warner Brothers. Shortly after the campaign it was announced that a UK channel was going to start airing *Supernatural* again—a success!

There have been so many other wonderful projects that I have been involved in, all introducing me to new friends and new aspects of fandom, plus showing me fandom's power and heart. It's crazy to think that this all started by watching a TV show and joining Twitter.

It was also through Twitter that I first interacted with Adam. He was great at responding to fans and chatting with them about the show or whatever other topics came up. After we had chatted for a while on Twitter we became friends on Facebook, where we could have more in-depth discussions about music, religion, or whatever else came up.

There is a particular moment during these interactions that really stands out to me: when Adam played me one of his old songs that he had written and recorded. It was so beautiful and deeply heartbreaking. This showed me a vulnerable and broken side to this man with the usually bulletproof egotistical persona that I had been so used to thus far.

As well as befriending Adam, I also found some other wonderful people that I know will be lifelong friends. These friends, and being a part of the fandom, helped fill my day and give me a purpose in life. But it wasn't until I took part in GISHWHES that the really big changes started happening.

I first learned about GISHWHES (Greatest International Scavenger Hunt the World Has Ever Seen) in May 2012. As part of the scavenger hunt, you are tasked with taking photographs or video of approximately

200 items with your fifteen teammates from all over the world. It's eye-opening, life changing, and one of the craziest things you will ever find yourself doing! Through GISHWHES I learned not to take life or myself too seriously, to be proud of my creativity, and not to be afraid to take chances. It helped me learn not to care what people thought of me getting involved in crazy things; they could accept that what I was doing was making me and others happy, or they could not—it was their choice, but it no longer influenced my goals.

It was taking part in GISHWHES that gave me the confidence to travel by myself across the world to a *Supernatural* convention in Vancouver. I chose the one in Vancouver because it is where the show is filmed, so I could visit some of the filming locations and take part in the tour hosted by *Supernatural*'s locations manager, Russ Hamilton.

It was also where Adam lived. As our friendship had blossomed throughout our chats, I was really looking forward to meeting him in person; I was not really expecting it to be a new romance as much as a great new friendship.

So, in August 2013, I packed my suitcase and nervously made my way 5,000 miles across the globe. This was the first time I had ever flown by myself—actually, it was the first time I had been on a vacation by myself. The thought of meeting up with Adam, and with the other friends I had made online, turned me into a ball of excitable nervousness during the nine-hour flight. I feel sorry for whoever was sitting next to me.

My first day in Vancouver consisted of the locations tour, so it was a whirlwind of busy. The tour was everything I had hoped for and more! We visited some amazing locations, including the outside of the Men of Letters bunker, and reenacted part of "Larp and the Real Girl" in the actual location where it was filmed. I also had the chance to get to know some awesome new friends, including the enigma that is Jules, Super-Wiki's administrator, and, of course, Adam.

Despite any nerves I'd been feeling, when Adam and I met in person, it turned out to be fantastic. We chatted like we did online and really enjoyed each other's company straight away. It just felt right.

We tried to spend as much time as possible together—as much time as attending a convention allows. We knew we both saw something very special in each other immediately, although it wasn't until my last day there that we discussed me coming back to Vancouver to see if we could make a go of it as a couple. By this point I just knew that I had to take a chance and see what happened; the way we both felt meant that not trying was not even an option.

But first I had a lot to sort out back in the UK. I had a very well-paying job as the manager of a company that I had worked my way up in over twelve years. I also had a stunning brand-new company car and a lovely little property that I owned and had decorated to my own personal taste, plus my family and a close circle of friends whom I would miss terribly. It was a huge and extremely risky choice, which was totally out of character for me, but I knew I had to follow my heart and just hope that everything else fell into place. So, without hesitation, I willingly gave up everything I had so that I could take this chance on a new and exciting life in Canada.

The day after I arrived back in the UK I went to visit my mother to give her the big news. I'd already told her through messages that I had met a guy in Vancouver, but still I don't think that helped to soften the blow that her baby would be moving 5,000 miles away to live with a man she had only just met!

The separation from my family was, by far, the hardest part of leaving the UK. I had never been very far from my family and friends for any great length of time. But they understood and could see how much Adam and the move meant to me. So, in November 2013, just two months after I returned from my Vancouver vacation, I packed up as much of my life as possible into two suitcases and headed back to Vancouver to live with a man I had spent barely a weekend in person with!

The flight this time was intense. Nine hours is a lot of time to contemplate your choices, but when I finally got through airport security and saw Adam standing there waiting for me, I just knew I had done the right thing. We didn't talk much during the journey to my new home, just held hands and kept stealing little kisses. I think at one point I asked if I was crazy for doing this, to which he grinned and said, "Yes!"

The next few months were a whirlwind of getting our apartment sorted and spending time getting to really know each other; luckily, we

Left: A sneaky kiss after a lovely day at Stanley Park in Vancouver.
Right: Hanging out near our apartment in our favorite spot
along the river, which we refer to as Adcy Beach.

found that we still had that initial attraction, which only increased over time. I was extremely homesick at times but Adam managed to help take my mind off of it, plus his parents, sister, and daughter made me feel welcome, like part of the family.

Because I was following my heart rather than my head, I hadn't really considered how difficult it would be to actually stay in Canada once I arrived there; the process of work permits, temporary visas, and eventual permanent resivdency status has been a huge trial that, at times, looked like we would not get through. I even had to return to the UK for a few months in 2014 when a temporary visa ran out, which was extremely difficult for us both. But with hard work, determination, and a lot of luck, in May 2016 I became a proud permanent resident of Canada, which meant that #ADCY (our ship name) could stay together.

We have had our ups and downs, which I think is to be expected for any "crazy rushed" relationship, but we worked on making it together and are now stronger than ever. I still question my sanity on occasion, as does Adam, but I also feel like miracles do happen. I found not only true friendship but also great love through taking a chance.

The *Supernatural* fandom is something that helped me through a time of great loneliness. With Adam in my life, I still love the fandom, but no longer rely on it to fill my time and quell my loneliness. I look forward to an exciting future together working on our own projects and having our own adventures.

If I have learned anything in my time in the *Supernatural* fandom, it is to embrace your passions, be proud of who you really are, and not let fear stop you from taking chances. You never know where it could lead!

THE ROAD SO FAR

LAURENA AKER, AKA "NIGHTSKY"

A s life-changing events go, *Supernatural*'s impact on my life may seem a bit ordinary. I wasn't pulled back from the brink of death, converted from a life of crime, or discovered by a Hollywood producer. Still, *Supernatural*'s effect on me has been profound, and it isn't only what happened but how it happened that is astonishing.

When I first discovered *Supernatural* in syndication, I was a stay-at-home mom, but it hadn't always been that way. For more than twenty years I had been a corporate executive who juggled the pressures of career and family with precision scheduling. Conference calls and international travel coexisted with soccer games and dance recitals . . . for a while. The stress fractures in my life slowly increased, until one day it became clear that I couldn't live two lives any longer. I ultimately made Sophie's choice and gave up one thing I loved, my career, in order to save the other thing I loved, my family. For the next ten years I was content and engaged with my new life, but I lived in a much smaller world than before. Where once I had interacted with people all over the globe, now everything I worried about pretty much took place within a twenty-mile radius of my home. My activities didn't require laptops or social media, so I fell way behind the technology curve. I didn't care about Facebook or Twitter, and I didn't have a smartphone or "apps." I expected that "someday" I would embark on a second career, but that was not yet a burning concern.

Supernatural began terraforming my world the moment I saw the back roads, Heaven-and-Hell conflict being fought by two striking young men who were dedicated to the concept of family. I eagerly awaited each day's reruns, but they were several seasons behind the prime-time version of the show and I was becoming increasingly impatient with the pace of network television. To accelerate my immersion, I did something inconceivable and unprecedented (at least for me): I bought the entire series on DVD and watched *Supernatural every night for months* until I caught up—130 episodes straight! Nothing had ever captured my imagination or *dedication* like this before.

When the binge marathon was over, I shifted my *Supernatural* obsession to the Internet. Imagine my relief when I learned that I wasn't alone in my passion for this show! A lot of *really smart* people were posting insightful examinations of plots and mythologies, cinematography and writing. Whereas I had originally been attracted to the show's complexity, I was now struck by a global following that was just as complex . . . and all interconnected somehow. Quite by accident, I had stumbled upon the vastly intricate *Supernatural* Family. Well, this was my show now, too, and I wanted *in*.

I enthusiastically embraced my new quest, but my outdated skills weren't up to the task of navigating the online realm, so I shed my stubborn resistance to the social-networking advancements that had taken place during my ten-year absence from the mainstream and taught myself how to use an iPad. I braved the unknown worlds of Apple, Twitter, and YouTube and investigated numerous websites, eventually finding the epicenters of the *Supernatural* fandom. It was a massive undertaking, and I accomplished so much so quickly, but the next rabbit hole was still ahead of me, just waiting for me to take one more step . . .

I learned about *Supernatural* conventions through my new online access to the SPNFamily. I was enticed by a chance to meet the show's cast, but being an online fan is completely different from going to a convention! Was I seriously considering becoming a pop-culture groupie? Internet browsing had allowed me to read about *Supernatural* from the anonymity of my living room. Going to a convention meant publicly admitting that I was fascinated with a television show! It was a completely unorthodox notion that would require a whole new level of commitment to this growing interest that I still did not completely understand. I was a traditional eldest child who had always done what was expected of me. I had never rebelled or hitchhiked or taken a summer off to go backpacking. I lived in a suburb with a family, a dog, and a white picket fence. I was scandalized at the crazy idea of going to a fan convention! No matter how hard I tried, though, I couldn't shake the magnetic pull of getting closer to the show that had ignited my life, so I took a deep breath and went all in . . . and bought tickets to my first *Supernatural* convention.

At this point I was sure of two things: I had absolutely lost my mind, and there was *no way* I was braving this adventure alone. Terrified by this countercultural lapse in judgment, I blindly contacted two people whose names were associated with websites I had come to admire, asking if they would be my lifelines during the convention. One was a professor and the other ran a review site. Surely with their positions they would be old enough for us to have something in common! They kindly agreed to try to meet me, yet despite that reassurance, when I arrived at the convention I nearly ran out the back door before registration even opened! I felt like a reserved, middle-aged interloper invading a world of young, uninhibited fans. I had come this far, though, so I nervously stood my ground.

This is where things start to get a little eerie. Amid the chaos of the convention, I managed to find one of the women I had hoped to meet. I apologetically introduced myself to the startled fan I had been frantically stalking all weekend. Her name was Lynn Zubernis (yes, the editor of this book!), whom I later learned was one of the most connected and prolific authors in the fandom. She was on her way to meet Alice Jester, the founder of The Winchester Family Business (The WFB) website, which I also discovered later was the largest review website dedicated to *Supernatural*. These were the people I had contacted! Out of the thousands of fans online, I had naively asked to meet two of the most active veterans of the fandom; then, out of the thousands of people at the convention, I met them together. As luck would have it, they were friends, and they asked me to join them for lunch. The ley lines for my new life had just

Part of the joy of a Supernatural con is the contagious laughter, usually started by Jared and Jensen having fun themselves. At ChiCon, September 2016.

been drawn, and no less than an act of God would intervene next to connect them.

Hurricane Sandy hit the East Coast of the United States on the last day of the convention, stranding Lynn in Chicago. Since hundreds of flights were canceled, the only hotel that still had vacancies was a seedy dive behind the airport. Lynn begged the *Supernatural* Family on Twitter to recommend better accommodations. I had only met her once, but she was desperate and "family don't end with blood," so I invited her to stay at my house. She enthusiastically accepted and we spent the next twenty-four hours touring the city, comparing notes about Jared and Jensen, and laughing until our sides hurt. Our day together was spontaneous and carefree. I had things I was supposed to be doing and she should have been on campus teaching classes, but there we were, discussing our love for *Supernatural* and just having *fun*. It was exhilarating and eye-opening. We became dear friends overnight.

Lynn eventually made it home, and I was left trying to understand the overwhelming experiences of my astonishing weekend. As the convention audience expanded with each successive day, I became increasingly more comfortable with the people who had spent their time and money celebrating a wonderful thing in their life called *Supernatural*. I witnessed scenes of fellowship, happiness, personal triumph, and compassion. Since I knew virtually no one at the convention, Alice took me to dinner with The Winchester Family Business writing staff (which was both intimidating and amazing!). The convention also gave me the euphoric experience of talking to the two actors who are the heart and soul of *Supernatural*, Jared and Jensen (which was utterly mind-blowing!).

The post-convention shock wave that hit me was much more than these individual moments, though. Words kept flowing through my mind to try to express the pure *joy* that I had seen and felt. The words became phrases; phrases became sentences; sentences became paragraphs. Night and day, these thoughts wouldn't let me rest. I *had* to write them down.

When I finished recording my experience of stepping through the looking glass, I shared it with my two new *Supernatural* comrades, Lynn and Alice. To my surprise, Alice liked my account of entering fandom enough to ask if she could publish it. I was thrilled by her reaction, but still much too embarrassed to admit my newfound obsession, so I tentatively agreed under the condition that I remain anonymous. I assumed my Twitter identity, "Nightsky," and a new chapter in my life began. My excitement the day my story was posted on her website was nothing less than what Pulitzer Prize winners must feel when they receive their award. I was unabashedly over the moon, elated by yet another completely unexpected adventure.

After that brief encounter with fame, my life slowly regained some semblance of normalcy . . . except now *Supernatural* and its fandom were firmly entrenched in my routines. It was three months before the urge to write struck again. I was driven to capture my thoughts about the current season of the show, and again I sent my observations to Alice, who graciously posted them on her website. I was catatonically nervous, hoping to receive at least one comment so I wouldn't be publicly humiliated by a complete lack of interest in my essay. After all, I wasn't a television critic. Why would people care what a new and virtually unqualified fan had to say? I didn't have to wait long before the first comment was posted, though. Soon more comments were posted, then more, and more. When it was all over, there were nearly 450 comments and the article had been read by 22,000 people in the first few weeks alone, far more than usual! I didn't understand what was happening but I remember thinking that something was starting. I was being sent a clear and unmistakable message that I should do this again.

I occasionally wrote about *Supernatural* in the following weeks, and each time Alice published my work. The last few articles convinced Alice that I had something to say, so she asked me to join her writing staff—an honor that required a commitment of writing a review every week. I was positive I didn't have *that much* to say and I was equally sure I wasn't capable of writing on demand! I had written because I felt compelled to express what I was feeling, not to play a more active role in the show's following. Still, thus far *Supernatural* had been tremendously good to me: new friends, the overwhelming response to my first article, and now a shocking invitation to be on the inside of it all. It sounds odd, but I sensed that I should follow wherever this show took me. I accepted the offer and began writing for The Winchester Family Business.

Then, only three weeks after I embarked on this new venture, the most extraordinary thing happened. I had just posted my third weekly article. It was an open letter to Jared in which I praised him for his performance in the season 8 finale, "Sacrifice." His wife, Genevieve, saw the letter and tweeted me, saying, "@Jarpad and I thank you. This is very special." Of course, I didn't see the tweet. I didn't consider myself to be of any consequence in the public eye. I had very few followers on Twitter and I could count on one hand the number of tweets I had sent, so I wasn't expecting anyone to tweet me, let alone Genevieve Padalecki! Alice sent me a very understated email that simply said, "Have you seen the tweet from Genevieve?" You know that feeling when the world goes into slow motion? Your mind stops being able to comprehend words. Your voice doesn't come out of your mouth, despite your jaw hanging open, allowing air to escape from your lungs. My hands were trembling and I no longer knew right from left, so it was impossible to type a response in a social medium with which I was barely familiar while my mind was still frozen on the thought that Genevieve and Jared liked my letter. *They read my letter.*

My Twitter account exploded. Everyone was trying to find out who I was, what Genevieve had read, and how they could get a copy of it. Links to the article were flying back and forth. The WFB website crashed with the barrage of hits that came at it out of the blue. I had only been on staff for *three weeks* and I had crashed the site! What was happening to my life? If I had thought the hurricane, the staggering response to my editorial, and the surprising offer to be on a writing staff were signs that I should trust where *Supernatural* was taking me, then these few days were the ensuing tsunami washing away all traces of my former existence, rebuilding my life from the ground up. The website had crumbled, and I couldn't ignore the symbolic irony that the same thing was happening to me.

Unbelievably, five months later, on Halloween of 2013, I received the following message:

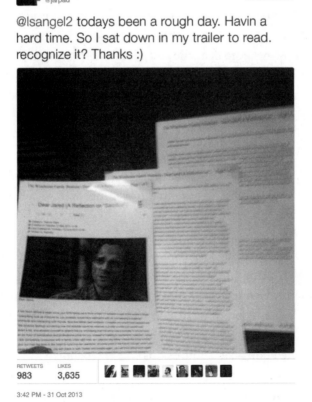

Jared had tweeted me. Personally. *My writing* had helped *him*. One of the stars who makes *Supernatural* and inspires hope, strength, and goodness in a worldwide family was helped by my writing. My mind went blank as my hands managed to type a reply. This straitlaced, overachieving career woman jumped out of her chair and ran around the house screaming. Over 100,000 people have now read that little letter I wrote to Jared.

If you're keeping track, so far I had stumbled into a serendipitous luncheon, been detoured by a hurricane, been possessed by a writing muse, caused a website to crash, and received personal encouragement from *both* Genevieve and Jared. I wasn't receiving signs; I was being hit over the head with anvils.

I spent the next six months cranking out weekly reviews. I learned more about online posting, the entertainment industry, and writing. Then, to notch it up one step further, both of The Winchester Family Business site administrators quit at virtually the same time and I was asked to become the managing editor of the site. It meant a much larger commitment to learning, well, everything, and more time than I truly had to offer, but I now believed that the cascading events were not mere coincidences. I said yes.

Lynn and I had stayed friends throughout this whole ride. She had encouraged and guided me through emails, but we had only seen each other once since our first meeting (at the next Chicago *Supernatural* convention, of course). It was now April 2014 and she was back in Chicago for an academic conference where she was launching her third book, *Fan Phenomena: Supernatural*. We wanted to get together, so she asked me to meet her at the conference. While waiting for her, I struck up a conversation with her publisher, who was displaying the entire *Fan Phenomena* series of books. I casually commented that one pop culture phenomenon seemed to be missing from their collection. The publisher acknowledged this gap, then offhandedly asked me if I would like to submit a proposal for that book. Come on now. Really? I was just a visitor passing the time with small talk! When I thought about it, though, in my managing editor role I had edited both staff submissions and independent fan fiction. I had a year of online publications to my credit and I understood the popular culture phenomenon called the SPNFamily. I had project management expertise from my corporate days and I had extensive experience in business writing, research, and marketing. I considered his offer and decided that this was another one of those miraculous moments. I was completely out of my element with the academic publishing process, but I sent him my proposal a few months later. To my amazement, they accepted my vision for the book over all the other proposals that were submitted. My first book, *Fan Phenomena: The Twilight Saga*, was published two years later.

How did all this happen? I don't think it was an accident that I found that *Supernatural* episode one morning. I rarely watched TV while I was working at home. I had never before, nor since, chosen to watch a horror show (I don't like scary things!). Even though I have been a science-fiction fan since the original *Star Trek* series, I never had any desire to become a member of a fandom, go to a convention, or write about a show. Despite having a leadership position in a management and technology consulting firm, I had never embraced technology as an integral part of my life. I had written volumes of marketing and business communications, but I had never considered the possibility of pursuing a career as an author. I now have a published book about *Twilight*, one of the largest pop culture series of our time; I'm a managing editor and social media manager for a prominent *Supernatural* website; I'm writing a chapter in a book about *Supernatural*; and the chapters of my second book are invading my thoughts. It won't be long before I have to write those down, too.

I also don't think it was an accident that two very young men named Jared and Jensen were thrown together into an audition for *Supernatural*. The two actors had never met, yet they had an instant chemistry, both personally and on camera. They would become lifelong friends and develop a rare professional bond that has become the cornerstone of a global franchise and "family." By all reasonable expectations, both the show they piloted and the struggling network that sponsored it should have disappeared into obscurity. Instead, *Supernatural* boldly exemplified the very best in risk taking, storytelling, and connecting with fans; reached a twelve-year milestone that is reserved for only the legends of the industry; and became a worldwide phenomenon that has changed millions of lives—and there's no sign of it stopping anytime soon.

"Nightsky" and Lynn in a squish hug with Jared and Jensen, September 2016, at ChiCon. Yes, I've come a long way since my first con!

The respect, dedication, and love that Jared and Jensen have for each other, the show they create, the people with whom they work, and the fans who love them has had a ripple effect of goodness in the world. I believe it is more than inspiration. In the real fight between good and evil, between complacency and action, between being ignored and being loved, between apathy and passion, between fear and courage, something dropped these two young men together into the ocean of the universe, generating waves of miracles that are radiating outward across the globe.

How has *Supernatural* changed me? Like so many others, it unleashed my creativity. A person who had lived each day with scheduled precision is now a writer, intuitively following inspiration. I've always accepted the unknown as being what was meant to be, but I never would have imagined this future for me.

In my first convention report, when these marvels were just beginning, I confessed that I wanted to work for Jared. I recognized the amazing effect he was having on the world, and I wanted to apply my talents and experience to help him extend his reach. I don't know; maybe, in a small way, that is exactly what I've ended up doing (or is that still in my future?).

I have no idea where this road might lead, but I've learned to trust wherever *Supernatural* takes me. It might be fate, God, angels, the universe, goodness, or just luck guiding me, but I know for a fact that *Supernatural* changes lives. I know because it absolutely changed mine.

WAYWARD AF

KIM RHODES

The first time I walked out onto a *Supernatural* convention stage, I was pretty sure I was on the wrong side of the equation. I was a fan. I was not an object of fandom. Pretty damn sure. I expected someone to tap me on the shoulder at any moment and say, "I'm sorry, ma'am, could you step this way? Those snacks are reserved for the talent. Who let you in here? And how did you end up with a microphone in your hand?"

I was born wanting a microphone in my hand. I needed to be heard. Hell, I just *needed*. That pretty much defines my memories as a child. Needing to be heard and needing to be something I wasn't. When I discovered things I could be a fan of, some of that lifted for a short while. I could watch *Wonder Woman*, then spend hours in the backyard with the cape my mother had knitted for me, trying to lasso the dog with my string lariat and force him to tell me the truth so I could save Lyle Waggoner. I still adore Lynda Carter for what she gave my tender young self. I may have not had a voice of my own, but I could borrow hers for a while. It gave me comfort and strength.

Then I got a little older, and my comfort in idolatry turned to despair. I realized I *wasn't enough*! That's why nobody wanted to hear me. Or play with me. Or put up with me. It had nothing to do with me being a bossy, selfish, and insufferable child. It was because I lacked what "they" had. The world became full of "they" and "them" and "those" and they were all on the winning side. I was on the side populated with home perms and hand-me-down training bras stuffed with socks. We were *not* the winners.

I tried so many ways to find a voice that would be deemed acceptable. I flirted with the popular boys and ignored their derision. I let people with criminally low IQs cheat off my papers so they'd quit pretending they didn't know me in the cafeteria. I stole money from my mom to buy kids candy. I got mad as hell and started wearing black lipstick, writing realllllllllly indulgent poetry and, I am not lying about this, even cut myself and drew a goddamn self-portrait with my blood. I was not a happy camper. Furthermore, I didn't know if anybody was listening or not at this point: because I was so desperate for something to be the magical bean that grew the stalk I could climb to a different life, I wasn't listening to anyone else. (God, my poor mom. She loved me so much. Must have destroyed her to see me so miserable.)

GOOD FUCKING TIMES!

In utter and complete despair, I became an actor. I thought maybe if I could put on *other* faces and voices and use words that had previously been approved, I might find some sense of worth. Plus, people had to clap for me. It was a rule. You have to clap after a play, so neener neener, you have to clap for me if I get into that play somehow.

It started to work. The soul will find a way out. Slowly but surely, I began feeling a part of something. It wasn't humanity yet. It wasn't a sense of acceptance yet. But I discovered a way to be of service, if not to myself, then to a story. To something bigger than me. I found a sense of ease and fun. I found a little self-worth and I gained some approval. I became a functional human, by all accounts. I still associated it with the characters I wore, believing my own truth and voice could never be met with accolades. Still, I was content to be the voice of others.

This was my state of mind when I arrived at *Supernatural* in 2010. I had made peace with my various masks, learning to mold them from bits of myself rather than grasping wildly at characteristics completely foreign to me. I had even learned to allow myself the luxury of laughter and including joy in performances. My acting was pretty mature. My life as an actor, however, was about to blow the hell open. I had no idea.

I stepped onstage at my first convention and realized I had no lines. I had no script. I had nothing but my own voice, dusty and rusty with lack of use. I didn't know what was expected of me. I didn't know what people wanted. I was *certain* it couldn't be me. But that's all I had to offer. So, by miracle, grace, insanity, or just utter bloody-mindedness, I did. I offered myself with as much honesty as I could muster through the bone-quaking fear. Honesty was not a practiced skill for someone who was as frightened as I was. Honesty, I thought, was for people who knew they were good enough. Honesty was for "them." But I gave it a shot.

No one threw anything. And some people clapped. Some even told me they saw my truth and felt it was theirs as well.

Well, *that* was unexpected.

I was fascinated. I was doing exactly the opposite of what I thought I needed to do to be heard and seen and loved and met with "Yes!" and here everyone seemed to be saying . . . "Yes!" So I kept trying. I am still trying. I offer a unique perspective that has shaped the character of Jody Mills. I offer the unique experience of my life and views when I interact with fans. But what I *receive* is priceless.

I have begun to feel the way I always imagined "they" feel. I feel good and worthy. I feel that I can speak my beliefs and release any need to define how they are received. I feel strong. I still feel terrified, but I can meet that terror with truth. The truth is, I showed a bunch of strangers the broken, fragile, cussing, awkward, overly energetic creature that is my heart, and they said "Yes!" and quit being strangers. I found the identity I had been searching for. It turned out to be me.

And that's when I wrap life up in a neat bow and put it on the shelf, right?

Life had other plans.

Finding "me" was just the start. It was the "suit up and show up" part. Life wanted me to stretch. Life wanted me to grow. Life apparently wanted me to learn this stuff just so I could share how it's done with others

who deserve to feel it too. The *Supernatural* arena is where it happened, because I sure as hell couldn't do that alone.

See, my head is still my head. It is not a place anyone would want to be in by themselves. Here there be dragons, trust me. Fortunately, a Higher Power or a Fate or unbelievable luck handed me a partner, and suddenly one plus one equaled Fourth of July sparklers.

Briana Buckmaster is the teacher who came when the student was ready. Full of gunpowder and lollipops, she announced herself as thoroughly on my team from the first moment we met. Here's the thing: as confident and affirmed as I may have become, I didn't have a "team." My comfort was being solo, though the fandom had already nestled into my heart enough to threaten that a bit. I have a husband, a child, a sister, and two best friends . . . yep, I'm good, thanks!

But here was this shining spirit proclaiming that, yes, I had changed, but now how about we change the world? How about we offer others what we have found here? How about we create a space for EVERYONE to play and expand and feel supported and we do that by making it ourselves? Whaddya say?

That's just crazy talk. Get off my lawn.

But the "me" I had found had a heart that grew three sizes that day. My friend Briana gives me courage to shout my truth and not just whisper it. She has strengths where I have weaknesses and because of the love we share, that gives me solace rather than jealousy. I got to know the me I was through the fandom, and now I am becoming the me I want to be because of the entire *Supernatural* experience. And I've chosen to make this journey public, because it is a loving offering to everyone. I'm finding the core of it is truth.

I think it's easy to look at someone onstage and let the umbrella of their image or persona overwhelm who they are as a person. What's more, when that person is you, it's easy to believe you're SUPPOSED to be that image. So Briana and I have made a conscious commitment to honesty. That's where the Wayward came from. We are on our own path of loving each other and loving ourselves. In this world, we are told that's not done. It is somehow disrespectful or dangerous to the status quo.

Know what? We think the status quo can make people pretty miserable.

It took a friend and the fandom for me to take the first step of, "Yes, here I am," and now the second step of, "I'm learning to love it, I invite you to as well." Briana and I are no different than you are. We are perfect in our imperfections. We are striving to improve through our mistakes. We are growing and learning and the strength we have in each other is available to every human on this planet. Embrace truth and love it. It can heal and conquer everything. Each unique voice singing the same song can change the world.

Maybe you're reading this and shaking your head. You hurt too much. I can't possibly understand, you think. You are too by yourself and too broken and too afraid and too sure I don't actually speak from experience.

I want to hold you and kiss the top of your head. I want to make silly jokes and make you laugh through your tears. I want to show you the stupid scars on my wrist and tell you of the *ridiculous* things I did when I felt the same way. But I can't. So I wrote this so you will know I know. And the pain I feel is delicious and worth every tear I shed, because it is the price I pay for finding my voice, as I know you will as well.

I have walked that walk. And I show you my blisters and my map so you can, too. You are loved. You are worthy. I am eternally grateful to you.

WAYWARD DAUGHTERS

http://waywarddaughtersacademy.tumblr.com

Wayward Daughters is a fan-led movement that sprouted from the *Supernatural* fandom in May of 2015. In the episode "Angel Heart," when Claire was sent off to live with Jody and Alex, the line "What is this, some sort of halfway house for wayward teenage girls?" struck a chord with the fandom. After the success of "Hibbing 911"—Kim Rhodes and Briana Buckmaster's runaway hit episode—it became clear that was exactly what the fans wanted to see: a spin-off starring Jody, Donna, Alex, and Claire.

Kim Rhodes replied to fans Riley Keshner and Betty Days's enthusiasm with helpful advice: TPTB (The Powers That Be) would need to see the interest behind the idea in order to consider it. The fandom definitely had the interest—they just didn't have any organization. Thus "Wayward Daughters"—a bid for a female-led *Supernatural* spin-off—was born. Social media pages and a petition were created to channel the fandom's disparate voices through a central outlet. The fans wanted better female representation on the show—they wanted their ladies not only to stick around longer but also to have more depth and be involved in better relationships with other women. What Riley and Betty didn't realize at first was that the fans didn't just want to see those positive relationships on *Supernatural*; they wanted to embody them in real life.

Fandom, like any group, can sometimes be divisive and catty. Thanks in large part to Kim and Briana's example, Wayward Daughters fans tossed that drama out the window. The Wayward community came to be a place where fans could meet like-minded, similarly offbeat (wayward) people and express themselves freely without judgment. (The WaywardAF line of clothing, also inspired by the Wayward movement, gives voice to that self-expression and empowerment.)

Through the advent of fund-raising campaigns and service projects, the community grew and evolved into something none of its organizers expected, and before long, Wayward Daughters had become an empowering force for social good. The campaign and movement eventually garnered enough interest to warrant its own *Supernatural* episode (season 11's "Don't You Forget About Me," nicknamed the "Wayward Daughters episode"). But above and beyond that, WD fans have raised thousands of dollars for charity, helped Random Acts in building a free high school in Nicaragua, and grown to be more loving toward themselves—and one another.

Content contributed by Riley Keshner and Betty Days

First-ever Wayward group photo op.

I AM YOU

BRIANA BUCKMASTER

What's a convention?" I asked, sitting in my chair while I waited for the crew to do their turnaround. Kim Rhodes sat next to me. We both had our cozy coats on and our daily 3 P.M. cookie-with-coffee. We were about halfway through shooting "Hibbing 911" and I was pretty sure I was in love with this woman, so I hung on her every word.

"Oh. *Oh.* Just you wait. They're *amazing.* You'll totally be invited."

"REALLY??!!" I said as I adjusted my drooping gun belt so I wouldn't have to buy it breakfast in the morning.

Kim then proceeded to fill me in on what sounded like all my dreams coming true. A stage. A microphone. A willing audience. *And karaoke.*

When a person decides to become an actor, there can be a little voice inside her head that tells her she is trite. Vain. Perhaps slightly useless. It's confusing to follow your passion and yet still feel like you have something more in you to give. A piece of you that's not being fulfilled. I had reached the age where, as a woman, you are taught to start settling for what life hands you. And then I got Sheriff Donna.

The role of Donna Hanscum was everything I could have dreamed of. From the beginning, she was a real woman: complex, with her light

disposition but also her sadness and low sense of self. And the best part is, because I am playing this role and a part of this show, I'm honored with a platform from which to talk to others who've experienced what Donna did. What I did. I can be of service! Something I never thought I would be able to be.

I grew up on a farm outside of a small town in Saskatchewan. I didn't have cable or satellite. But I had a fireplace bench that very closely resembled a stage. So I was constantly performing. My parents were farmers and, while they didn't dissuade me from pursuing my dreams, they were not huge influences in what would be my biggest passion in life. I had older twin brothers (to whom I credit my high threshold for J2 shenanigans), and most of our days were filled with things such as bale jumping, rock picking, and cornfield mazes. Sounds pretty picturesque, doesn't it? It was, for the most part, but the schools weren't great and my father was losing his eyesight due to a brain tumor he'd had most of his life. So we had to make some changes.

We moved to the city, where life was very different. Kids spoke to one another differently; they treated one another differently. Girls really wanted to wear the "right" clothes, and I had no idea what those were. To say I was bullied is a massive understatement. I was always much heavier than other girls my age. My family didn't have the resources to live in a nice house or buy nice clothes. Often I wore my brothers' hand-me-downs. Discovering that I didn't fit in, I went inside myself and became an introvert. "Shy and quiet" was the phrase often used to describe me (if you can believe it). I thought, *If they can't hear me, they can't make fun of me.* It didn't quite work.

That lasted until high school, when I made the new realization that if they were going to laugh at me I would make them laugh *with* me first. That was the beginning of finding the real me. She just needed to figure out what it was she wanted to say.

Fast-forward some more. When I was in my second year of theater school, I worked really hard and lost a substantial amount of weight (pretty much to the size I am now). This is what I like to call the shedding of the skin. I still wasn't what would be considered thin by Hollywood's standards, but I was being seen. Like, *actually seen.* People looked me in the eye, and they listened when I spoke. So I strived to make sure the things I was saying were thoughtful. Not perfect, but actually things I meant. And I made sure that I saw everyone, no matter his or her size. Fast-forward to SPN conventions. Whether I am speaking with the fandom from the stage, during a meet-and-greet, or while just passing by to go to the loo, I try to make sure I am hearing them. Seeing them. Because really I am one of them. *I was you, I am you, and I aspire to be just like you.*

Sheriff Donna, as many people know, was only supposed to be a teeny-tiny one-off character, a lighthearted woman with a broken sense of self. The audition sides were such fun to me that I couldn't wait to get in the audition room. That's not very common for actors. Phil Sgriccia was in there and had a few notes for me based on my first audition. He made it very clear that the accent was important. Since I'm from midwestern Canada, the dialect was directly in my wheelhouse. I did the audition and then we spent a few minutes talking about football. I think that miniscule exchange gave both of us a good feel of what it would be like to work together. I like to think it solidified my winning the role. Go Riders!

My first day on set was thrilling and terrifying. I'd only been doing TV for about six months prior to my first episode. Most of my acting training and experience is in theater and comedy. So I was very well behaved on set. I didn't want to fuck up, and when people said things like "I need you to hit your original marks" or "First team coming in!" I had no fucking clue what they were saying. I would ask once and remember forever. I was in no position to waste professionals' time. The first person I met was Jensen. He was everything I imagined he would be: funny, gentlemanly, and handsome as all hell. When I met Jared the first thing I thought was, "Holy shit, he's tall." The second thing I thought was, "How does anyone get any work done with these two in the room?"

As we dove into first-team rehearsal for the now-infamous doughnut scene, they called "Action!" and I dug my chompers into that doughnut like my life depended on it. When they yelled "Cut!" the crew burst out laughing, and the boys looked at me, saying, "Wow. You really went for it." I thought I was in trouble and had made a big mistake, but it was actually the opposite. Like I said, I don't mess around.

Filming the last day of that episode with the boys was magical. We laughed more than I had laughed in a long time and the boys at one point looked at me and said, "We're stealing you away to Los Angeles to make you famous." What more can an actor ask for? Phil had mentioned to me the idea of bringing me back. But in my fifteen-year career I had heard such words uttered more times than I cared to remember, so I

wasn't holding my breath. But look at Donna now—a full-fledged hunter. I know I have Phil, the boys, and the fans to thank for that. And thank them I will, for the rest of my life.

The magic that has come into my life because of this beautiful, simple, and yet complex character is hard to describe in just a handful of words. One afternoon in an audition has completely changed my life forever. And it almost directly coincided with the birth of my daughter, so the probability that there was some kind of lunar shift is highly likely. If that sounds hippy-dippy to you, I don't blame you. But COOOOME OOOOON. Three seasons later I'm now completely entrenched in the SPNFamily. The actors who regularly attend the cons have become some of my best friends, and I'm slowly getting to know more and more of the fans through our brief but substantial encounters. Every word they say to me affects me, teaches me, and becomes a part of me. Meeting all these people has been the most incredible experience of my life. Every day I count my lucky stars that I have had the honor bestowed upon me to be a part of the SPNFamily.

FEEL WHAT
I FEEL, SEE
WHAT I SEE

KIM PRIOR

I came to *Supernatural* knowing how to be a fan. After all, I'd spent the last twenty-plus years in the oldest fandom in the history of fandoms: Parenthood. As a mother, I have fangirled for my children from the very start, from saving art pieces drawn by tiny hands, to sitting at soccer games, to saving my pennies—literally, pennies—to buy gaming systems and new clothes and new shoes and tickets to concerts and, oh yes, taking more than a few pictures along the way. Little did I know that the *Supernatural* fandom would be so similar, from fangirling over—well, everything—to fanart, to taking pictures, to saving pennies for conventions.

Twenty-plus years in Parenthood, and then the day finally came: the day when my youngest child was about to graduate from high school, soon to leave home for college. While I would always be a member of Parenthood, it was going to be in a different way from then on. The thought of being an empty nester brought all those ugly feelings of shame I'd battled

73

for the past twenty years to the surface again: the shame of being a stay-at-home mom. What would I do now that they were gone? What *could* I do? I'd been a stay-at-home mom for over *twenty* years. I was just a mom, just a soccer mom, just a mom with a camera taking pictures of all the things my kids did, a part-time videographer of team highlights. Although I did have a college degree, I knew I didn't have any actual skills. I had done a fair amount of volunteer work, but I didn't have any actual work experience. Realizing that I was about to become a stay-at-home mom with no kids living at home, it hit me hard that I had nothing to offer to anyone. And I began to think that maybe I never had.

A television show changed that.

I initially started watching *Supernatural* with my son a few years before his graduation. I was drawn in by its strong element of family, and I knew I'd continue to watch it even after he left for college. Though I'd been watching the show since 2012, it wasn't until the 2013 season when some sort of divine intervention guided me to the SPNFamily, showing me this online community of support, something I would need as my son's graduation approached.

I sat quietly in the shadows at first, observing and learning the way this fandom worked. I soon discovered common elements between this new fandom and the Parenthood fandom with which I was so familiar. Both are wonderfully diverse. We are soccer moms, band moms, working moms, and stay-at-home moms. Moms who cook and moms who don't. Young moms and grandma moms. Biological moms and adoptive moms. We are Mary Winchester, who cuts off the crusts on the sandwich, makes pies, and whispers to our children as they fall asleep, "Angels are watching over you." We are Ellen Harvelle, willing to give our lives for the sake of our children, praying that we will be by their side when our children pass through the veil. We are Jody Mills, stepping up to be the parent to all the wayward kids who come our way.

We are also dads who coach, dads who never miss a game or a recital. Dads who change diapers and dads who teach their kids how to ride a bike and drive a car. Dads who painstakingly teach their sons how to tie a perfect knot in their tie. We are John Winchester, just doing the best we can for our children. And we cannot overlook the Bobbys in both of these fandoms either: the honorary parents, the stepparents, the not-so-biological parents, the parents who step in and step up and never, ever, let our children down. Kudos to all of the Bobbys in this world, who personify one of the greatest lines of the show: "Family don't end with blood."

Another common element between these two fandoms is the concept of fangirling. In Parenthood, we share our thoughts on pediatricians and teachers and hot new toys just like the SPNFamily shares their thoughts on the cast, the characters, and the episodes. In both fandoms, we share funny stories, weird stories, pictures and memes, hospital trips, deaths, and sometimes we just share that we are having a rough day . . . which leads us to sharing love and hugs and prayers, gifs and more pictures.

In both fandoms, we celebrate together. We rejoice together. We excitedly share with one another new pictures and new stories. We applaud the achievements, whether a child's first steps or first date, or a first time in the director's chair or perfectly played photo op. We celebrate birthdays, the ones we knew you would have and the ones we prayed you would see; we trend birthdays too, with #HappyBirthdaySam or #HappyBirthday-Jensen or #HappyBirthdayJJ. We are together for the highs, like kindergarten graduations and weddings, like "The French Mistake" and "Fan Fiction." Hugs? We have those in both fandoms, too. Big, squishy, mishy hugs at airports upon seeing your child return home safely from deployment, or the equally emotional hug at the end of "Mystery Spot," when Sam realizes Dean won't die yet another time.

Unfortunately, as any member of either Parenthood or the SPNFamily will tell you, it isn't always about happiness and joy. In both fandoms, we experience disappointment and sadness, too. We have learned to lean upon one another during the tough times, like stitches or broken arms or broken hearts . . . like Hell or Purgatory or "Bloodlines." We support one another, with prayers and hugs during the rounds and rounds of tests or diagnoses or meds, or with prayers and hugs during the bloody fight scenes or the trials or the season finales. We carry one another through the lows, like lost championships or fights with a best friend, like "Heart" or "Swan Song." We comfort one another at tear-filled funerals that came too soon . . . in real life, or for Bobby, or Kevin, or Charlie.

As I came to know this SPNFamily, I began to see one common thread over and over and over again. We are all incredibly, painfully human. We all have issues. It doesn't matter what your issue is; the point is that we all have them. While there is a measure of support for one another within Parenthood, it doesn't quite compare to the unconditional love and support of one another within the SPNFamily.

I also began to see more and more "fanart" on Twitter. This was something that piqued my own creative interests as a longtime photographer of my kids. I did a bit of digging into the subject: How are people doing this art, through what mediums, what are the restrictions and limitations? I did what any good fan would do, and I contacted Jules at Super-Wiki. I cannot say this plainly enough—Jules not only encouraged me to dive into the fanart arena, but she also breathed life into me. I didn't know where my fanart experimentation would lead, if it would even lead anywhere, but I knew that I had found something that would allow me to continue with my own creative interests now that my children were gone. (The people I've met in this fandom, the friends I've made—they have all played a part in that divine intervention I mentioned, they have all played a role in helping me find my way as a new empty nester—but I will be forever grateful to Jules, for her kind words of support and encouragement.)

As I combined these things—realizing that everyone has issues, then adding my years of experience with photography and editing, then realizing that I could do my own piece of fanart . . . and *Demons* began to take shape.

The words had been floating inside my head for weeks. I needed to get them on paper, to share them with others, somehow, some way. So one day in late May of 2014, I sat down at my computer and I poured it all out. The words flowed easily, as did my own tears. The artwork wasn't as easy, but I did my best. After several days of thought and rethought and more overthinking, I finally let it fly. I posted it on Twitter.

Demons remains out there, in cyberspace. It still shows up on my Twitter timeline. Some person, someone I don't even know, will tweet it, saying it is a reminder for him/her that there is always hope. I never dreamed it would touch so many people. I'm no artist, not like Petite-Madame or

Demons are Everywhere

Abuse - Addiction - Anxiety
Depression - Disease - Failure - Fear
Heartbreak - Jealousy - Madness
Neglect - Pain - Racism
Sadness - Self-loathing - Violence

Then two brothers came along...

Teaching us how to Fight.
Teaching us how to Survive.
Teaching us how to move past
the Apocalypse that is our Lives.
Teaching us to be Proud of Us.

They Give Us Hope.

Written & Illustrated by
@MamaPrior
kpedits~   © 2014
Revised 2015

Denise Ferragamo or Anne Kirn or Kaiya or Sherri or too many others to name—they are *artists*. But if I can pull a photo into Photoshop, artsy-fi it, and add a phrase to it—and if that photo makes just one person smile, helps just one person make it through a rough day, gives just one person a reason to crawl out of bed, drives just one person to #AlwaysKeepFighting . . . well, that's what matters. And that makes me wonder: Maybe I do have something to offer? Maybe I can soothe someone's pain, be someone's friend? In the grand scheme of life, isn't that what it's all about—helping each other, lifting up one another?

I have been practicing my art—photography, videography, and editing—for more than twenty years. I have taken thousands upon thousands of pictures, spent thousands upon thousands of hours processing pictures, learning Photoshop, learning new techniques in both shooting and editing. I understood long ago that I have the ability to let go, to drown out the white noise of the cheering crowds, to twist and turn and stretch and lean without actually moving an inch, to allow the moment playing inside my viewfinder to consume me, and yet remain acutely aware of my surroundings. I have found that I can walk the delicate line between enjoying the moment as it happens and maintaining a calm-focus-on-the-moment-so-as-not-to-miss-the-shot. I have learned how to "play" through the pain, whether it's a migraine or a broken arm. I have learned to tune in to my instincts, allowing myself to literally feel the moment coming—and then when the moment hits, and I click the button, and in that split second I've captured a moment that everyone can *feel*: joy, excitement, pain, sorrow. I have filled the frame with my own breath, slow and measured, patiently anticipating that one shot, that one shot that is so clear, so technically right, so full of emotion.

Sometimes I allow myself to dream of seeing one of my shots as a poster adorning bedroom walls and office cubicles all over the world. Sometimes I even dream I'll take a photo good enough that maybe Rob would use it as his next Louden Swain cover art, or maybe Jared would use it as his Twitter avi, or maybe Jensen would use it as his Facebook profile pic. I do not say that in vanity, "Oh, hey, look at the great thing I did," but rather as an acknowledgment that all my years of being "just" a mom with a camera was actually time well spent and not something to be ashamed of. Maybe, just maybe, the cast and the fandom understand what I intend to do every time I pick up my camera—I want to share and savor this moment together, I want you to feel what I feel, see what I see.

Many years ago, a woman who was not a member of Parenthood asked me this question: What do you *do* all day? The disgust and the judgment in the tone of her voice cut me to the very depths of my soul. She judged me for being a stay-at-home mom, judged me for not having a "real" job, judged me for what she assumed was sitting on my ass all day doing nothing, judged me for basking in the joy of Parenthood. I chose to be a stay-at-home mom, believing that dedicating my life to my husband and my children would be a wonderful thing. But with one question, with just six words, that woman poured such shame onto me, a shame that I have carried upon my shoulders and in my heart to this day.

Jensen, Vegas Con 2015

Jared, VanCon 2016

Rob, JaxCon 2016

Jensen, JaxCon 2016

On every form that came home from school, every form at the doctor's office, every form in buying a new car or a new home, on every friggin' form, there is that line: "Employer." Every time I couldn't fill in that line, I felt that shame all over again. With every new person I met there was that moment of shame and judgment when he/she asked me what I did for a living, and the only answer I could give was "nothing." Six little words and years of judgmental looks had taught me that I was a lame, pathetic, unproductive person.

Staring at my newest path, as an empty nester, I struggled with knowing how much more pathetic and unproductive I would become. I wondered how I could ever feel useful again.

Until I met the SPNFamily.

How has this show, this cast, this fandom, this family impacted me? Although I am a proud member of Parenthood, although I love my kids and my husband to the moon and back, I have never, not ever, felt as accepted and valued and validated as I do right now. Am I a gifted artist? No way. Am I a great photographer? Certainly not. But this show, and this cast, and this fandom, and this family—you support me, and encourage me, and believe in me anyway. The SPNFamily appreciates me for my little bit of talent, in ways that no one else ever has. It is because of this show, this cast, this fandom, and this family that—for the first time in my life—I can say out loud that I am a photographer, an artist, and it is actually okay.

So many of us take the exact same shot at the exact same time. My posts may not have thousands, maybe not even hundreds, of favs or RTs or shares, but that's okay. Some of my real "omg" moments come when Matt, or Kim, or Briana, or Ruth, or anyone from the show favs or retweets one of my photos . . . and when Gil uses one of my photos as his profile pic, well, that's a joy that carries me through my darker days. But it is because of this SPNFamily that I even have the courage to put my photos and my fanart out there publicly. It is because of this show, this cast, this fandom, and this family that I actually feel—oh, what's the word?—*self-confident* when I post a new photo. And you know what else? Sometimes, I can look in the mirror and not see the shame. Sometimes I can look in the mirror and I can see the years of preparedness joining forces with opportunity, and suddenly there is an artist reflecting back at me. Because of this show, this cast, this fandom, and this family, I can begin to heal the years of shame. I can perhaps hold my head a little higher. I can say with pride that I Am a Mom—and I am the luckiest person in the world.

Jensen, NashCon 2016

CONVENTION PHOTOGRAPHY: KIM TALKS THE BASICS

One: Know your equipment. Cell phones and point-and-shoot cameras have very limited abilities within a convention setting. Even a great DSLR camera has limitations. Read your manual. Know the buttons on your camera, know what each one does, and know that each little variation can drastically change your picture.

Two: Where you sit within the hall matters. Your cell phone may take a great group selfie at lunch, outside, in the bright afternoon sunshine, but that same cell phone will not capture the changing color of Jared's eyes as he moves under the lights if you are sitting any farther back than the first two or three rows of Gold. If you have a DSLR but you don't have a great lens, you probably won't see those subtle changes of color with any sort of clarity.

*Jared, ChiCon 2014, shot from Gold Row L with a
Canon Rebel XTi using a 70-300 mm lens.*

Three: Know your purpose for taking pictures at a convention. If you just want to snap a few pics to show you were there, then any camera will suffice. And you can sit in any seat. However, if you want to see Jensen's freckles in detail, then using your cell phone or point-and-shoot camera from Row S won't give you what you want. Make sure your level of expectation matches both your equipment and your seat.

Left: Jared, DenverCon 2015, shot from Gold Row F with a Canon 70D using a 2.8 70-300 mm lens.
Right: Misha, PittCon 2016, shot from Gold Row B with a Canon 70D using a 2.8 70-300 mm lens.

THE POWER OF A PICTURE

STACEY ANDERSON

When the idea came to me, about using a photo of my mother and me in the photo op, I went back and forth because I wasn't sure if it would spook the actors or make them feel uneasy. The tenth anniversary of my mother's death was coming up, and since we were celebrating ten years of *Supernatural*, I figured it was fitting to thank the actors and let them know how much they helped me to move past the pain of losing my mother when I was fifteen. So I emailed Creation's photographer, Chris, and asked if this would be okay. He said yes and actually printed out the photo I wanted to use in my J3 photo op.

I got in line with specific instructions to go last or as close to last as possible. The volunteers were very helpful. While hanging out at the end of the line, I met Lynn (author of *Fangasm* and the editor of this book) and she saw that I was nervous. I told her I don't normally get nervous but this was a memorial tribute to my mother. So she kind of took me under her wing and asked if I would be more comfortable if she introduced me to the boys. I said "Sure," since the boys know her pretty well.

When it was my turn and we walked up, I was so nervous that I was barely looking up at the cast. I heard Lynn tell the boys who I was and Jensen said, "Oh, that's nice of you to introduce her. She's pretty hard-core shy." Then I glanced at Jared and Jeff, my mom's photo grasped tightly in my hands, as I moved out of natural instinct right up to Jensen. I took a deep breath, though it didn't help, and started to explain my op.

"My mom died nearly ten years ago, the summer before the pilot aired. The show gave me something to look forward to and helped me with my grief. It was a way to distract me from everything." (It came out a lot more choppy, but it all came out somehow.) Then I turned to Jensen and said, "I really gravitated toward Dean because he used to be funny." Jensen smiled big and Jeff laughed and said to me, "You're right, he used to be funny. Not so much anymore." I glanced at Jared and his expression was full of sympathy. I glanced back at Jeff and asked, "I was hoping we could have my mom in the photo, too?" And Jared replied, "Yes, of course," as Jeff took the picture frame from my hands.

I was so out of it when Jensen said, "Come here, sweetie," and gathered me into a huge, comforting hug. I had no idea what Jared or Jeff were doing. All I can remember is being engulfed in Jensen's warm, protective arms and scooting back to get closer to Jared or Jeff when Chris motioned to Jensen to move back a bit.

Chris took the photo; I can't even remember it being taken. All I can recall is grasping onto Jensen's shirt as he held me, trying to smile to look somewhat decent. As I started to back away from him to thank him, he once again pulled me into a protective embrace, saying, "Hold on, sweetie, let me give you another hug." I wasn't expecting him to brush my hair back and press a kiss against my forehead.

After getting a kiss from Jensen I am not sure how I functioned. But I thanked Jared and he gave me a really big hug. Then I thanked Jeff and he also pulled me into a hug and kissed my forehead as well.

At first I was nervous to post my picture on Creation's Facebook page because I was afraid I'd receive hate for sharing a "sob story." But the feedback I received was full of support, understanding, and kindness. It was a relief to finally have my story out there. It felt good to share it. I hope, for those fans who aren't able to share their stories with the boys, they can take from my experience that Jared, Jensen, and Misha really do care about their fans and the circumstances that led them on their *Supernatural* journey.

Though it's very unlikely Jared, Jensen, or Jeff remembers my story, what matters is the impact that moment made in my life. Now, when I look at a picture of my mother and me, the photo op brings a sense of closure—it brings back happy memories that my mother is included in. Before that moment in Vegas, it was hard to look at photos of my mother . . . now, when I do, I have a reason to smile.

These men are so humble and respectful, and they truly do care about their fans' lives. I cannot thank Chris enough for helping make this happen. I feel so relieved that J3 took the time to listen to my story and show interest in what I had to say even when I was scared to death. I have never shaken or stuttered as much as I did during that moment. It wasn't because I was nervous to be in these men's presence; no, it was because I was afraid that they would be uncomfortable with me telling them my story. I was a fool to be nervous. As you can see in the picture, I was a wreck and Jensen was pretty much my lifeline.

So thank you, Jared, Jeff, and Jensen . . . thank you for not rushing me through my story. Thank you for making me feel like you truly cared in that moment. And thank you for making me feel a bit more at ease while I told you my story . . . even if my focus was mainly on you, Jensen.

And thank you to everyone online for your kind words when I shared my photo op of Jensen, Jared, and Jeff with y'all and for taking the time to read why that photo was so important to me. The love the SPNFamily shows each other is mind-blowing and it truly touched my heart.

A MESSAGE FROM
MISHA COLLINS
(IT'S FUNNIER IN ENOCHIAN)

I think it's an amazing thing about this show, to find that it has served as a lifeline in many ways for a lot of different people for a lot of different reasons. People identify with the characters, or something that an actor on the show has said resonates with them, or the community that has evolved organically around the show has served as a safety net for so many people. That is something that I feel truly blessed to be a part of. It's just an amazing phenomenon that is very rare, very precious, and I think we're all very lucky to be a part of it.

I've heard a lot of people say that they've struggled with feelings of worthlessness or self-harm, and somehow some thread that they pulled from *Supernatural* and its expanded community has provided comfort, that in this community there are a lot of people willing to help. I think it's very common for people to struggle, that most people have some struggle in their lives. I know that I did. Our family didn't have a lot of money, we were homeless a lot, and we struggled with some of the issues that come with poverty. But we had a loving nuclear family that was very important to me, and I think that helped me a lot getting through hard times. Not everyone has that. But luckily, in this SPNFamily, you may have landed in a supportive and loving community—a community that has your back.

SPREADING KINDNESS LIKE CONFETTI

CLAUDINE HUMMEL

Misha Collins is so unassumingly good he makes you want to be a better person. Between his character Castiel on *Supernatural*; GISHWHES, the Guinness World Record–breaking scavenger hunt that he runs; Random Acts, the nonprofit he founded; YANA (You Are Not Alone), a social movement for crisis intervention that grew out of Random Acts; and simply having the courage to be himself, openly and honestly, he has inspired me and changed my life. It is difficult *not* to be inspired by someone who is so passionate about everything he does.

I can't really pinpoint a specific moment when Misha changed my life because the improvement has happened a little bit at a time, every day. I didn't have the greatest childhood and had a tendency to get angry and hate myself whenever I "failed" at something. I felt ugly, and I felt alone. On a good day I would wake up and say, "I'm a fat loser, but that's okay," and go about my day. I let society and relatives dictate my self-worth.

Then Misha Collins came along, essentially saying that our worth isn't measured by our looks or success, but by our actions. I don't know why a stranger changed my life—maybe it was his strong positive energy that I wanted to wrap myself in like a blanket—but somehow his words and actions spoke to me. He is so encouraging and active in so many endeavors that I can wake up almost every day and see his kind words and feel his positivity. He isn't afraid to say he messed up or to make himself look foolish. He isn't even afraid to say he is afraid. This was a message I needed when I started watching *Supernatural* five years ago, two years out of college, without a job, and feeling afraid.

Watching Misha portray Castiel on *Supernatural* was just the beginning of how he moved me to become a better person. Castiel always strives to be the best he can be and to do the right thing. He often makes the right decisions, but despite his best efforts, sometimes he doesn't. We've all been there. At times, life throws us into places where we don't want to be. But Castiel teaches us to find the strength to persevere no matter how bleak things appear. His innocent optimism and belief that things will always work out mean he has yet to give up hope. No matter how hard it has gotten. No matter what he's been through. We have to always keep fighting, despite the odds, and Castiel inspires us to do so.

Shortly after discovering *Supernatural* and becoming enthralled by Castiel, I started to follow Misha and the rest of the cast through various social media. From there I discovered and started going to *Supernatural* conventions, where I've met wonderful people and started the truest, most meaningful, life-changing friendships I've ever had. Conventions, of course, are also where I was able to meet Misha.

Specifically, I first met Misha at Creation Entertainment's Las Vegas convention in March of 2013. I bought a duo op with him and Jim Beaver, which I shared with a new friend whom I had met a few days before at the convention. It sounds silly as I write this now, but I wanted to hug Misha while Jim held up a sign that said "Idjits!" next to us, and I was truly worried Misha wouldn't hug me. I was afraid I was asking too much. It turned out I had no reason to worry at all. Both were game for the photo op, and Misha hugged me tight. When it was done, he said I looked pretty in my dress and he hoped I had a great rest of the convention. No one other than my parents had ever said I was pretty before. *Me, pretty?* I tear up even now, thinking of that moment: how low my self-esteem was, and how that simple statement helped change the course of my life.

That weekend started a snowball effect. I felt better about myself, so I was willing to get out more and try new things. I'm lucky and fortunate enough that I get to go to a few *Supernatural* conventions a year, where I can get more hugs from Misha during photo ops or a quick few seconds to talk to him while getting his autograph. Each time I feel happier, more confident, more *me*. I've also started visiting the world, specifically Europe. Doors I had let society close on me I've now kicked open and explored.

Supernatural conventions introduced me to GISHWHES (the Greatest International Scavenger Hunt the World Has Ever Seen). I adore everything about GISHWHES. The list is always challenging, thrilling, and absurd, ranging from items that make you tear up to items that make you laugh out loud. GISHWHES likes to have participants break out of their comfort zones, think outside the box, and perform acts of charity. GISHers believe that "normalcy" is overrated, and that we are all artists with gifts we can give society, no matter what our talents or capabilities.

Participating in GISHWHES is an emotional roller-coaster ride. You go from a completely stressed "There is no way I can do any of these items! I'm going to let my team down!" to "This is the best week of my life! I can't believe I actually accomplished all that—I'm so proud of myself!"

GISHWHES is about art; it's about random acts of kindness; it's about stepping out of your comfort zone, making friends, and making yourself feel more alive . . . and the ripple effect those things cause in everyone around you. The number of people willing to go out of their way to help you do something utterly ridiculous is amazing and will restore your faith in humanity. GISHWHES not only accepts your weirdness and life's absurdity but also celebrates them.

Continuing the chain of inspiration, through GISHWHES I discovered Random Acts, a nonprofit Misha founded. Random Acts' mission is to conquer the world one random act of kindness at a time. It aims to inspire acts of kindness, both big and small, around the globe. And it provides a vast network of caring people who encourage and support changing lives for the better.

Misha demonstrates that the most effective way to make a difference is to lead by example. Kindness and generosity are infectious, and a small act can have an exponential effect. That small gesture can be a seed from which empathy blooms, and empathy is a very powerful healer. It's all about getting people to care . . . and Misha gets people to care.

Random Acts does so much every year. There's AMOK (Annual Melee of Kindness), a global day for kindness. There's E4K (Endure For Kindness), an endurance and stamina event and fund-raiser. There is the #SPNFamily Crisis Support Network/You Are Not Alone, a community support system to which the SPNFamily can turn for help for themselves or others suffering from mental health issues, such as depression, self-injury, or addiction. And there are the Dreams to Acts projects, which helped children in Jacmel, Haiti, after the devastating earthquake in 2010. It raised hundreds of thousands of dollars to build the Jacmel Children's Center, in addition to supporting other sustainable local projects. Dreams to Acts also helps support the Free High School in San Juan del Sur, Nicaragua, which provides access to education for adolescents and adults who are excluded from regular schools, including women with children, anyone over eighteen, people who work on weekdays, and those who live too far from the city to attend daily.

Random Acts has motivated me to volunteer more. I sign up for AMOK and E4K every year, and each time I participate in those events, I spread kindness like confetti. It feels as if life is a party and I'm not the person hanging out in the corner by the snack table; I'm the person dancing, talking, and living.

At San Diego Comic-Con 2016, after visiting the GishBus (a mobile humanitarian art project) on Saturday and waiting in line for Hall H to see the *Supernatural* panel Sunday morning, Misha, with some of the Random Acts staff, came by the long line to pass out granola bars for breakfast. When Misha saw me, he smiled and said, "You again? You're everywhere!" I laughed and said, "Yeah, I am," and that's thanks to you, Misha. You inspire me to live courageously and with kindness.

Saying "thank you" will never do justice to the magnitude of the positive change Misha has made in my life. His attitude, style, spirit, emotions, heart, and hard work have given me the desire to be all I am capable of being and the knowledge that what I am capable of is much more than I ever knew. Misha, for all you do, and for who you are, I will be forever grateful you entered my life.

You, too, can inspire like Misha does. So get out there and start inspiring people with who you are and how you live your life. And remember always to have courage and be kind.

MY TOP FIVE INSPIRATIONAL MISHA COLLINS QUOTES

"I want to live in a world where the word 'normal' is an insult."

"Don't pressure yourself. Don't worry about what others think you should do or what the social norm is. Do what moves you and makes you smile and the good will follow."

"We are bound only by the limits of our imaginations."

"Be kind to yourself so you can be happy enough to be kind to the world."

"It's fun to see people blow through their own perceived limitations."

RANDOM ACTS

http://www.randomacts.org

Random Acts had its humble beginnings in 2009 when actor Misha Collins asked his Twitter followers to join forces with him and find ways to fund-raise and do some good in the world. Early on, the movement saw an immediate need for assistance following the 2010 earthquake that devastated much of Haiti, and rallied to raise money for the victims, initially bringing in a total of $30,000 for a UNICEF-based aid effort. It was on the foundation of that early act of kindness that Random Acts first began to take shape.

Today, Random Acts is a registered 501(c)(3) nonprofit, organized under its parent company, The Art Department. Its mission is to conquer the world one random act of kindness at a time, and with the support of its numerous amazing followers, Random Acts has taken many steps toward that goal.

It was with those same supporters' help that Random Acts was able to create sustainable programs in Jacmel, Haiti, to help the children there gain access to basic needs, such as food, water, health care, and education. Over the course of several years, hundreds of thousands of dollars have been contributed for those affected by the earthquake. Random Acts is also currently building a new campus in San Juan del Sur, Nicaragua, for the local Free High School, so that students who wish to continue or complete their unfinished secondary education may do so in a space that is conducive to learning.

Every year, Collins also organizes a worldwide Guinness Record–breaking scavenger hunt benefitting Random Acts, the Greatest International Scavenger Hunt the World Has Ever Seen (GISHWHES). The weeklong hunt encourages people to step out of their comfort zones and challenge themselves to undertake, as Misha says, "the bizarre, the beautiful, and even the impossible." GISHWHES aims to foster creative expression and random acts of kindness, giving "Gishers" explicit permission to play and leave "normal" behind. Perhaps equally important, many fans have made close and enduring friendships on their GISHWHES teams.

Random Acts supporters have gone on to perform incredible acts of kindness in their own communities, crafting blankets for homeless children, creating sustainable gardens, utilizing Random Acts funding to purchase new water purifiers for neighbors recovering from surgeries, and distributing care packages for the homeless.

By purchasing this book, you can count yourself among those supporters: a portion of the proceeds from the purchase of this book go directly to Random Acts, and will be used to carry out all the aforementioned projects, and so much more. More important, the Random Acts staff is grateful for your support and hopes you'll join us in our mission to conquer the world with a spirit of kindness, generosity, and compassion for all.

Content contributed by Jennifer Willis-Rivera and Melanie Schmitz

THE OPPOSITE OF FAN FICTION

The Extroverted Adventures of an Introvert

OSRIC CHAU

You agree to way too many things," a friend told me recently.

"I do!" I responded overenthusiastically.

My behavior is often at odds with my logical thinking, and that's because deep down I'm still in favor of a lot of the things I've taught myself to avoid. Things like comfort. I associate comfort with that year of my life when I stayed in a basement playing video games all day while feeding on chips, salsa, and shepherd's pie. And while I was one of the happiest people on the planet that year, I know I can't let myself do that again. When a similar opportunity presents itself, my brain will tell me that a quick "no" is the best decision because it brings me closer to that wonderful basement again. Usually that's about the time I impulsively chime in with a "Yes!" before I get the chance to think myself out of it.

Ignoring your common sense comes at a price, though. And that would be finding myself in situations where I'm a bit over my head—or, in the case of agreeing to write a chapter in this book, way over my head. I'm

not a writer, and I haven't written an essay in . . . well, I think any English teacher I've ever had will tell you that I've never written an essay, certainly not an essay that was structurally sound or had any kind of point to it, anyway. The one thing I've got going for me this time is that this is a subject I actually care about, and that subject is more than just how *Supernatural* changed my life, or my immersion in the fandom. This is about how *Supernatural* continues to change my life and how the fandom continues to help me in my lifelong pursuit of stepping out of my comfort zone.

Ten years ago I took a Myers-Briggs personality test as part of a career preparation course, and among other things it identified me as an introvert. A lot can happen in ten years, though, and these days I had just assumed that I'd made some sort of transition to being an extrovert. I'm an actor, after all, and it's my job to get in front of the camera knowing that millions of people will see my every move. I'm also a guy who goes up onstage in costume for no apparent good reason before meeting and talking to hundreds of people without hesitation. I've made it my job to be out there and to try and inspire others to do the same, but something I noticed in these last couple of months of self-reflection didn't quite add up. So I started to dig deeper into the recesses of my brain in the hopes of uncovering some of those less-than-comfortable memories we're all so good at suppressing.

My first thoughts were of the Friday-night karaoke event at the Salute to *Supernatural* conventions here in North America. You'll notice that most of the following accounts will be of my time at these conventions. That's pretty much the only time I meet and interact with new people, so it's a good measure of my true mettle. Most days for me are spent in a nook at home in front of my computer, and it's not very accurate to test courage while you're behind a keyboard.

If you've never been to a Matt Cohen and Richard Speight Jr. karaoke party, here's a quick rundown: It's your normal American-style karaoke you'd find in the corner of a bar, except it's in the main convention hall where the panels are held, it's the only free event at the convention, people who were unable to get tickets for the convention are able to attend as well as anyone else who happens to wander by, it's getting bigger every single time, and it already has the energy of a rock concert's mosh pit both on and off the stage. Throw in a majority of songs from your *Supernatural*-themed playlist and it is a really fun event. So, even apart from the sheer amount of respect I have for Matt, Richard, and Rob Benedict— they're kind of a trio, so I throw Rob in there, too—not only as performers, but also just as good, honest people whom I'd attend any event for just to show my support, it is the nonmandatory event I go to every single time because it's a fun event. And I'm far from the only one. Even after a long day, since joining the convention circuit, Rob's Louden Swain bandmates have always come out, and most of the guests from Friday and even the Saturday guests who fly in early enough will join in or at least make an appearance. It's a giant party where we can pull down the veil a little bit further and interact with people in a much less formal way. That's something I really enjoy, and for that reason it's been one of my favorite events since my first convention appearance.

The last couple of Friday-night karaoke parties really had me thinking about stage dynamics, though. I have no problem being onstage on my own. A duo panel has proven to be quite fun, especially when you're both getting going and bouncing things off of each other. But when it gets to be a group thing where there's up to ten people onstage just hanging out, many of whom are performers—and that includes members of our multi-talented fan base—my self-consciousness shoots through the roof as I start comparing myself to everyone else and I start feeling the dark corners of the room calling out to me. I remember one night I was watching Matt and Rob getting the crowd going between songs while Richard was running his always witty commentary. I was standing onstage with them, admiring their showmanship and wishing I could do the same. And then my mind kicked in, as it usually does, and reminded me that of course I could do the same, and I often do. So I decided I would join them and gave it a 1-2-go! But my mind and body were at odds that night and my body would just not agree with what my mind was willing it to do. Shortly after that, I realized just how long I must have been standing up on that stage spacing out. Hoping I didn't look too dumb, I retreated backstage to recover.

That memory reminds me of much of my childhood. I was never the cool kid, though I did hang out with the cool kids every now and then. They would do their antics and I would sit back and try not to draw too much attention to myself. I never felt like I had much value to add to the conversation or anything funny to say that would make anyone laugh. For most of elementary school, my identity came from martial arts and being a fighter, but that just made me someone people wanted to talk about, not talk to. By the time I was smart enough to teach myself how not to fight, I found my new thing, and that was being a student activist, school president, and participating in as many clubs as I possibly could. It was an incredibly social lifestyle, polar opposite from the years prior, and I was spending upward of sixteen hours a day at school. That life gave me purpose; it made me important—I always had somewhere to go and something to do. But I also stretched myself too thin and turned out to be mediocre at everything, a master of nothing. And that included my social skills. I never got to know any group of friends well enough to get all the inside jokes or be able to find those clever moments to throw in my

two cents. I was arguably the social butterfly of my year, yet I didn't really know how to socialize. I was used to being needed somewhere and rarely had to stay in any conversation for too long—certainly not long enough to get into any deep discussions. In those rare moments when I did, I was left standing awkwardly, with only my thoughts of how I wished I had something clever to say or somewhere else to go.

The Saturday-night Louden Swain concert, which would eventually become the "Saturday Night Special," made its debut in 2014 at that year's Salute to *Supernatural* convention in Washington, D.C. I had recently started playing the guitar and I made the impulsive decision to say yes when they asked me if I wanted to perform something onstage. I had the runs the entire weekend up until I stepped out on that stage, and when I was done I had to lay myself down on the floor for a couple of minutes for my mind to readjust itself. While writing this piece I decided I would find and watch that video again, and felt my heart racing in anticipation of watching myself perform. To this day, performing any type of music in front of an audience still brings up the most intense feelings of anxiety I've ever experienced. And if it weren't for the warmth and acceptance that I knew existed in the *Supernatural* fandom, I would never have put myself in such a vulnerable position.

The safety net that is this fandom allows me to do these things that I would otherwise be too afraid to do. I've been able to turn off the part of my brain that used to yell at me, frantically waving red flags, once it calculated the impending doom that was fast approaching in the form of embarrassment. Well, maybe that part of me isn't turned off, but the part of me that's yelling "This is going to be so much fun!" seems to drown it out.

People will say no to you when you say "I want to be in that movie." There will be thousands of people who'll say "No, you can't be in that movie." But *you* can't say "I can't be in that movie"; you have to say "I'm going to be in that movie," and walk ahead until you can't anymore. Taking these chances has taught me a very valuable lesson that I often preach to anyone willing to listen. There are hundreds, even thousands of people who readily say no to things. You can't be one of those people. This mindset has opened a lot of doors for me and has led me through some of my favorite adventures.

For my involvement in the live-action *Halo* web series, I was invited to go to San Diego Comic-Con in 2012. It was my first time attending this convention, and it blew my mind. I remember telling numerous people that the experience had changed my life forever. I was hooked, and so in anticipation of returning in 2013, I spent months preparing one of the most elaborate costumes I'd ever worn, even enlisting the help of friends and other third-party sources.

On Friday, September 20, 2013, I arrived in Dallas ready for another *Supernatural* convention; this was to be my third appearance onstage. There I was in my hotel room, looking into the mirror, adjusting my tiara. San Diego Comic-Con had come and gone, and due to a last-minute scheduling conflict I had been unable to attend. My Princess Bubblegum cosplay was to be my pièce de résistance for Comic-Con and I'd been fully ready to strut through the crowd there like nobody's business, covered head to toe in pink. Not wanting to wait a year or put a good costume to waste, I brought my Princess Bubblegum outfit with me to the other convention I was going to, Dallas Con, not considering the fact that I was a guest at this event and not an attendee.

I can still remember the overwhelming sensation of regret and shame when I saw the look of shock on my handler's face. At that moment I had every intention of slamming the door, disrobing, and scrubbing off the pink before excusing myself for my tardiness later. It was a moment of truth, and that's when I heard that inner voice of mine again. "Just go for it, Osric. People like *Adventure Time*. It'll make it easier for the shy people to talk to you if you're more embarrassed than they are. If you could do this in front of anyone it would be this group of people. You know you want to." And then the years of acting finally paid off and I just committed to it. I stepped out that door with a grin, and I blew past encounter after encounter with full confidence, staring right back into the eyes that were staring at me. The response was a mixture of bewilderment, laughter, and, I'd like to believe, awe.

This happy accident started something. It gave me something I could do that was enjoyable for many of the fans attending the convention. It offset my fear of becoming desensitized to conventions, were I to attend so many that it became routine, since the constant wondering about people's reactions to my costume kept me far from my resting heart rate. Doing a new costume at every convention gave me an objective, something to obsess over, something I could get good at and progress at, in levels you could say, with increasing challenges as I escalated the difficulty in design and materials I was working with. Very quickly I had to start enlisting the help of cosplayers from all over, and the selection process of my cosplayers eventually evolved to the point where I started to look for specialists: Finding a leather specialist for a leather-based costume. If there were electrical components, enlisting the help of an engineer. In cosplaying, it turns out, I found something like a real-life role-playing game, and that got me really excited. It was not only fun, but it also gave the attendees and me an icebreaker. If there was nothing to talk about, we could at least talk about what I was wearing, and since I hadn't redone a costume yet, it was always topical.

I cannot emphasize enough the importance of a good icebreaker followed by pleasant small talk, a painful lesson with awkward repercussions that I am still figuring out. I would argue that the amount of times we're able to execute both an icebreaker and small talk smoothly could be correlated quite proportionally to both social and professional success. In this day and age, networking is closer to a necessity for success than simply a recommendation. Even if you're good at what you do, unless others like you as a person, they're not going to want to be around you for eight hours a day Monday through Friday; they would rather hire someone less skilled whom they don't have to worry about. Of course, smooth is a relative term, and some of the most awkward introductions could be charming to a kindred spirit who might end up being your best friend. That best friend could end up leading you to the career you were hoping for.

I first realized this about eight years ago when I was starting out as an actor and all I could say was, "Hi, my name is Osric, I'm an actor." That was usually followed by a "What have you done?" which I answered with silence, or sometimes I would get lucky and somehow be able to start talking about martial arts. I bring all this up because I am so aware of it now. And if I were to look at this like a game, with this fandom, it is kind of like playing in Chuck mode. I know the fandom well enough that I know every single person could very well end up being my best friend, and I have no fear of breaking the ice or talking to them about any random topic that comes to mind. There have been so many conventions and I've met so many thousands of people with this "cheat" in hand that it became the only way I knew how to introduce myself, and I ended up kind of relying on it.

A couple of months ago I attended a birthday party where I only knew the birthday person, and so I understood I couldn't be clinging to the only person I knew. But in the name of adventure and because I had it in my mind that I was good at meeting and talking to strangers, I attended. That night I found myself sitting in an empty corner observing the guests coming in and out before quietly sneaking away. I was out of my element; I didn't have the benefit of people knowing exactly who I was, and I learned that I was unable to fend for myself in some social situations. Of course, I kind of erased that memory and feeling of helplessness and chalked it up to the event being an industry party and just not liking those in general.

With all that in mind, and to further dive into self-discovery and personal development, I decided to take that same personality test again to see just how much I had changed in the course of a decade. The results came in, and lo and behold, I was still an introvert, but this time around I came with very strong extroverted tendencies. So I will keep making myself go out to these parties that I would have avoided ten years ago. I might be better at handling myself at them, but I still could use a lot of work. As a performer, I've learned to turn it on or my brain off when I need to go onstage. But unless facilitated to do so, or unless I have some sort of leg up by being known, put me on the spot out of nowhere and I regress to my natural state of being an introvert.

Knowing all this and tabulating the wealth of experience I've collected and adventures I've had that I would otherwise have missed without the safety net of this fandom, I can only be grateful. I receive amazing messages from fans every single day thanking me, but it really is a two-way street and a wonderful symbiotic relationship. Because of you, I allow myself to do the things that I do, and then you thank me for it. And so I respond with the most honest and straightforward answer I know: "No, thank *you*."

Osric and Rob Benedict at the Saturday Night Special.

A PIECE OF MY HEART

SABRINA GREENWOOD-BRIGGS

t would be hyperbole to say that my life started when I found *Supernatural*, but it is true that the life I live now is a direct effect of finding the show. Every bit of where I am today can be traced back along a path to *Supernatural*.

Ten years ago I was miserable in the life I was living, with what looked to be a boring (and long) road ahead of me. I had made the choice to relocate from my dream city in California back to my New Hampshire hometown in order to save money so I could pay off my debt and move in with my boyfriend once he returned from his military post overseas. I was staring down the path of what I thought I should want: a husband, children, a stable job. But I was making all of my choices based on what others around me were doing and what I thought I should be doing with my life, with no real concept of where I was headed or what I even truly wanted for myself. I was drifting along, life a movie I was watching instead of living. I felt completely alone in this dissatisfaction, like I was the only one floundering and confused, even though I was surrounded by amazing friends and family.

I found the online world through a complete accident, when an acquaintance emailed me an invitation to join a Yahoo! Group about *Star Wars: Episode I – The Phantom Menace*. There, I made some fascinating friends who helped me mentally escape from the swamp of my day-to-day existence. That group led to others, which finally led to me joining an online fanfic writing community I called home for nearly nine years. The whole of that sounds melodramatic when written out, yet I can still recall the hopelessness and aching I felt in those years.

When one of these online friends suggested I watch *Supernatural*, I thought she was crazy. I was and am no fan of horror, and the few times I had glanced at the show in passing while channel surfing made me think that the show was nonstop scares and gross-outs. But this was the same woman who had turned me on to *Firefly*, *Sports Night*, and too many other wonderful shows to name. She was one of the first people to encourage my fannish side, which has made all the difference in my life. So I decided to trust her and ordered the first disc of season 1 from Netflix (at this point, season 2 was headed into its midseason hiatus). Against all my expectations, I was hooked. So hooked, in fact, that I watched the entire first disc in one nail-biting sitting, only managing a handful of hours of sleep before work the next day. I sent that disc (and all others in the house) back the next day and reordered my Netflix queue to send me the whole season as quickly as possible. I lost myself deep in the world of Sam, Dean, and the idea of saving people and hunting things. This purpose of theirs resonated deeply with me. I wanted to do something that mattered and, watching this show, I realized that while I was purposeless, it was absolutely within my power to change that.

Over the next couple of months, I bought season 1 and then found torrents to mainline the first half of season 2 so I could be caught up and ready to go when the season restarted. I even roped my roommate, along with several of my friends, into watching with me. We would have watch parties at home every week, starting with the new season 2 episodes after the hiatus. Our group devoured the show and spent hours discussing it. I also spent time and energy on the annual campaigns to get the show renewed. I was refreshed and galvanized, and the love I felt for the show pushed me to make changes in my own life. It made me take a long, hard look at what I was dissatisfied with, what I really wanted, and what I could do about it.

I was no longer hiding from the fact that everything was within my control, if only I was willing to take the time and do the work to make things change. So much of life is about taking stock and then acting on it, a theme that was hammered home in nearly every episode of those first seasons. By the summer of 2007 I made some major changes: dumped the boyfriend, made more friends both online and in my local area, went back to school, and finally got a new job, which had me packing up to relocate back to Southern California. I knew it was where I belonged, where I needed to pick up my story and write new chapters.

From the moment my plane touched down on that July 4th, I knew everything was going to change. It was akin to the way I knew which college to go to and whether or not to study abroad. I felt it in my bones: a complete rightness that had been absent from the last few years of my life. That summer I did everything I could to forge a new life I was happy with. This included going to San Diego Comic-Con for the first time (I was planning to sleep on the floor of my work the night before until I met this anthology's editor, who was gracious enough to offer me a place to crash), seeing a screening of *Ten Inch Hero* with new friends, watching music gigs around LA starring Jason Manns and Steve Carlson, and challenging myself to apply for an entry-level accounting job that has turned into a nine-year professional career in finance and human resources. I never imagined my life taking the turns it has when I was sitting in my old New Hampshire living room. The process of this life change was something I finally felt capable of doing, and felt as though I deserved. I owe so much of that to *Supernatural.*

Through all these adventures I met amazing women, ones so much more like me than any I'd known before, who helped shape me into the person I am today. Each experience with them has continued to add to my life. They helped buoy me through all kinds of roller-coaster experiences, and they have taught me valuable lessons about being a great friend, having true friends, and what it means to be a single adult woman with passions and interests just that little bit outside the mundane.

And I would not have known any of them without *Supernatural.* I can say that with certainty because I met the first of these women (along with this anthology's editor) at 4:30 A.M. in line for the 2007 *Supernatural* San Diego Comic-Con panel. This was back when the show was featured in a modest-size room (not the largest hall, as it is now) and most of the other people waiting in line were there to see other panels. We waited from the early hours to score our front-row seats, battled with people trying to save those seats for friends not in line, and sat through an entire day of programming we knew nothing about just to see the guys and the team walk into that room, present us with some exclusive clips, and talk to us about their love of what they were doing. From there, this new friend invited me to join her group of friends a couple of weekends later at a music gig where she introduced me to the women she knew . . . most of whom were people she had met either as fans of the show or from other fandoms. It was a transformative summer.

For what seemed to be the first time in my life, I was immediately accepted in a non-online space. These women took me in; they celebrated my fannishness, shared their passions, and helped me find additional outlets through this amazing thing we all loved. To this day I remain connected to these people through the experiences we've shared; I've taken a part of them into myself and been shaped and changed. And the whole *Supernatural* Family has been along for that ride, even if they had no clue they were part of my journey. The show was there for me in my time of greatest need, it helped me develop my creative side through the fanfic I wrote, and it gave me some of the most amazing, important people in my life, including several women who are like sisters to me.

Do I think I'd have had a decent life without *Supernatural?* Of course I do. But that life would not have been nearly as full, nearly as exciting, or nearly as rewarding as the one I enjoy today. I deeply appreciate the love and energy everyone connected to the show puts into it, be they part of production or part of fandom. And, while I may no longer participate in the fandom the way I once did, this show will forever claim a piece of my heart and soul. It has left an indelible mark on the person I am, and I will carry that with me through the rest of my life.

FINALLY ME

MATT COHEN

My name is Matt Cohen. I was born in south Florida and I was raised by a single father since I was about eighteen months old. My father and I have a great relationship; we are more like best friends than father and son. He did a fantastic job raising me and gave me all I could ever ask for in life. I did not start acting until 2004 or 2005 when I was about twenty-two or twenty-three years old.

I spent most of my life trying to figure out who I was and what I wanted to do with myself. I was a pretty popular kid in high school. I played football and I ran track and I participated in all the dances and all the homecoming courts, etc. My dad was in auto racing his entire life, so naturally he tried to steer me in that direction. I raced everything from motocross and dirt bikes to stock cars and go-karts. I enjoyed auto racing and motorcycle racing; it came to me very naturally and I was quite good at it. The problem was that I was torn between being the popular football star and taking a different route. My dad was thrilled that I was racing, but as much as I loved it, I never knew if it was where I was going to fit in.

As I got older and being cool started to matter more, I veered away from my racing background and more into being a football star. Now, while

110

I was torn between auto racing and trying to be a football star—which I never actually achieved—I had every other life stage under the sun. Seventh, eighth, and ninth grade I was doing a lot of skateboarding and inline skating and I shaved my head and tried to be a full-on punk-rock skater bad boy. That was followed by tenth and eleventh grade, when I thought I was a rap star. Baggy pants, braided hair, and loud rap music everywhere I went.

I never felt really comfortable in any of these stages of my life. I always found myself trying to be something for somebody else. I'm not saying that I didn't thoroughly enjoy racing, but I wanted to be the best race-car driver because my dad loved racing. Football was another experience altogether. I learned a lot of the discipline that I carry through life on the football field, but I wanted to be the star of the football team because, well, let's face it, who doesn't like the popular star of the football team? I was never the best football player, but I tried super hard.

Not being the best at something can make you want to go against the grain. So then I wanted to be a skater punk just to rebel against the norm. It was never for me; it was for the idea of me, to other people. I wanted people to think of me in a certain way, so I became all these other things. Senior year of high school I was all over the place. I was playing football and I was doing a little bit of racing and I was skating whenever I had time. Never in my high school career did I want to be an actor. I did take an acting class with a fantastic drama teacher by the name of Jim Usher. He was a great teacher and, sadly, I didn't take his class very seriously. I would do monologues that were just lyrics from songs that I memorized to get by.

It wasn't until I went off to Florida State University that I took my first theater class. Looking like Mr. Joe Jock, I wasn't welcomed right away by the other students. And to be honest with you, I can't blame them. They probably thought, *Look at this jock trying to get an easy grade by taking a theater class that we all care very much about.* And the truth of the matter is, maybe I was trying to get an easy grade; I'm not sure, just like I wasn't sure about everything else I did in my life up to that point. The scary thing about discovering yourself is that you might not like what you find.

Needless to say, the theater class didn't go well for me. Soon after that I was at a crossroads where I was trying to decide again what I wanted to do with myself. I was fortunate enough to meet a talent manager in Miami by the name of Sharon Lane. She told me that I had no acting chops, I couldn't act my way out of a hole, but if I really wanted to give acting a try I needed to move to LA for pilot season. That didn't go over very well with my father. I happen to be the only one in my family who ever got into college and attended college. I added one more first to that list: I was the first one to leave college without graduating. I wanted something else in life, but I had no idea what it was. The only thing I knew was that I was done studying all night and taking tests. Where was the creativity in that?

Just a few months after I met Sharon Lane, who still manages my career to this day, I moved to Los Angeles. The problem with being in your early twenties and moving all the way across the country to try to figure out who you are is that it is like high school all over again. I remember my first interview at a big talent agency in Los Angeles. My manager coached me on who to be when I went into that room: how to act, how to speak, the things I should and shouldn't say. So I became that guy for the time being. Shortly after getting an agent I remember studying for roles and going on my early auditions in Los Angeles. I would go to auditions and try to dress like the other guys I saw at the auditions—not the character that I should be dressing for, but trying to be like the other *actors* who were in the room. I wanted people to look at me and go, "That guy must be an actor." And then there was the nightlife: beautiful bars and clubs and many, many young, talented, beautiful people everywhere. I would go to a bar or nightclub and I would look at all the people around me and I would try to become more like them. The problem with all this is that I was never able to be myself. Probably because I still had no idea who I was or who I wanted to be.

Let's fast-forward a little bit. I began working as an actor, and a few years into my career I booked a role on *Supernatural*. Performing on *Supernatural* gave me the opportunity to do fan conventions. The first convention I ever went to happened to be in Birmingham, England, and it was absolutely terrifying. I was with all these famous actors and I never thought I was good enough to hang out with any of them. I was extremely intimidated by the talented people surrounding me. I was extremely intimidated by the thousands of fans and what they wanted from me. I was so confused about where I was in my life, but I was also at the most successful point I had ever known. If I hadn't had my wife with me, I might have just imploded. I remember sitting on that stage for the first time, terrified. I remember blushing and sweating and shaking. It wasn't until later on the convention circuit that I learned these people are fans of what I do. That basically means they are there to support me. That made me wonder why so many actors tend to act so famous when they're around their fans. These fans support me and love what I do; that made me feel as if I should be more open with them. I think at some point I decided to slightly erase the line between fan and actor. This allowed me to relate to the fans and to be more open with myself.

From that point on, life started to get really good. Being an open book and simply showing appreciation for people is a lovely thing. I started to realize that the little things I did for the fans were huge things in their eyes. I found out that sending a "happy birthday" tweet to a fan made them feel really great. I found out that if I hugged every single fan I could at a convention, there would be smiles for miles. I found out that if I danced around and sang poor versions of karaoke covers, fans would dance and have a great time. I found out that when I opened my heart to the fans and told them my personal stories of both triumph and tragedy, we could relate. The fans gave me an opportunity to examine myself publicly without being judged. That is a rare thing.

All these new experiences made me step back and examine why I was so happy. I sat and thought a bit. I was happy, truly happy, for the first time in my life. The reason? I think I figured out who I am. I think I want to be the person who makes people feel good. I think I want to be the ear to listen to people who need someone to talk to. I think I want to be the person who proves a hug can change your day. I was having a fucking epiphany! I want to be the man who changes lives while changing his own.

I started to realize that we are all here for the same reason: to help one another and to teach each other. Now, I'm not saying I can teach you much academically, but I may be able to teach you how to have a happier existence. The fans were unknowingly teaching me and making me a happier man. The funniest part about all of it is that none of the fans ever knew they were making me the man I always wanted to be. Through me opening up to them and them finding their happiness, it allowed me to find happiness. The fandom was teaching me to let loose and have a good time and smile. They were teaching me we're all the same in this giant world. The fandom knew who I was coming in, and they accepted me. We all grew together and continue to grow every single day. The constant excitement of preparing to go on a trip to a convention is amazing. Not only do I get to go to a place where I can be the man I am proud of becoming, but I also get to go hang out with the people who are responsible for it: the fans.

In addition to seeing all of the fans who draw a large smile on my face, I have the extraordinary experience of working with a group of people I consider my mentors. Mentors I wouldn't have ever met had I not been invited to a *Supernatural* convention. An invitation that I only received because of the fans' positive feedback. So not only have the fans helped a boy become a proud man, but they have also helped provide the instructions on how to be a quality husband and father, by bringing me together, weekend after weekend, with the great group of people I work with at the conventions.

I've learned what a good husband, a good father, and a good friend really are. In addition to that, I've learned what hard work and dedication drenched in talent look like. I have watched the men I work with respect and love their wives while continuously working and traveling. I have had the rare opportunity to have a preview into fatherhood before I became one myself. The guys that I work with at conventions have shown me what it takes to be a fantastic father. When we all get together on these weekends it's kind of hilarious. There's about five or seven guys all showing one another pictures of their children. And not only are they great fathers and husbands, but all of us are damn good friends. We have all been through life's ups and downs together. Some of us have almost died together and some of us have celebrated life's greatest gifts together. I am just a touch younger than my core group of convention buddies. I became a husband during my time at conventions, and I became a father during my time at conventions. I can say with all sincerity, I hope I die next to these guys. The fans allowed me into their kingdom and because of them I have found myself, my friends, and new meaning. Maybe meaning for the first time.

So let me try this again:

Hello, my name is Matt Cohen. I am from Florida and have been confused for most of my life on this planet. I have realized some things in the last four or five years. I am a very happy man. I love my son very much. I love my wife very much. I love my father and family very much. I love my friends very much. I love going to conventions and hugging thousands of people because I love seeing thousands of smiles. I know that it is okay to dance awkwardly and sing poorly as long as you're doing it with people who accept you. I have learned that dressing up in women's costumes, as well as vegetable costumes, makes life a whole hell of a lot more fun. I have realized that crying with a couple hundred more people makes the tears sting a lot less. This is my thank-you letter to the *Supernatural* fandom. I am so grateful you have taken me in and made me feel at home. I am so grateful you have allowed me to find me.

I am finally me.

Matt and Rob at the Saturday Night Special.

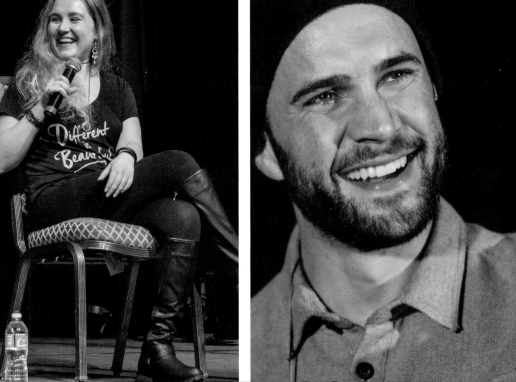

AT THE CROSSROADS WITH
MARK SHEPPARD

These are some very disturbing times in the world right now. It's not as kind and gentle a place as I think it was when I was a kid. In the middle of all that, what's been fascinating for me is this sort of secret thing that we do—this fandom thing, for want of a better word. This fandom thing has brought people together.

The fact that Jared and so many of my fellow costars are willing to talk about their journeys in life means that it no longer holds the same stigma as it used to. It's a massive catalyst for change. I'm proud of Jared especially, talking about issues of depression and anxiety. You can't go through life without mental illness having an impact on you, your family members, your friends.

What I love is what happens when you put large groups of people together, unified behind a positive thing—the love of the show, the love of an idea about the show, or what the show stands for. The fact that it stands for family, the fact that it stands for togetherness. Fighting demons—while I personally (as Crowley) hate the idea—fighting our demons is a very important thing. And to watch people come together behind that, to use the show and the meeting points around the show, like conventions, to come together and help one another is a massively humbling thing.

We would try to make change anyway, but the fact that when we broadcast that we're doing something, that you guys get behind what it is that we do, is amazing. Look at what Misha does—schools and hospitals and helping people, the beautiful things that go on. We talk about how it's wonderful that people with a little power and influence do the right thing, but I think what astonishes all of us is the fact that you guys are so willing to come in behind what we do and push it and drive it to be something bigger and something incredible.

I am so proud of you guys because I can remember a time when being a fan, because it was of course related to the word *fanatic*, was looked down upon. A fan was somebody who was not of the norm, somebody who had an irrational like of something. Like, "Oh, those weird people who read comic books." But now, we drive television, we drive the Internet, we're a force. We have changed the way things are being watched and the way things are being absorbed and looked at. It's almost like the geeks have inherited the earth.

I think we're used to being outcasts; as geeks and weirdos we're kind of used to being on the outside, being on the periphery of the norm. And so, as the type of people we are, I think we tend to be a lot kinder toward other people who have more difficulty than most. I see that groups of people who feel different and set apart from others tend to love to get behind causes and make a change and make things happen. And so I'm proud of you guys for wearing your hearts on your sleeve and coming out and showing people what it is that you love, what you enjoy. And I'm proud of the fact that you stand up for those who can't necessarily stand up for themselves.

FANGIRL

LYNN ZUBERNIS

There's a reason I wanted to write a book about how a television show has changed and even saved lives: *Supernatural* changed mine.

I'm a different person than I was before a sci-fi genre show on the CW network kidnapped me and decided to never let me go. Before I discovered this amazing community of fans called fandom and let it inspire me to put some of my fears behind me. All my life, I've been afraid. Afraid to fail. Afraid to be anything other than perfect, as though that were ever achievable in the first place. Afraid to be myself, and instead investing way too much time and effort figuring out who others wanted me to be and then struggling mightily to be it. My parents, my partner, my friends, my bosses—I spent so much time figuring out who they expected me to be that I nearly lost myself in the process.

As a kid I hid behind my mother's skirts—literally—and hardly said a word. I'm not sure most of my teachers even knew I was there. When they did, they weren't exactly happy about it. Sure, I got good grades, but class participation was a different story. I still remember my humiliation when my mother marched into the school to protest my C in Geography. Mr. Ritts, my seventh-grade geography teacher, stood his ground.

"I'm sorry, but she's never spoken in my class. NOT ONE WORD."

Even my mother was speechless at that one.

For most of my life, I tried to fit in and not make waves. To be invisible. Fear kept me from doing a surprising variety of things, from talking in front of a crowd (even a small group of neighbors) to traveling places on my own. Fear of not being accepted led me to cut myself off from many of the things I'd loved as a kid (like sci-fi television shows and obscure rock bands), allowing myself only "serious pursuits" like grad school and work and mom responsibilities. I'm fairly certain I spent most of my early adult life being constantly anxious and vaguely dissatisfied—and pretty boring.

Until *Supernatural.*

You might be thinking, how the hell could a television show change that aspect of someone's personality, especially for the better? Fans are more often thought of as losers obsessed with a fictional character or a celebrity, or geeks who need to "get a life." Being a fan conjures up images of hysterical girls screaming for the Beatles or grown-ups spending their hard-earned cash on trips to Harry Potter World. Certainly fans aren't immune to making bad choices; passion can inspire you to take risks you might not have otherwise, and sometimes the outcome isn't pretty. But other times? That's the risk that changes your life for the better.

Like many people who find fandom, I've always felt different, which I'm sure contributed to my pursuit of invisibility. I was the shy, skinny girl with glasses who wanted to hide every time people called me a "brain" or snickered something worse under their breath. I quickly learned never to raise my hand or draw attention to myself, hiding the fact that I had a brain in order to stay safe. I hid the things I loved, too; the things I now recognize as inspiring my first fannish passions: *Star Trek, The X-Files, Buffy.* After all, it was unlikely to make me any cooler in the eyes of my peers to confess that I had a thing for Spike, or that I imagined he might have a thing for one of the other characters (maybe even Angel instead of Buffy). The fact that some of my fantasies about my favorite fictional characters weren't exactly G-rated just made me more convinced of my weirdness. Most of us are easily shamed when it comes to sex, women and girls in particular. No wonder my real self went underground, and my voice with it. On the surface, my differences were erased; in truth, they were just covered over by a false persona who wanted to please and was happy to sacrifice being genuine to do it. I married, had children, worked hard, went to grad school. Fantasies? Fun? Who had time!

It wasn't until I fell head over heels for *Supernatural,* many years later, that I remembered what it felt like to be passionate about something. To love something so much you can't sit still while watching it. To be so excited you can't stop yourself from screaming when the good guy goes down—and shouting even louder when he staggers back up, bruised and bleeding, and saves the day anyway. For the first time in a very long time, I was doing something I wanted to do . . . something for myself.

I was terrified. And I felt guilty. Could I really allow myself to do this? Have *fun?*

I tried to talk myself out of it, to go back to being a hardworking, serious-minded woman with a PhD and a lot of carpooling to do. Yet, as uncomfortable as I was with my newfound frivolous pursuit, I found I couldn't give it up. *Supernatural* had a hold over me stronger than the show's villainous Yellow-Eyed Demon had over poor Sam Winchester!

I went online searching for more, more, more about the show I loved, and realized to my surprise that there were other people who were also passionate about television shows. Lots of them. Many were women, and while some of them struggled with the same shame and guilt I did, they were also determined not to give in. Online, we formed our own fandom communities, with norms that were vastly different than the ones in the "real world." Here women spoke up, not with what others wanted to hear, but saying what they really felt. Here it was okay to scream your passion instead of suppressing all that emotion. It was okay to fantasize, too, and not just about things that were vanilla and socially sanctioned. Here you could share your real fantasies and be validated instead of shamed.

Fandom, for me, was a revelation. In a matter of weeks, I took a crash course in all things fan (which I'm pretty sure I aced). I learned about fan fiction in all its glorious permutations. I learned about fanart and fanvids and manips and gifs and social media. I learned about shipping and wank at the same time as I saw how supportive and giving fans were with one another. This was a community that threw out the customary norms most of us—especially women—live by. Norms like "Don't tell the truth; say what they want you to say." "Don't love too much or want too much or, God forbid, desire too much." Fandom said nope. Talk about what you really feel, what you really want, what you really like. Talk about it here and we won't judge you or scold; we'll chime in and say *OMG, yes, me too.*

Within fandom's safe space, I also unlearned the lessons of my repressive past and began to learn new ones. I found my voice, quite literally, through fandom and *Supernatural.* Within the fandom community, I toyed with being genuine for the first time. I felt less different than ever; or, more accurately, I began to cherish my differences instead of hiding them. I began to speak. And I began to write. I've been writing all my life, but in secret. In multicolored dog-eared journals penned before bed each night, I imagined the adventures of my favorite characters from television and books and films, and kept the results hidden in a box under the bed. (Like many others, I was writing fan fiction long before I knew the term existed.) But that was just for me. I never considered that anyone else might want to read what I had written . . . until *Supernatural.* The depth of my love for this television show was an unstoppable force insisting on expression. It wasn't so much that I decided to write about it; I *had* to. When I discovered the enthusiastic creative space that was online fandom (and discovered that what I'd been writing for decades had a name and an audience), I held my breath, whispered a prayer, and dove in. Posting something I had written was terrifying. I obsessively checked the post every two minutes, hoping against hope that there might be a comment. And that it wouldn't be, "What sort of shite is this?"

The first time someone said, "This story really rings true," I had tears in my eyes. Slowly, as people commented and encouraged and gave me feedback about what worked and what didn't, I began to think, *Yes, I can do this. I can write.* Something else happened, too. The people commenting on my fan fiction, and the people writing the fan fiction that I read and commented on, became my friends. I learned from them, and I got to know them. Their struggles and their triumphs, their families, their loves and losses. They shared their fear and rage, too: all those things we'd been told to keep hidden. Sometimes they displaced those forbidden feelings onto fictional characters; sometimes they spilled it all directly. I did the same. Like a giant, multinational, gloriously diverse online therapy group, we helped one another figure out who we really were and then find the courage to live that truth.

I met my friend Kathy Larsen in that group, and together we embarked on an unexpected road trip through *Supernatural* fandom. We were both academics and had written articles before, albeit in academic journals read only by other academics. Now we wanted to write something very different, to say something we felt was even more important. We had the crazy idea that we could write a book about what it was really like to be a fangirl—one that would set the record straight about fandom and challenge the negative stereotypes. After all, we knew firsthand how powerful and positive fandom could be! We also suspected, even then, that *Supernatural* was something special.

Of course, nobody believed us.

"You want to write a book about *what* TV show?" publisher after publisher said, frowning. "How about doing one on *Star Trek*?"

I love *Star Trek*, but it's not exactly underresearched. Even in 2007 we knew *Supernatural* was going to be a phenomenon. Unfortunately, nobody else at the time shared our conviction. But Kathy and I didn't give up. Partly through beginner's luck and partly because we didn't know any better, some of our clumsy attempts to reach the show's cast worked. To our surprise, the *Supernatural* actors were interested in our project. No one else had asked them the sorts of questions we were asking, and they were all thoughtful people who enjoyed tackling topics a bit deeper than journalists' standard "What's your favorite color?" Warner Brothers got wind of what we were writing and, since nobody else was paying any attention to their little show at the time, they decided they'd support what they could get. They invited us to the *Supernatural* set and behind the scenes to talk with the actors, which was pretty much our Fangirl Fantasy No. 1 come true.

We managed to keep calm, more or less, when chatting with Jensen Ackles in his trailer. We managed to stay articulate when Jared Padalecki started taking off his clothes in the middle of our interview. (Wardrobe, folks; wardrobe.) We interviewed Misha Collins in a bar and got him in trouble for being late to his next interview; we like to think it was because the conversation was so compelling. Alarmingly often, we flew back and forth across the country to *Supernatural* conventions and Comic-Cons, meeting up with the fans we'd gotten to know online and interviewing the actors.

Left: With Jared at the very first Creation Supernatural convention in 2008.
Right: My first awkward photo op with Jensen (in which
I stealthily bumped shoulders with him . . .).

The actors kept agreeing to interviews even as Kathy and I repeatedly proved ourselves woefully inept as amateur journalists. During one of our first times in the cloistered greenroom (the room at conventions where the actors are allowed to go and fans are not), Kathy and I were jittery with nerves. I was trying hard to look like I belonged—and feeling like I most definitely didn't—while our interview subject chatted with some of his friends. There was a carafe of wine sitting on a table in the back, so I casually poured myself a very large glass.

"What are you doing?" Kathy hissed.

"Having some wine," I hissed back. Wasn't it obvious?

"That's bourbon, you idiot," Kathy said way too loudly, grabbing the giant glass from my hand. "If you drink all that, you'll keel over," she continued, with an eye roll for good measure.

She was right. I'm a lightweight under any circumstances. And the liquor was probably top shelf, so I would have wasted more money than I can even estimate. Attempting to pour it back into the carafe didn't help my quest to fit in.

Later that night I was glad Kathy had spoken up, so I could be sober enough to remember Jensen Ackles teasing us with his freaky ability to cross *one* eye (the only time in my life I have ever told him to get away from me). We also got to witness Jared Padalecki starting his Twitter account, which turned out to be a rather significant moment for the *Supernatural* fandom. We even managed to conduct a halfway-decent interview.

As we road-tripped and continued our clumsy attempts at research, our book began to take shape—an unusual shape that confused most prospective publishers. Still, the fact that our interviewees had so much to say, coupled with the confidence we'd gained in our fandom community, kept us going through repeated rejections. Eventually, a small academic press agreed to take a chance on our book. That turned out to be Book No. 1. Our original idea was to write a hybrid book: one that told the real, joyous, squeeful story of being a fangirl, along with all the research we'd done on the psychological benefits of being a fan. Unfortunately, although we knew from personal experience that fans were smart and analytical and inquisitive, nobody believed fans and academics would read the same book and enjoy it. We did, however, manage to sneak some decidedly nonacademic anecdotes into that first book, *Fandom at the Crossroads*. (Fandom had also taught us how to be subversive in order to make our voices heard, which came in handy.)

The publisher was so obscure that we weren't sure if anyone would ever read the book. And yet I found that didn't matter as much as I'd expected. *Fandom at the Crossroads* was a love letter: to fandom, with its community of women and its invitation to be real; and to *Supernatural*, which had so inspired us. If nobody read it, at least we'd done what we set out to do: we'd said what we wanted to say.

I brought a copy through the autograph line at the next *Supernatural* convention, placing it in front of Jensen.

"This is for you," I said, relatively calmly. As calm as I ever am around Mr. Ackles. "Thanks so much for all the interviews you gave us for it."

Jensen looked up, those big green eyes making me pause and stare, because *damn*.

Then he pushed the book across the table, back toward me.

I froze in horror, my stomach flipping wildly. Did he hate the whole idea of the book? Was he sorry he'd given us those interviews? How would I survive this rejection?

"You know," Jensen said, oblivious to my panic attack in progress, "I've signed a lot of autographs for you over the years."

I nodded, my throat too tight to speak.

Jensen calmly opened the book to the author page, then looked up at me. He pointed to the page and smiled.

"I think it's about time you gave *me* an autograph."

If there were an award for keeping your composure under impossible circumstances, I should have won it. The rush of relief that flooded me left my eyes so watery I could barely see the page where he wanted me to write. My fingers fumbled as he handed me the Sharpie he'd been using to sign autographs, and somehow I managed to sign my name, probably illegibly.

Jensen picked it up and put it beside him. I think he said congratulations, but by that time I couldn't really see or hear very much. I have no idea what I mumbled in return or how I made my way back to my seat. If someone had told me at the start of this crazy journey that Jensen Ackles would ask for my autograph, on a book about *Supernatural* that I had written, I would have offered them some free therapy, since they were clearly living in a fantasy world.

We gave copies of the book to Jared and Misha, and several of the guest actors who had contributed, too. At the next convention I brought a book through the autograph line again, this time to have the actors sign so we could donate the book for a charity auction. When I placed the book in front of Jared, he stopped and looked up, a serious look on his face.

I began to panic. Had he looked it over and hated what he saw? Once again, fear slid down my spine, leaving me mute.

"I just wanted to thank you," Jared said, "for writing this book. It's really important to me to understand the fans, and reading this book really helped."

I recovered the power of speech a little more quickly this time, though not the ability to be tactful. "You read it?" I blurted.

Jared laughed and nodded. "Cover to cover. Go ahead, ask me anything."

I can't remember what I asked him, but he answered it. Correctly (and rather eloquently). Huh.

Later that day, we met up with Misha at a local Starbucks for an interview and he mentioned the book.

"I've read some of it," Misha said. "But Jared read it all."

"Really?" I asked, still having trouble believing it.

"Every bit," Misha assured us. "He's an avid reader."

We nodded, on cloud nine. Then, predictably, Misha couldn't resist adding a jab.

"And Jensen looked at the pictures," he said, with a sly grin.

Fandom at the Crossroads didn't exactly make the *New York Times* best-seller list. But the fans and cast (and our fellow academics) who read it seemed to like what it said. What reviews the book garnered were positive. I had dared to speak up and be real, and the world hadn't ended. In fact, it looked a little safer. Meanwhile, we had an entire other story that hadn't made it into that book: *our* story. To be honest, Kathy and I had been reluctant to share that one. Who wants to tell the entire world the true story of *you*, warts and all? What kind of fool would put that out there—with their real names, no less—for all the world to see (and inevitably tear apart)?

But some people wouldn't leave it alone.

"Write yourself back into the story," our friend, director and producer Tony Zierra, said. We had met Tony through Chad Lindberg, who memorably played Ash on the first few seasons of *Supernatural*. Tony's documentary indie hit, *My Big Break*, had at first been focused on Chad and three other actors living in a house in Hollywood trying to make it big. They challenged Tony, who was also living there, to tell his own story in the film, too—and that made all the difference.

We knew a few other people who also knew a thing or two about writing. Writer/director M. Night Shyamalan has been a friend for many years, long before *The Sixth Sense* made him a household name.

"Write about your own experience," Night said. "Here you are, two smart, accomplished women. And you find yourself on the couch with a bag of Doritos watching episode after episode of *Supernatural*, and you think, how did I get here? Write about that."

The idea was terrifying. It's one thing to do research and theorize about why some of us are so passionate; it's quite another to confess your own passions. We waffled. Could we really speak up that much, that authentically? Who would publish that, anyway?

A funny thing happens once you start to express yourself, though. You can't just shut your mouth and stop. We decided Tony and Night were right, and we went in search of a publisher who would believe in our voice. Eventually, *Fangasm* was published as a memoir. Who knew they published memoirs of nobodies? It was terrifying. Everything was in there. Not just my obsession with *Supernatural*, but also my fears and insecurities, passions and fantasies. Fights with my kids; a breakup with my long-term partner.

Perhaps, I thought, no one will read it. Certainly not the actors. I had no plans to hand them a copy like I had with *Fandom at the Crossroads*, that's for sure. Jensen didn't need to know the details of my appreciation of his . . . acting.

In an unfortunate lapse in judgement, I failed to tell other people not to tell Jared and Jensen that I had a new book out about their show. Shortly after *Fangasm*'s publication, they stopped me to chat, looking surprisingly affronted. I panicked, unsure what they wanted to talk about. Had I inadvertently let my hands wander during a photo op or something?

Jared fake punched me in the shoulder and demanded, "You have a new book out and you didn't even tell us? We're in it and we haven't even read it yet!"

Jensen just grinned at my gobsmacked expression.

So much for the actors not reading it. They did. Even more improbably, they liked it.

Falling into *Supernatural* fandom had already changed me. Writing *Fangasm* changed me again, because—miraculously—it changed other people. In emails and tweets and in person at fan conventions, fans told me that *Fangasm* was important to them. That reading our story let them know they weren't alone. They weren't weird, or psychologically flawed, or losers. They were okay. *Fangasm* did for them what discovering online fandom did for me, which is exactly why we wrote it. Every time people tell me that reading the book helped them leave that nagging internalized shame behind, I'm thankful we wrote our story the way it really happened, with all the ups and downs and embarrassing and exhilarating moments.

At a *Supernatural* convention shortly after *Fangasm* came out, a middle-aged woman approached me in the ballroom with the book in her hand.

"Are you one of the authors?" she asked. I said yes, and she reached out and shook my hand. It was only then that I noticed a teenage girl behind her.

"Thank you," the woman said. "My daughter is too shy to tell you, but she read your book and then she shared it with me, and now I finally understand her. I finally get it."

The daughter nodded, and the mom's eyes began to water. My eyes began to water. The daughter's eyes began to water. I'm sure everyone around us was wondering why the three of us were smiling and crying simultaneously, but it was a wonderful moment. It's why we write: to touch someone else.

My experience with *Supernatural* has had a snowball effect. A little bit of confidence allows more self-expression, which builds a little more. Kathy started the *Journal of Fandom Studies* with Intellect Publishing, with me on the editorial board. In one of our meetings with Intellect, I heard about their Fan Phenomena series, each focused on a book or film or television show that was a bona fide phenomenon. Why, I wondered, was *Supernatural* not on that list? Intellect informed me that the shows in that book series had been around a long time and were no longer on the air, which had given them time to accumulate large fan bases.

"But *Supernatural* already has that," I argued. "It's been on the air for eight years and has all the fan support and Internet awards that qualify it as a phenomenon!"

I think the publisher got tired of my emails arguing the case (another benefit to finding your voice). They agreed to let us edit a volume devoted to *Supernatural*. Misha Collins wrote a chapter, about how being cast as Castiel and having fans had changed his life for the better. Richard Speight wrote a chapter, about how the experience of doing conventions had changed his understanding of both himself and fandom. Serge Ladouceur, the show's brilliant cinematographer, contributed a chapter. We had essays by fans and by academics, too; *Fan Phenomena: Supernatural* has the multiple perspectives we thought were important.

I brought a copy to the Vancouver *Supernatural* convention that year to give to Serge, to thank him for his contribution.

"Are you coming by the set while you're here?" he asked, as though that were the most ordinary question in the world.

I managed to squeak out an okay and we returned to the studio for another set visit, once again struck by the warmth and friendliness of the cast and crew. Much like my first set visit, everyone went out of their way to make us feel welcome. During the lunch break, the guest actress showed us exactly how *Supernatural*'s brilliant makeup person makes an attractive woman look like the wicked witch. The script supervisor explained her job and asked us all about our books. Best of all, the episode's writer, Robbie Thompson, sat next to us all day. He shared insights about the episode and his writing process, and when he found out I wrote books on *Supernatural*, he said he would go right out and get them. *Mm-hmm*, I said politely, in response to what I was quite certain was his graciousness. It's no secret that I fangirl the show's actors, but I fangirl the writers almost as hard. Interviewing Eric Kripke and Sera Gamble gave me as many butterflies as chatting with Jensen, Jared, or Misha did. So let's just say I sat there rapt. (And, oh yes, Robbie bought all the books. And read them.)

Robbie was called in to consult on dialogue several times, and the changes needed were made on the spot. That's the handy thing about having a writer on set! Between shots, he showed us around the bunker, which is an amazing set that takes up most of one of the gigantic sound stages at the studio. Most sets don't seem real once you stand inside them, but this one does. Protection sigils carved into the ceilings and doorways. Pots and pans and cans of pie filling on the shelves in the kitchen. A plethora of mad-scientist-type supplies in the room outfitted as a lab: beakers and test tubes half-full of colorful liquids, microscopes with something disgusting-looking on a slide, shelves of jars and cans and notebooks. We happily perused the library with Robbie, looking at book after book to see what Sam and Dean might be reading. I was particularly thrilled to find an old psychology text on the shelves—they clearly need that! The hallways are actual hallways, and the rooms are actual rooms (albeit with removable ceilings to allow for overhead shots). In fact, the set is so large that once or twice I found myself a bit lost trying to get to the bathroom or outside to grab a snack from craft services. Lost in the Men of Letters bunker—could there be a better problem?

Every time the "video village" (the cameras and monitors, along with chairs for the director, cinematographer, script supervisor, writer . . . and, in this case, us!) moved, we were stunned by how quickly and efficiently they went from one place to the next.

"Moving on," director Bob Singer would say, and they would.

Thompson is the writer who created the character of fangirl and geek heroine Charlie Bradbury, so I think he understood our fangirl priorities: he made sure to take us to see Dean's bedroom before we left. I sat on the bed for a few minutes, awed. It wasn't the memory foam I was expecting, but it was still a moment. Hey, it was the closest I'm ever going to get to being in Dean Winchester's bed, so allow me my flight of imagination.

In season 11, I was able to visit the set again, this time on location, to watch Jensen and guest star Rob Benedict film some of their powerful scenes together (while they fought off the rampant mosquitoes between takes—did you know that Jensen can clap his hands together and take one out in midair?). Jensen apologized for not having something "more exciting" going on that day, and I shook my head. This show? Every single thing about this show is fascinating to me. Watching Rob and Jensen share laughs between takes and toss around the popcorn. Chatting with guest star Emily Swallow (Amara) about the challenges of wearing the same dress for an entire season (either Amara had a major dry-cleaning bill or that dress was pretty disgusting by season's end). Watching the cooperation, mutual respect, and affection between director Tom Wright and the actors, as he popped in and out with notes and the actors subtly changed their acting in response. Not exciting? I was mesmerized.

They were filming that day in a beautiful Vancouver woods, the tall pine trees seeming to reach halfway to heaven and a thick bed of twigs and broken branches beneath us. Those twigs unfortunately made a loud crunching and cracking sound if you walked on them, which meant I stood frozen every time they started filming, terrified that I'd shift position and the crackle of branches would ruin a take. I remember vividly a moment when I was walking behind Jensen and Emily as they crossed to a different part of the woods, staring at Jensen's feet—because those were Dean's boots he was wearing. The sun was streaming through the tall trees and the sky was blue above and I was following in Dean Winchester's footsteps, feeling almost as if I were walking with the fictional character who has meant so much to me. Not exciting? I was smiling to myself as I tried to commit that image to memory.

Later that day, they filmed a scene with Rob and Jensen (as God and Dean) talking on a park bench. Jensen told us that the giant old tree we were standing under as we watched was the one that the cast and crew call "Kim's tree" in memory of their beloved executive producer and director, Kim Manners. It seemed fitting that we had ended up there, and I remembered the first time we'd been on set, when Kim was still with them. I was overcome with emotion about this show that has changed my life in so many ways over the course of a decade.

The confidence I found through *Supernatural* and fandom changed my professional and personal life, too. I'm not the sort of person who can just say, "Oh, cool, let's change jobs." I get attached. I like security, not risk. And we've established that the last thing I'd willingly volunteer to do is get up in front of a hiring committee and give a job talk! But my experience in *Supernatural* fandom had been all about risk: taking a chance, throwing caution to the wind, daring to do what I *wanted* to do! I took a deep breath and put in my application for a faculty position at a nearby university. I was so nervous during the interview that I brought the wrong version of my PowerPoint presentation, and then stared at the screen in horror for a good two minutes while I tried to figure out how to reconcile my carefully prepared notes with the non-matching slides. Internally, I was cursing myself for taking such a risk. Outwardly, I managed to wing it. The hiring committee told me part of the reason they gave me the job was because of my ability to keep my wits about me during a crisis.

I found my voice in my personal life as well. The validation I gained in fandom and from writing the books turned out to be helpful in my love life. Once I found the guts to get out of a relationship that was anything but validating, I was determined to be as real with my next partner as I'd dared to be with my online community. My new partner got to see the real me from the start, fangirling and all. He read my writing, professional and fan fiction, with equal interest. He also learned very quickly that suggesting, "Hey, wanna watch some *Supernatural?*" was a more potent aphrodisiac than the best bottle of wine or my favorite chocolates.

Once I'd found my voice, I discovered other ways to use it. In public, no less. Considering my long history as an introvert (and that humiliating seventh-grade-geography debacle), speaking up in public was a significant challenge. After the release of *Fangasm*, we started to get some press and people began requesting interviews. Print interviews? No problem. We happily answered everyone's questions in long, detailed emails and loved the printed results. Radio and podcast interviews? That was a different story. I was sure I'd end up babbling nonsense, but consoled myself with the thought that at least nobody would see me turn red while I did so.

We were beyond thrilled when we were asked to do a piece on *Supernatural* for National Public Radio. It was exciting enough to know that the show had become so popular that it was being recognized on NPR, but the idea that we would be the "experts" they'd want to speak to? Almost as thrilling as meeting the actors and writers. So I took a train down to Washington, D.C., to record the segment, even though I had injured my back two days earlier and was in tremendous pain. Pain doesn't stop a truly passionate fan, after all!

The trip down wasn't too bad; it's a two-hour train ride, and as long as I stood up, I was more or less okay. The NPR reporter came to Kathy's house to record the segment, and began with, "So, this show must be pretty special. Show me why." We spent the next few hours watching episodes and regaling her with all the reasons why *Supernatural* is the best show ever. By the time we taped the actual piece, I'm pretty sure she was a convert.

The trip was worth it. I can say that now. Unfortunately, the return train to Philly ran into track problems (whatever that means) and ended up stuck without power for *five hours*. That's a long time when you're in pain and can't sit down! The conductor eventually took pity on me and cleared off a table in the dining car, saying, "Here you go, ma'am; you can lie down." I'm sure I looked like an idiot splayed out on a table in the dining car, but desperate times call for desperate measures. Even with the euphoria of knowing we'd just done a segment on *Supernatural* for NPR, that trip was not fun. But worth it? Hell, yes. Misha Collins caught the segment when it aired live and sent his congrats. Even Warner Brothers was impressed, sending us a lovely email congratulating us on the success of our books.

PR was going well, we thought. No problem. Then we were asked to shoot a piece on fandom for a documentary film. Kathy and I were both close to panic. Kathy refuses to even have her picture taken, let alone speak on camera! But how could we turn it down?

Luckily, the filmmaker was patient. She taught us how to sit so we didn't look like posed mannequins.

"You can move, you know," she assured us repeatedly. The end result is still two rather stiff women, but at least we were able to smile.

By the time I filmed my fourth documentary (about fangirls), I was laughing and enjoying myself as I recounted one of my fangirl adventures. I took another risk and signed on to be a writer and associate producer for that film, which is soon to be released in online episodes as *Squee! The Fangirl Documentary.* That brought me back to Comic-Con, where my fangirl adventures had begun eight years before. If someone had told me pre-*Supernatural* that I'd be coordinating shoots with celebrities and a film crew—which requires a fairly high level of outspokenness—I would have said they were nuts. But there I was, pulling together the *Squee* shoots in between the *Supernatural* panel and Nerd HQ. The highlight of my weekend was helping the *Supernatural* cast give back to their fans, handing out pizza with Misha Collins and Osric Chau to the long line of fans waiting in line overnight.

The next summer I returned to Comic-Con again, this time to sell *Fangasm* and *Fan Phenomena: Supernatural* with pop-culture vendor Cinequest. Going back as a vendor felt surreal, and seeing our books for sale at the booth across from Warner Brothers even more so. Comic-Con has taught me a lot over the years; that year, it taught me that finding and using your voice doesn't necessarily mean you'll get what you want. I have always, like many people, had a hard time not falling into depression when faced with disappointment. Fandom and *Supernatural* have taught me to Always Keep Fighting. They've also pushed me out of my comfort zone repeatedly, so that I could have lots of practice taking risks and then coping with the disappointment that sometimes follows.

On the afternoon of the Comic-Con *Supernatural* panel that year, I settled in at the Cinequest booth, thinking I'd have a ringside seat to say hi to Jared and Jensen and Misha at the WB booth ten yards away, where they'd be signing autographs. I'd forgotten that the convention floor turns into a solid mass of people once the *Supernatural* cast arrives at the booth, packed so tightly together that raising your arm becomes an impossibility. The crowd stretched at least forty yards in all directions. The only way to get anywhere near the WB booth was to start "upstream" at the edge of the crowd and then go with the flow. In fact, you had no choice *but* to go with the flow once you moved into the mass of people. It was like being caught in a swiftly moving river; you couldn't really move of your own volition, but had to let the current carry you.

Of course I had to give it a try, even though I'm not known for my swimming prowess. I waded in, twenty yards upstream from the WB booth, and held my breath as the crowd's current took me. As people were swept in range of Jared, Jensen, and Misha, fans predictably stopped to stare and attempt a picture. The security folks were less than happy about this idea.

"MOVE ALONG!" the tall, burly security man behind the railing yelled, only inches from my face, as I was swept into range. As though there were anywhere for me to move. I was still caught in the mass of people, and no one around me was moving. "THAT MEANS YOU, LADY!" he reiterated, and gave me a helping hand in that direction, none too gently.

I used my fandom-honed speaking-out skills to yell back.

"WHERE THE HELL DO YOU THINK I CAN GO?" I demanded. Then added "SIR" as an afterthought.

The river of humanity resumed its flow and I was carried away before he could answer . . . and without getting more than a fleeting glance at the actors. Not a single photo, much less the chance to say hi. I gave up, discouraged, and headed for the ladies' room behind the booth.

"Oh no you don't," a security woman said, motioning me away from the restroom line.

"Excuse me?" I managed, confused.

"You don't have to use the bathroom," she accused, glaring. "You're just trying to stand there so you can see them."

Them? I looked up. Sure enough, there were the boys on the second-floor VIP area of the WB booth—where Kathy and I had interviewed Eric Kripke four years earlier.

Priorities, though. I really had to use the restroom. Once again, I managed to speak up.

"How about if you curve the line around so we're waiting *inside* the restroom?" I suggested, starting to hop up and down a bit.

The security woman was skeptical, but agreed, so I did get to pee. Never got a photo, which was definitely disappointing, but I attempted to shrug it off with at least a bit of success. At the end of the day I made the long trek back to my hotel. "Well, that's probably my last Comic-Con," I thought, with a mix of resignation, relief, and sadness. "And my last book on *Supernatural*."

Obviously, I was wrong. In the last several years, something extraordinary happened. As the fans and cast of *Supernatural* got to know one another over the course of a decade, fans drew inspiration and support not only from one another but from the actors as well. When fandom organized to counter a rash of online bullying, many fans re-blogged Jared's words to a fan struggling with depression: "Getting rid of yourself isn't going to help anybody. Just keep fighting the fight." Soon it wasn't just fans trying to get that message out; the cast joined in. That quote turned into Jared and Jensen's "Always Keep Fighting" campaign, bringing awareness to and shattering the stigma of mental health challenges. Fan after fan dared to talk about their own struggles with depression and anxiety and suicidality, and in the process managed to keep fighting. Misha and Jensen started the "You Are Not Alone" campaign, and all three actors recently launched the #SPNFamilyLove initiative. Mark Sheppard posted a photo with the message "Family don't end with blood," an iconic line from the show and one of its primary messages. "If you hurt right now, please share your story," he said. "Let someone help you, love you. Our secrets are what do the most damage."

He's right. That's what I discovered on my twelve-year (and counting!) road trip through *Supernatural* fandom. Finding my voice and using it, refusing to keep secrets based on shame and doubt, and believing I had something to say that was worth listening to have been life-changing. I'm still an introvert, but I'll be damned if I'll let other people—or the shame or doubt imposed by them—keep me quiet. And that has made all the difference.

With Laurena Aker and "the boys" at ChiCon 2014.

TONE DEEF*: THE STRUGGLE IS REAL

(*Tone deaf as said in "Scottish")

RUTH CONNELL

My mum has a lovely melodic singing voice. I remember her singing "Memory" very well when I was wee; very musical is my mum.

My dad is tone deaf. I mean literally unable to repeat accurately a single note just blasted at him. Not for want of trying, mind you; my dad sings around the house almost constantly things like, "Who's sorry now . . ." at full tilt. It often amazes me when I hear old songs on the radio and I somehow know the lyrics but the tune is strangely unfamiliar . . .

I live somewhere in the middle.

When I was nine years old I was given a song-and-dance routine to perform at a dancing competition. I wasn't aware of any competitiveness or of winning medals, just that I had a dance to learn and somehow a song that went along with it to sing: "The Chattanooga Shoe Shine Boy." The rendition I had to go on was all played in the minor key, on an old piano, on a dodgy recording that was never broken down for me audibly, never note bashed or shown to me as sheet music on paper. I never saw the notes or understood the tune in that way. Or any way! I couldn't hear the tune on the recording, either. These are all my excuses.

I was sent out in front of an auditorium full of people in my Little Lord Fauntleroy–style burgundy velveteen jodhpurs (clearly the go-to gear of shoeshine chaps in old Chicago town in the 1920s) to belt out said song for one minute and thirty seconds, on my own.

I came offstage and my mum said, "Oh, hen!" She said this not in a good way with a joyous tone; it was more a perplexed, anguished tone. That I *could* hear. (Mum, I know you were just concerned—I love you, and ALL the costumes you made me were amazing and I couldn't have done ANY of this without you.) You know in nightmares when you are naked at school or with all your teeth crumbling out of your mouth and out on a date? That slow-motion surreal knowing that something is not quite right and yet there is nothing you can do about it whatsoever except try to live through it. That, onstage, in front of all my peers.

I wasn't used to failing that badly at stuff. I felt ashamed and confused that I had somehow messed up and done such a bad job. More so, that I had had no control over any of it. I got a fright to the point where I refused to go onstage and do it ever again (or until the next festival at least). I admitted defeat to myself in the song-and-dance arena, which had meant a lot to me, as musicals were in my brain and in my blood—I adored them, was weaned on old movies, and really all I had wanted out of life was to be Michelle Pfeiffer in *The Fabulous Baker Boys*. So the dream died.

The wires in my brain don't easily mesh to remembering sequences of musical notes. It feels a bit like pitch-blindness. Show me a sequence of dance moves and I'm your lady, ALL OVER IT. Tunes . . . not so much. Confusing, because I knew my voice could be pretty loud when it needed to be! This singing malarkey was my Kryptonite. And we always want what we don't have.

I of course compared myself to the girls around me, which is *always* the smartest move to make in any life situation, I don't find! To the left (to the left) my friend Alison singing a beautiful soprano. To the right my friend Sarah belting out Michael Jackson. In front my friend Jo as Barnum: a one-woman spectacular song-and-dance sensation in all areas, including the odd backflip!

(This is perhaps an opportune moment to put in perspective that which only hindsight can give a person: Alison Connell went on to work in *Phantom of the Opera*, Sarah Gardiner worked as a professional singer, and Jo Gibb played Roxy in the West End in *Chicago*. It's all relative; I sure was a duff singer compared to them if comparison is what your bag is, and don't we all fall into that trap?)

Compounding the terrible tragedy that I was not the best at something I wanted to be good at, I was then shamefully given the one *speaking* part (i.e., non-singing part) of a song-and-dance trio routine with the aforementioned Alison and Sarah. *Okay, so everyone knows I'm bad at this and can't be trusted to hold a note,* ran my inner monologue. My icky feeling knew no bounds. There is something so personal about our voices, right? It's hard to hear ourselves back on a voice mail or on a recording. Singing is opening up that soft spot of the core of who we are, and it's vulnerable-making. Even the best singers I know still get nervous before a performance. Super-tough for the rest of us who want to make like Barbra Streisand.

By the time I was fifteen, my teacher Joyce Paterson suggested a great old song for me to perform for the Edinburgh Festival competition coming up: "If There's a Wrong Way to Do It," which I choreographed into an old-school vaudeville, comedy-schtick routine. Quite talk/singy, loud and brash and proud: "If there's a wrong note I sing it—nobody does it like me!" Weaknesses into strengths, people, weaknesses into strengths. I fell over a few times in the routine, tripped up deliberately and all that. Comedy gold. Winner, winner, chicken dinner; I won the Song and Dance trophy for the entire festival. I was now Rocky. And nearly ready to work alongside Bette Midler.

Which brings me leaping forward in time to a later pivotal point in my singing odyssey; age twenty-three and I'm doing a summer season as a dancer down in Devon, England. They had an Eternal tribute band as part of the Saturday-night show (please tell me some of you are old enough to know this band?). Anyway, they needed a Louise to be cast from the company dancers, as they were a singer short for the quartet. "Don't let go!

Pictured backstage as "Macavity," the fierce yet only non-singing cat in a Cats song-and-dance act.

'Cause we're just a step from heaven." Um. More like hell. The auditions went great and I was riding my song-and-dance trophy memories like an actual surfer *dude*. They picked me! To be a singer. In a professional show.

Then they put me onstage, live, with one of those Madonna head mics in an all-white trouser suit to sing the lowest part of a four-part harmony . . . that I had never really been taught. Oh, dear. Car crash. No fold back. Couldn't hear myself. It was "Chattanooga" all over again. Minus the jodhpurs, but still . . . I came offstage mortified as the massive audience had probably all winced at the sound and seen me not have a clue what to do about it, like a pop-wannabe bunny in the headlights and then with the choreographer looking at me like I'd licked her cat's poo as I passed her, side stage, gulping my mortification down.

The course of true melody never did play out smooth. Life gives us setbacks, right? One step forward, two back. Not every path or story has a beginning, a middle, and an end (pretty sure this chapter might fail that template, also), but rather is like a bumbling little lane with boulders and puddles to negotiate, with the end not quite in sight and a hole in our socks to boot. The relationship with my voice was once again an uneasy grumbling of discontented discord. I was quiet for quite a while after that. No more singing in the shower. I knew my voice could fail me at any point.

The real point of all this, the place this story is leading me to, is cons. Conventions. The SPNFamily live! Saturday Night Specials! Louden Swain. Richard Speight. Rob Benedict. God is good, it seems . . . And here is the "rising from the ashes like a phoenix" epiphany in my story. Or maybe more like finding a reasonable place of self-acceptance, the middle ground.

The first *Supernatural* US convention I did, I watched the Saturday Night Special, the concert Louden Swain gives to the con guests on Saturday night, and was amazed. The SNS is a real coming-together highlight of the weekend; we, the lucky actors, get to guest sing a song with the band. Sometimes there are kazoos involved. Richard asked me to introduce Osric. He later caught me practicing my words side stage under my breath, something like, "Fresh from the yellow-brick road, Mr. Osric." Like about twenty-five times in case I messed it up. Not sure I filled our Dickie with the utmost of confidence at that moment! To then see Jensen perform like the utter rock star he is (pitch-perfect of course, even in playback) blew my mind. At that moment I thought, *I will never do this.* By the end of the concert and one (or two) whiskeys from Chris Schmelke along, I joined in the group rendition of "A Little Help from My Friends." Rob heard me sing a line of the chorus (it's the same line over and over and pretty much one note, so I had it *down*). He said after the show that I must sing with the band and that it wasn't about being perfect, just to get up and do it. He followed through with emails about song suggestions and didn't flinch when I said "Son of a Preacher Man" as a possibility.

When I came into the greenroom one day at the next convention, the band had worked on the song and there was no way I could bow out and have wasted their time. Billy and Stephen, Robot Mike and Robert (I like to say Rob's name in as thick a Robert the Bruce–type Scottish accent as possible), Mark Sheppard volunteering to drum, and Adam Malin, the co-owner of Creation Entertainment, playing keyboards. Can't back out of that, girl!

The first sound check was a little dicey. And I had to consciously talk myself down off the ledge when people started suggesting that I turn up my earpiece so I could hear myself better (it was already up very high, it's just that I become tone deaf with nerves).

I remember walking out onto the stage when it was my turn and the crowd went crazy! Now I was Beyoncé. You guys are amazing. A wall of sound, light, and intensity hit me. I felt better straight away as the audience was so loud I thought, *Great, they'll not really be able to hear me too clearly anyway!* I started to digest the support that I was being given by the fans. Almost deafening. Not many people get to experience that in a lifetime, right?

Then the band started. And stopped. And started again. Then stopped again. Third time lucky! Don't you just love it when other people don't get it right the first time? Must try to remember that next time I get it wrong!

Lucky lass getting to play with Louden Swain. Pictured with Billy Moran, Rob Benedict, and my belly button, which I use to divert attention from pitch.

A weird calm settled on me and somehow I sang the song through, fans sang along with me, and people cheered at the end. Every time I looked at someone in the band playing with me, their eyes and smiles were egging me on. Nobody died. I got hugs leaving the stage. Then I retired my career. Moved to a sheltered house in Palm Springs and married my much-younger butler.

I'm writing this on a plane on the way to a convention and I know that tomorrow I will sing with the band again—a great band; I love Louden Swain. And I will more than likely be okay, and I know that it doesn't matter anyway, as it's not about me, it's about joining in the party that the SPNFamily throw themselves at the cons. Giving the fans the best show we know how to on a Saturday night. I'm such a lucky lady to be a guest on this crazy SPN road trip around the States and the world. A wee secret part of me knows I might actually/probably enjoy myself. Maybe my Achilles' heel ain't so wobbly after all. It's getting stronger, thanks to the fandom and my fellow players on the stage.

(NB: Editing this chapter on the plane on the way back from JaxCon and I can indeed report that I loved Saturday night—including *during* my performance. Onward! Upward! Madison Square Garden, here I come! Maybe I'm not tone deaf after all, just "pitch challenged" and coping.)

When I first started the cons, in Detroit, I couldn't believe someone would put a microphone in my hand and let me speak for an hour. Fans asking me questions about Rowena and me. Here I was talking a lot, more and more openly, and on record, judging by all the videos online that spring up (something that in previous years would have given me cold shivers of fear). However, the fans at conventions are the best audience a person could hope for. So in love with the show and the boys, I get to ride on the coattails of all their previous years of work and shared history. The love is there in the fandom, and amazingly for me I have a character who has been accepted and seems to be cherished by the fandom (as much as I cherish her) and so I am given the confidence from the fans to take up more space. (This is where Mark would call me "Wee Bit.")

It's only because of the unerring love and support of the SPNFamily that I am able to get up in front of a room full of over a thousand people (who knows how many more via the interweb thingy) and talk and sing. Out loud. Live. Repeatedly. Without falling over. Aw, I realize writing this I'm like a wee delicate flower opening up because of the fandom compost. Or, um, more like a chatty know-it-all hydrangea with new boots and a blowout.

The job of playing Rowena has expanded my life in so many wonderful and amazing ways. I'm so grateful that the show exists and that I can be a part of it. Then there is this whole other world, which runs concurrent (like in *His Dark Materials*): this world with the fans, and the conventions, cosplayers, and mini rock star bit. I hope I never look back. Maybe I will make it to Broadway one day after all . . . or perhaps just be able to handle myself in a big interview situation because I've gained so much positive interactive experience within the fandom. I'm coming for ya, James Cordon.

To put the public-speaking aspect more into context, I used to almost stammer as a teenager, tripping over my words and failing to catch my breath, I could get so anxious. My doctor gave me an inhaler at one point. I had two actual panic attacks, so nervous of my own self and voice—paradoxically one of the reasons I am an actor. I feel I have stuff to say, things to get out there, but I like lines. I like other people's words. I managed to complete a three-year degree course in acting without once "devising" or really improvising a piece . . . at a college known for its improv. I was so terrified of putting my foot in it (as I often do), but the encompassing love and acceptance within the SPNFamily have allowed me to begin to develop my own voice, not just singing but as a person who sometimes has opinions and is now less afraid to share them. And to sometimes just talk bloody nonsense, too, and for it not to matter a whole heap.

Con audiences may be dangerous, I realize writing this! I sometimes come away actually thinking I'm funny . . . because everyone is such a good sport (and I put a spell on them to laugh at my Dad-type jokes). Ocht and it doesn't matter anyway as long as we are all lifting one another up and having fun, which is what I see at the cons and online: the amazing support and joy we all give one another in the SPNFamily.

Perhaps it's being in America, too, this ethos of freedom of speech, perhaps also in gratitude to women like Jennifer Lawrence who speak out more and more unapologetically. Certainly I'm inspired by the women around me now at the cons: Alaina, Sam, Kim, Briana, Katherine, Emily, not to mention the Osrics and the Gils, the Manns and the Tylers, the Travises and the Curtises and the Tims. Also the people who get up to ask questions. I know how much my heart pounds when I ask a question at a film Q&A. On the other hand, I also know what a nerd Misha is, and if he can do it, well . . . (I love you, Misha.) Jared and Jensen—let's speak no more of the gods of charm and wit. Rob and Rich are off the scale. Mark could teach blades of grass to converse. (I think at times I've seen him try. It looked cute.)

When I get up onstage at a con with a microphone in my hand for the panels or karaoke or to sing, the energy that I'm given or that is transmitted through me via the fandom is like rocket fuel and I can't believe some of the antics I have gotten up to. Disco ball–change anyone?! VClub Mega?! I'm not usually a very karaoke-type person in real life (flashback to karaoke with Erica Carroll and a *Thelma and Louise* bra-flinging moment, screaming, "Give me the mic!").

The empowerment to be oneself and to bloom in public is at once terrifying and intoxicating. I hope to encourage more and more others to do the same. Introvert or extrovert, we can all feel the same shame at a faux pas. I'll probably go too far. Fair warning: I hope you catch me, forgive me, and prop me back up.

Writing this chapter I still dodge in and out of self-consciousness a bit but I want to "gie it laldy," as the outpouring of encouragement from the fans has meant so much to me.

That I get to meet the fans and grow in the ways I've described and hopefully give back a little is miraculous/genius. Thank you to all the organizers of the conventions, amongst them the lovely Adam and Gary, Wayne, Bill, and the many others I've yet to meet . . . and to Julie, my convention agent. Mainly, though, to you guys, for buying the tickets and

When we "played Vegas" and I mounted Kim Rhodes,
and we were henceforth rock stars.

for tweeting, Facebook-ing, Instagram-ing, and Tumblr-ing me. You make my life amazing.

I learned from a wonderful lady called Maria Nemeth to focus on what's important and positive and thus my life has improved immeasurably. She is a clinical psychologist and life coach/financial coach in her seventies, and she took me under her wing in 2013 during a particularly rough patch. She is amazing! And now watches the show, by the way! Thanks to her, I don't give a monkey's about being "cool" anymore. Having gratitude is the coolest vibe ever and one I see ever-present in the fandom. You guys thank us for the episodes and for turning up or interacting with you on social media. I'm like, "WHAT?!" It's a privilege. It terrifies me a bit that some of you on Twitter say I'm your mentor or that Rowena is! If it's Rowena, I'm less worried . . . I'm actually trying to take a leaf out of her book with the unapologetic-ness and all that. If it's me, well then I shall do my best to be graceful and grateful and to keep on singing regardless of flat or bum notes.

Back to the completion-not-perfection idea; perfection is so boring. We are such an inclusive and brilliantly dysfunctional family—it's

Thanks as always to Megan, a.k.a. Stardust and Melancholy,
for making me look like a good singer.

familiar and fabulous. We know who we are and it's awesome. I'm not a bad enough singer to be funny, nor a good enough one to be great (like Stephanie Dizon—WOWSERS). I don't go up there to be the best or to show what I've got. I go up there because it's a bloody gift that you guys want me there and that the Saturday Night Special includes me. Don't get me wrong, though; I'd still cut off a pinky to sound like Briana Buckmaster. Damn her eyes.

Being part of a successful show like *Supernatural* is opening so many doors for me. It's wonderful and an amazing step in my life path of being an actor. In the same breath I'll say I know whichever new doors I step through, I will never now *not* be in the SPNFamily. I know this for sure because one Scottish fan warned me at Asylum: "Once yer in . . . ye canne get oot!" I'll proudly wear my SPNFamily badge wherever I get to in this careering career that I hope continues like Baby. In 2014 I landed *Supernatural*. Everything changed. Then came the fandom . . . all I can say is thank you. Thank you. Thank you.

ALMOST
SUPERNATURAL

GIL MCKINNEY

As I enter the thirty-sixth year of my life, I have learned that the greatest gifts on this earth are often the most unexpected. The ideas or plans I may have of where I should be personally or professionally have often been met with disappointment and confusion.

Don't get me wrong. I think it is important to hope, dream, and plan for the things you want. And no matter what your chosen field, getting into action to achieve those goals is crucial if you want a shot at success. There is no substitute for hard work, so when that moment comes, you are prepared. However, every so often, I believe there is something bigger than me at work on my behalf. The stars align in a way that I find hard to explain. The humdrum becomes extraordinary, as my life is catapulted into moments of unexpected joy and fulfillment. In a way, it almost seems *supernatural*.

Back in the spring of 2005, I was beginning my career as a professional actor when I auditioned and subsequently tested for what was then the WB Network's pilot of *Supernatural*. Though the role of Sam Winchester went to the extremely talented and very deserving Jared Padalecki,

I received an unexpected letter from the pilot's director, David Nutter, thanking me for going through the testing process and encouraging me to continue on my path as a young actor. Maybe he sent this same letter to all the actors who tested, but it meant the world to me. I framed the letter and have it to this day.

Eight years later, I received a call from casting to go in and read for the role of Henry Winchester, Sam and Dean's paternal grandfather. Even though it took them almost a decade to get back to me, I was thrilled to have the opportunity. Maybe, just maybe, I was meant to be a Winchester after all.

As I walked out of the Warner Bros. casting office and headed toward the bank of elevators, my head was held high and my breath was steady. I had done my job: prepared and delivered to the best of my ability in that room and in that moment. Not to mention, I felt pretty cool wearing a sharp suit with my hair parted to the side. The rest was out of my hands. It took a day or two for the word to come through my manager that I had landed the role of Henry Winchester. Thrilled to have a job and to get the chance to travel to Vancouver, I began to pack my bags. Little did I know the adventures that awaited me.

About halfway through shooting my first episode, "As Time Goes By," written by the wonderful Adam Glass, Jared and Jensen pulled me aside and informed me that there was a strong chance I would be invited to attend some of the many *Supernatural* conventions that take place all over the world. Though I hadn't even finished shooting my first episode, the boys insisted that me being a Winchester was the most important thing. I mean, the show is about family, right? At the time, I was merely flattered and excited about the prospect of being paid to travel, something I hadn't had the chance to do much of at that point in my life. I hadn't a clue of what the conventions were all about or how incredibly loyal and intense the fan base is. It wouldn't be long before I would be given a crash course on the *Supernatural* fandom.

In the spring of 2014, as I somewhat timidly stepped through the curtain and onto the stage at Creation Entertainment's Washington, D.C., *Supernatural* convention, I was met with a standing ovation and screams that shot right through me. I'm sure I was beaming ear to ear as I dove into my first panel with arguably the greatest fandom on earth. I did my best to answer their questions in an open and honest manner, attempting humor where I found it appropriate. I will never forget Richard Speight Jr. pulling me aside as I stepped off the stage and saying, "That was great. You're a natural." All I knew was that I had a blast. As the weekend rolled on, I met fans, signed autographs, took pictures, sang karaoke, and prepared for what was then being called "The Saturday Night Cabaret." The cabaret was in its early stages of development, and I informed the heads of the convention that I was a singer and would be happy to participate. They said yes, and I prepared a song or two. While appearing confident on the surface, I was quite nervous, as it had been years since I had performed live in front of an audience.

Alone onstage with a microphone in my hand, I finished my song and was instantly reminded that I was not alone. I was once again met with a

wave of cheers. I'm not sure if I surprised the audience, but I know I surprised myself. I was met backstage with an overwhelmingly kind response from my fellow cast and crew, and I felt an excitement that I hadn't felt in a very long time. There is nothing quite like singing in front of a live audience. And I have found no better audience than the fans of *Supernatural*.

A spark had been reignited. Something forgotten had been rediscovered. You see, I have been singing for as long as I can remember, but somewhere along the way my confidence had been injured, my hope all but shattered by rejection and deep frustration. I had auditioned for many musicals early in my career and had once even come close to landing a Broadway national tour. But these jobs just never came my way. And then, at some point, the auditions just stopped coming in. I continued to study with a voice coach and sing at home, but opportunities to perform were nonexistent. The stage was dark until the *Supernatural* fandom came along.

Fear of failure is something I think many of us battle. How do we not only face that fear but also work to get over it? I'm not sure I have the answer to that question, but I know it is almost impossible to do alone. I never would have imagined in my wildest dreams that working on *Supernatural* would be the impetus for me to face my fears. The support and encouragement I have received from the fandom is without a doubt one of the greatest gifts of my life and something I will always be grateful for.

Since that first show, I have performed at conventions all over the United States and Canada. I have future shows scheduled, and am now lucky enough to be backed by Rob Benedict and his band, Louden Swain. Their musical talents far surpass mine and only inspire me to work harder and dream bigger. I have no idea how much longer I will have the privilege of performing on the *Supernatural* convention circuit, but I will be there as long as they will have me. I will continue to work to hone my craft, and, who knows, maybe give Broadway a shot in the near future. For the first time in a long time, I feel like my story is just beginning. The unexpected gifts *Supernatural* has brought me may very well have begun to change my life. I have the fandom to thank for that.

If you are feeling alone, discouraged, or lost, remember this: the *Supernatural* family is there for you. And also, never forget, as a wise man once said:

"As long as we're alive . . . there's always hope."
—Henry Winchester

MY HERO WEARS A BEANIE

KRISTIN LUDWIG

I have been an extremely anxious person for most of my life, ever since entering school. Before that I was a fairly free-spirited little girl, but once I got put into the school environment everything changed. I was labeled early on as a daydreamer and somehow different from everyone else, so I felt isolated and constantly wondered what was wrong with me. I was never very good at socializing, so I usually latched onto one person . . . which always ended in disaster, leaving me with feelings of abandonment and a sense of not belonging. Between fifth and sixth grade I experienced a traumatic event from which I suffered significant PTSD that has stayed with me ever since. Due to that event, I became even more fearful and withdrawn, building a shell as a way to shield myself from ever getting hurt again.

All through middle school and high school, I continued to withdraw and my life became more and more unbearable. I never hung out with anyone or did much of anything. I just stayed home, becoming more reclusive with each day that passed. I was terrified to be around my peers. I couldn't sit in classes without panicking and feeling the need to escape. I didn't know how to relate to other students and constantly felt they were making fun of me. Some days I sat in the detention area instead of going to class. Other days I screamed and held on to my bed as tightly as I could so I wouldn't have to go to school, putting my family through a lot of turmoil. I feel tremendous guilt for that, even though I was mentally unhealthy and didn't mean to do what I did.

I don't know how I graduated from high school, but thankfully I did. After that I tried my best to venture more into society and do what "normal" people do. I had a number of different jobs through the years, but what happened to me in high school happened again when I tried to hold on to any job. My insecurities and my fears of being away from home grew. I became paranoid, thinking everyone was laughing and talking about me. I couldn't concentrate and all I wanted to do was get out of the situation. The overwhelming anxiety resulted in a permanent disability, and I haven't been able to work for some time. I don't know how to be a person. I have been trapped ever since that life-altering event took place, and have not been able to move past it. In many ways I am still that ten-year-old girl, too frightened to move forward, to let anyone in again who might hurt or betray me. I have been in therapy for many years and tried multiple medications, but I was never able to escape the feelings of self-loathing and inadequacy.

Flash-forward to 2009 when I discovered *Supernatural*. I was immediately drawn into the story and the characters. I could relate to both Sam and Dean Winchester for different reasons, but instantly connected with Sam/Jared. Escaping into Sam's world helped me cope with the chaos of my own. Sam felt like a freak and like something was wrong with him, exactly the way I always had. I shared that longing to be normal, so it was natural for me to bond with him. His love for his family and his willingness to sacrifice anything and everything to save them brought tears to my eyes. I don't have much family myself, so I lived vicariously through Sam and his close relationship with Dean. Jared drew me in by portraying Sam with such caring and compassion, and the more I watched, the more I fell in love with him, in a spiritual sense. He gave me hope and an inner strength I didn't know I had.

I began watching con videos and, in doing so, had the privilege of witnessing Jared's true character as he interacted with fans and displayed incredible compassion while talking with them. I knew that, whatever it took, I had to get to at least one convention to thank him for giving me the strength to keep fighting. It took almost two years, but in October of 2010 it finally happened. Those few days were a blur, as I was so scared the entire time. On Sunday I got the chance to meet Jared and briefly tell him about myself, thanking him for helping me. I was a bundle of nerves and almost felt as if I were out of my body. I couldn't believe I'd made it there, and I was doing everything I could to keep it together. He was very sweet and held my hand while I was fighting to tell him what I'd wanted to express for such a long time. I could tell how much he cared as he listened to every word. No one had ever shown such interest and consideration toward me. I felt at peace for the first time in so long and an instant connection was formed. Jared was the first person I had let down my guard with and allowed into my heart in so many years. I trust him implicitly and I am so grateful to him for being the kind of person that he is, who we should all strive to be.

I get extremely anxious leading up to going to a con. I get physically ill from worrying, as I tend to overthink and obsess about everything. I worry that something will happen to ruin the experience, and I anticipate all the things that could go wrong. What if my flight gets delayed? What if I get sick? What if I make a fool of myself? What if people don't accept me? What if I can't sit in the theater or wait in the lines? What if I embarrass myself in front of someone? All these thoughts play over and over in my head to the point that I'm a complete wreck.

In 2011 I went to my first full con in Boston, which was one of the hardest things I've ever done. I still look back and can't believe I was able to accomplish being away from home for four days. I was fortunate enough to win a coveted seat for Jared's meet and greet and I felt so blessed to be there. I was also terrified, as I'd only briefly shared with him my struggles in Chicago, and this time, in this more intimate setting, I wanted to tell him a bit more. My stomach rolled through almost the whole thirty minutes until I finally raised my hand to speak. I was able to say that I had extreme social phobia/anxiety/depression and that being there was inconceivably hard, but he had helped me find the strength to do so. As I was speaking, my emotions took over and I started crying—an ongoing

trend, I'm afraid. Everyone clapped and seemed proud of me for having
the courage to speak up, which helped a great deal. The SPNFamily is
such an amazing group of people. I am so thankful to be considered a
member. Jared gave me a hug when I finished, and I can say with absolute
certainty that that moment was a turning point in my life.

Since then I've been to a number of cons, both with my dad and
then on my own, which is something I never dreamed I'd be able to do!
I think knowing that I'll get another chance to see Jared is what gives me
the strength and motivation to go through with it. That is what gets me
through the anxiety and the crippling fear I have about doing something
of that magnitude. I keep telling myself I have gotten through them in
the past and everything will be all right. When I do get through them, I
feel a sense of accomplishment and self-worth, which are things I haven't
experienced in many years. It feels good to get out on my own, for a bit,
and feel like a normal person.

In 2012 another traumatic event happened in my family. My brother,
who had gotten married in 2011, decided he no longer wanted to have a
relationship with my parents or me. It was a devastating blow for us, and
we still don't understand his reasoning behind making such a heartbreaking decision. Since that day, we haven't seen him in person and have only
talked on the phone a few times (very unpleasant conversations). Watching my mom suffer has crushed my heart, and I'm helpless to do anything
about it. This has increased my depression to epic proportions and the
only thing that has relieved my pain is watching *Supernatural*. Being a part
of the SPNFamily has been such a comfort in dealing with this. I've been
able to talk about it with the friends I've made through the fandom, and
they give me strength to keep going.

I thank God for Jared Padalecki, who has also been a constant light
in my dark life. I am so grateful for the times I have gotten to talk with
him. He has helped me more than any therapist I've ever been to, just by
being himself. I cherish every precious second I am given with him; it has
meant everything in the world to me. Every day of my life is a struggle not
to give in to the demons that plague me. I ask myself on a daily basis if I'd
be better off not being in this world any longer, so I have to credit Jared
with saving my life. I realize that it is actually *me* who has kept going, but

when I think of him, the self-degrading thoughts that plague me dissipate and I'm reminded that he truly cares about every one of us. Whenever I am having a particularly difficult time I repeat "Always Keep Fighting" over and over, and it keeps me grounded. I haven't words to express how blessed I feel to exist in a world that has Jared in it. He will always have an indelible place in my heart.

Feeling safe, accepted, and at my happiest.
Pasadena, California, November 2015.

HELPING PEOPLE, SAVING LIVES: THE FAMILY BUSINESS!

KARLA TRUXALL

September 28, 2010. It was a Tuesday. We were all in the living room when the phone rang. It was my husband's parents calling, so I handed the phone to him. Within seconds I knew something was wrong and I hurried to the kitchen to grab another phone so I could hear what was being said. There is nothing in this world that could have prepared me for what I heard. My jaw dropped. I tried desperately to make sense of what my ears were hearing as my eyes filled with tears. My gaze shifted from my husband to my children, who were sitting on the edge of the couch, desperate for clues as to what was going on. I had no words. My brain was too paralyzed to allow them to form, so I slowly raised my hand to my head in the shape of a gun and pulled the trigger. My nephew, Mason, was dead from a self-inflicted gunshot wound at the age of nineteen.

This could not be real. Obviously, there had been a mistake. Why would he do such a thing? I spent the rest of the evening, and many weeks after that, stunned and in disbelief. How could this happen to our family?

I remember feeling dazed, confused, hurt, shocked, incredibly sad, filled with overwhelming grief, and alone. The emotion I never felt, though other family members showed it, was anger. How could I be angry? My heart had shattered into a thousand pieces at the thought of how much pain Mason must have been in for this to be his course of action. But I could cry, and I cried a lot in the weeks, months, and years that followed.

I also knew I needed help of some kind, but I didn't know what that looked like or where to turn. Thankfully, I found my way with a little assistance and inspiration from an unlikely source—a television show.

What is it about *Supernatural* that draws you in like a moth to a light, with a force so strong "resistance is futile"? It's just a TV show, isn't it?

My husband, Dave, started watching *Supernatural* in season 3; however, I didn't fall under the show's spell until I stumbled across the pilot episode one morning in 2011, roughly one year after Mason's death. I was immediately taken in by how the scenes were lit and the creative use of shadows and reflections. I was drawn to Sam and loved Dean's comedic timing. But that wasn't enough to explain the impact the show had on my life. Unlike the other shows I watched for entertainment, this show lingered.

I began to wonder, who were these people writing this show? How did they consistently reference my entire life? Did they grow up with me in my small Midwest town? The show's use of classic rock, movies, cultural references, the Impala (my dad worked for GM for forty years!), the two-lane roads in the middle of nowhere, and the wonderful use of zingers and sarcasm were like pages ripped out of my life story. To find answers to my questions, I turned to the Internet.

First I found videos from the 2006 Paley Festival. I was thrilled to be able to see not only the two lead actors, Jared Padalecki and Jensen Ackles, talk about the show but also hear from *Supernatural*'s creator, Eric Kripke, producer Robert Singer, writer/producer John Shiban, and director Kim Manners. Watching them interact solidified my love for the show and left me with a hunger to know more, especially from behind the scenes. Next I found videos that *Supernatural* fans had posted from Creation Entertainment's Salute to *Supernatural* conventions. What? Conventions? Really? A month later my husband and I were purchasing tickets to attend one of these conventions. I had to see for myself what they were all about and hopefully find the answer to my lingering question since being drawn into the show: "What the hell is happening to me?"

Dave and I hadn't been on a weekend getaway in years, so we were both more than ready to go to the *Supernatural* convention in Chicago (ChiCon) and do things that had nothing to do with our real lives. It was wonderful! We thoroughly enjoyed the panels on Friday and signed up for karaoke. I have sung in public many times in church and at weddings but never in front of a highly energized crowd. Wow! What a difference the energy of a crowd can make!

On Saturday, we were entertained by Richard Speight Jr.'s quick wit and banter as he roamed the ballroom during his panel. Two things stand out from what he shared that day. First, it was a big election year, so he reminded us of our civic duty to vote. And second, he informed us that he was there to have fun and, by golly, we were *all* gonna have fun! He went on to stress the importance of having fun in life because, without it, what do you really have? That was a message I needed to hear. Richard helped me realize I was *not* having fun. I was miserable.

Not only had Mason's suicide ripped a hole through my heart and knocked me off my feet, but we had also lost my father-in-law to aggressive bladder cancer six months before ChiCon. He'd been diagnosed only eight months after we lost Mason. Despite initially successful surgery and chemotherapy, and three days after winning a golf tournament in Florida, my father-in-law's health started declining so fast the window of opportunity to bring him back to Michigan was in a constant state of flux. Everything was stressful, stories kept changing, and my head was spinning.

We finally got my father-in-law medically flown home, and within twenty-four hours we were calling my husband's sister to fly home to say good-bye to her dad, only eighteen months after she had lost her son. I was not prepared *at all* to handle the speed at which my father-in-law's health deteriorated. As a wife, I was trying to be there for my husband. As a mom, it was very important to me that my daughter be able to have a happy fifteenth birthday. I was also trying to minimize the level of stress in my children's lives. They had papers to write and exams to take and my job was to keep them focused on their studies and sheltered from the chaos.

I was in no condition to deal with problems or drama from anyone else, not even my younger sister. She demanded my attention anyway, and I reached my breaking point. I had an ugly emotional meltdown at the hospital the night before my father-in-law died. Thankfully, my older sister offered me an emotional lifeline and talked with me by phone until I was able to get myself under control.

And the hits kept coming. My relationship with my parents has never been that great, and I *thought* I had come to terms with that fact years ago. However, the process of raising my own children and having to deal with them being typical teenagers exposed my old emotional scars at a time when I was in no condition to properly handle them. In an effort to cope, I found myself using *Supernatural* as my escape from reality. It became my happy place, as I could always count on the show to make me laugh.

So by the time ChiCon 2012 rolled around, it had been two years since my nephew had died and I was a very broken version of myself. Now, the question was, what was I going to do about that?

By Sunday morning, I was very much in love with the wonderful weekend I was having with my husband surrounded by all things *Supernatural*, and I was also very aware that we would be returning to our real lives in less than twenty-four hours. That reality forced me to be honest with myself and with Dave over brunch. Shedding tears over a meal, or anywhere else, had become a common occurrence in my world, but this time was different. These tears weren't just filled with pain, despair, or anger. They were also filled with hope, because I could see myself standing at a crossroads and choosing to walk down a different path. By the time we headed back to the hotel for the day's highly anticipated panels and photo ops with "the boys," I had agreed I would seek counseling when we got home. I had been trying to deal with everything on my own for two years and I needed someone to help me find my way back to the fun side of life.

Jared and Jensen did not disappoint that day. We were smiling and laughing from the moment they stepped onstage. As soon as their panel was over, I had to find my way to the line for my photo op with Jared, Jensen, and Misha Collins.

When it was my turn, I walked up to them and said, "Hi, it's nice to meet you," locked eyes on Jensen, who was in the middle, and said, "I don't have a creative pose." At this point my brain started to float away as I realized I was standing in front of Jensen and he was smiling at me. Suddenly I heard in my right ear Jared's voice saying, "Good! We don't like those anyway," and he grabbed my shoulders and spun me around toward the camera. Jolted out of my dreamlike state by Jared's unexpected declaration, I found myself off balance, falling backward, screaming, landing on Jared's foot and immediately trying to get back on my own feet. At the same time I could hear Jared saying, "I gotcha. I gotcha," very confidently in my left ear as I became aware of Jared and Jensen's muscular arms holding me up from behind. And then I heard the click of the camera as the photographer, Chris Schmelke, took my picture. In my head I exclaimed, "WHAT? You took the picture NOW? I barely have both feet on the ground and you thought *now* would be a good time? What the hell just happened?"

I walked away in complete shock and disbelief, convinced my photo was going to be a disaster. How could it not be? Too many body parts had been out of my control when Chris took the picture. But when the photos were ready, I discovered I had nothing to worry about. Chris Schmelke is a wonderful photographer who prides himself on capturing the emotion of the moment. There was certainly a lot of emotion running through me in that photo op, thanks in large part to Jared, and he captured it beautifully. Thank you, Chris!

After returning home I found a grief counselor, since Mason's death seemed to be the tipping point of my emotional downward spiral, and

I started on the path to recovery. One of the first things I learned in my counseling sessions was that I WAS NOT ALONE! For the first time, every emotion I had ever had surrounding Mason's death was being validated. It was like a weight being lifted off my shoulders, and it felt wonderful! Unfortunately for me, one of the first steps toward recovery is being able to talk about your loss. This was very difficult for me. In the two years since Mason's death, I had progressed to being able to think about him without being reduced to a puddle of tears (for the most part), but I still could not even begin to talk about him without becoming an emotional mess.

The following year, my wonderful husband suggested we return to Chicago for the next *Supernatural* convention and this time go Gold: the weekend package including autographs and some extra events. Really? Sold! We added Jared's meet and greet and a few extra autographs to our weekend schedule, which gave us wonderful opportunities to meet some amazing people and have intelligent conversations about our favorite TV show.

Dave and I were having a great time together and, in contrast to the previous year, I made it through about 80 percent of the weekend before tears were shed. This time I was a much healthier person. Little did I know that all my progress was about to be put to the test.

As Jared and Jensen's panel was coming to a close on Sunday, a young girl approached the microphone to ask the last question. She asked if Jared and Jensen thought Sam and Dean would ever give up on life. Did they think their characters would ever feel so overwhelmed as to consider suicide? I was immediately jolted out of the happy place I had been in all weekend. I could feel my entire body become engulfed by a wave of emotion as tears began rolling down my cheeks. I reached for my husband's hand and braced myself for how Jared and Jensen were going to handle such a serious and sensitive question. To my surprise, Jared answered the question beautifully.

The first thing he told that young fan, and all of us in the audience, was, "Getting rid of yourself isn't going to help anybody." You have to "keep fighting the fight." The fan said her family had been going through a very difficult time, and Jared went on to explain how when he's struggling, he has learned to take the focus off himself and look for ways he can help someone else. You help yourself by helping others. When Jared finished speaking, I was in awe. I wondered if I was strong enough to share with him my gratitude for his heartfelt answer.

After the panel I tried to find the girl who had asked the question, though I didn't know what I would say to her other than to try to encourage her. Despite my efforts, I never found her.

A few hours later I was trying to decide what to say to Jared while getting his autograph. The entire time I was in line, I debated with myself. What were the odds of my being able to thank him for his answer to the suicide question without falling apart in front of him? I decided to go for it. It took every ounce of energy I had to remain in control of my emotions while I spoke to Jared about that moment and my suicide loss. Rising above my fears and seizing that moment was a huge step on my path to recovery. The look on Jared's face while I spoke to him was very compassionate and I will never forget it.

Between that interaction with Jared, the brave fan who asked about suicide, and the emotional events of Vegas Con 2014, where Rob Benedict made his first appearance since his stroke five months earlier, and where I spoke with Kim Rhodes, who lost her dad to suicide, I realized I needed to take my journey and pay it forward to help others. Three months after returning from Vegas, and as part of my ongoing homework assignment from my counselor to look for opportunities to talk about Mason, to talk about suicide, and to share my story, Dave and I started designing a website and creating a support group, which has now grown into a nonprofit organization called SPN Survivors.

Our mission is to reach out, offer support, and bring people together through education and awareness while shining a spotlight on suicide prevention, self-care, Mental Health First Aid, and local, state, and national resources. Our motto is *Helping People, Saving Lives: The Family Business!*

We all have struggles and challenges in life, but we do not need to fight these battles alone. SPN Survivors' website and programs, including our Battle Buddies, Comfort Kits (for hospitals and schools),

Original logo, created by my daughter Natalie Truxall.

Misha, Jared, and Jensen showing support for our motto, DC Con 2015.

Community Ambassadors, and our annual events, March for Hope and #YouMatter! Day, were all created as ways to reach out and help others in our community. We also promote education and awareness about good mental health and the resources available to those struggling with mental illness and suicide loss. Our purpose behind everything we do is to provide encouragement, community, education, kindness, and, most importantly, hope!

In September 2014, I had the privilege of participating in an SPN Road Con, where three books traveled from state to state (one for Jared, one for Jensen, and one for Misha) collecting messages from as many *Supernatural* fans as possible. I wrote the following in each book: "*Supernatural* is a wonderful place where the fans can escape to, and while there, find the courage and inspiration to fight the monsters and demons in their own lives. You have played a significant role in that journey for so many fans, myself included, and for that I am eternally grateful!"

SPN Survivors was launched a few days before I attended ChiCon 2014. I was able to have wonderful conversations with each cast member who had played a role in my journey as I thanked them and told them about SPN Survivors. Everyone I spoke to that weekend, fans and cast members alike, was so encouraging and supportive of my vision that I knew I was on the right path. I also started looking for the young fan who asked about suicide the year before. Since I do not know her name, I have written an open letter on our website in hopes of finding her (www.SPNsurvivors.org).

One week after Jared launched his Always Keep Fighting movement in March 2015, SPN Survivors had its first suicide prevention table at Vegas Con. It was an emotional weekend filled with hugs, tears, and support from the SPNFamily as I shared my story and listened to others share theirs. That experience inspired me to create our Battle Buddies—cute and cuddly stuffed animals, with words of encouragement (from several *Supernatural* cast members) printed on a custom-designed bandanna, whose mission is to encourage you to *Always Keep Fighting for better days ahead because #YouMatter!*

For a long time, my photo with Jared, Jensen, and Misha, from my very first convention, sat on my nightstand, where I could look at it every

September 28

#YouMatter! Day

Creating Ripples of Kindness Across Our Communities

SPNsurvivors.org

Graphic by Natalie Truxall.

day and smile. The parallels between that photo-op experience and my life offered me encouragement. In both circumstances I had lost my balance and felt out of control. In the photo, Jared and Jensen are literally holding me up, but as I got stronger the message changed from Jared reminding me, "I gotcha," to *me* telling myself, "You got this!" The feeling of empowerment that those three words gave me was life-changing. That is why "You got this!" is one of the many encouraging messages found on our Battle Buddy bandannas.

Since 2010, September 28 has been a big, black, ugly cloud in my world, but I've had a growing desire to replace that cloud with something positive. In 2016, SPN Survivors decided it was time to make September 28 #YouMatter! Day. We asked everyone to join us in "Creating Ripples of Kindness Across Our Communities" during Suicide Prevention Awareness Month by reaching out and reminding those around us that they matter. As author T.A. Garcia once said, "It's amazing how kind words and actions can create a ripple effect and many others will benefit from the positive things you say and do."

We encourage everyone to be *that* ripple effect and make a difference in your community because YOU have . . .

- A voice to be heard
- A kindness to be shared
- A contribution to make
- A gift that others need

These are the things that give you the ability to make a difference, today and every day, because #YouMatter!

Today I am a much happier, healthier person. I am standing on my own two feet, both physically and emotionally. To celebrate, I attended a *Supernatural* convention with my husband, daughters, friends, and SPNFamily *on* my birthday. I can't think of a better way to celebrate my life than with the people and the show that helped me find my way back to the fun side of life!

This photo op from DC Con 2015 was my birthday present from my good friend and SPN Survivors board member Soncea (on the left), whom I met in a parking lot on our way to a cemetery in Ohio to pick up the SPN Road Con books!

SPN SURVIVORS

www.SPNsurvivors.org

SPN Survivors is a nonprofit organization that came to life out of the incredible relationship that exists between the cast and crew of *Supernatural* and their fans. The willingness of the SPNFamily to trust us with their personal stories and to share our message to "Always Keep Fighting for better days ahead because #YouMatter!" provided the inspiration for our Battle Buddies and Comfort Kits that are truly "Helping People, Saving Lives: The Family Business!" Thanks to the generosity of the SPNFamily, we now have partnerships with local hospitals, schools, and counseling offices where we donate our Comfort Kits (which include a Battle Buddy and other items) to kids and teens ages eight to eighteen in need of some extra love, support, and encouragement as they battle various obstacles in their young lives.

Our name, SPN Survivors, has special meaning. SPN is not just the abbreviation for our beloved show, *Supernatural.* It also stands for **S**uicide **P**revention **N**etwork. Through our community outreach, we hope to spare other families the devastating pain of losing a loved one to suicide. We also find it empowering to identify ourselves as *survivors*. After all, survivors continue to function and prosper despite hardship. In other words, we Always Keep Fighting!

For more information about our programs and community events, as well as how to get involved and become a Community Ambassador, please visit our website.

SOBER FOR SAM

HALLIE BINGAMAN

My name is Hallie (many of you in the fandom know me as Elle, from my middle name, Michelle), and since February 8, 2014, I am a recovering alcoholic. I often say that *Supernatural* and Sam Winchester saved my life, and I believe that to be true. My life has been saved over and over and over again through identification with Sam's character as well as through the supportive friendships I've made via the show. This time, with my journey in recovery from alcoholism, has been the most public, but it is just a (very large) chapter of the war I've been fighting for many years and against many different attackers, all of which come from within myself. This is the story of why I'm "Sober for Sam."

You may be expecting me to spill a lengthy, horrific rendition of all the terrible things that happened when I was drinking, and I'll touch on bits and pieces, but that's not what I want this essay to be. My story isn't a sad one anymore; it is one full of hope and gratitude. Yes, Sam Winchester saved my life, but the friends I made saved me, too, and they deserve all the praise I can fit into this love letter of a chapter.

I've been asked innumerable times what was my "rock bottom," or my turning point that made me realize I needed help. Ironically enough, it happened on a Tuesday night after a new episode of *Supernatural*. I used to celebrate new episodes by drinking an entire bottle of Champagne to start off the night, so I drank through the episode, and then a good bit more, and then decided it would be a smart idea to drive to the bar. I remember leaving my friend's apartment, and then suddenly I was sitting at the bar table with no recollection of how I'd gotten there. I had driven on the highway in a major city blackout drunk. I couldn't drive myself home, I couldn't speak, I could barely walk. Though that wasn't the first time I had driven while intoxicated, it was a wake-up call for me. I needed help. It's a miracle that I never received a DUI and never was in an alcohol-related traffic accident. It's another miracle I never hurt anyone else on the road as a result of my selfish actions.

I remember several people telling me I needed to "just ease up on the drinking, Hal," or maybe try AA, or even flat-out saying I had a serious problem. I became incensed with those people, most of whom were simply trying to be good friends. They didn't understand, you see. I had everything under control (so I thought). I was fine, I was just being a normal twenty-something, right? Hella wrong. I used to deflect the worry of others by joking that I was an alcoholic without letting myself absorb the weight and reality of those words. The way I was abusing alcohol to cope with my pain, my anxiety, and my emotions in general was anything but normal.

When I finally decided to get help, I Googled AA meetings in Austin, Texas, found one that was meeting that night, and made a post on Tumblr asking for good vibes and encouragement to push me into attending. Support flooded in. Turns out, more people were worried about me than I thought, and most had been too scared to come forward and risk a blowup on my part. Remembering the empty husk of a girl I was then haunts me.

I soon began chronicling my progress on Tumblr, using the tag "recovery" to keep it all organized. Amidst the messages of encouragement were a couple that said, more or less, "Sam Winchester would be so proud of you." While I couldn't fathom how that could be true, I clung to it. Somewhere along the way, the "Sober for Sam" tag was born.

Sam Winchester fought every step of the way, believing his self-destructive habit to be for the greater good, while I indulged in my addictions for purely selfish reasons. Addiction, however, doesn't discriminate based upon intent. Sam and I felt the same cravings, the same withdrawal, and the same self-loathing at the monsters we had become. I cringe when I go back and watch Sam choose Ruby over Dean, when I see Sam's powers increase and his lust for blood grow hungrier. I cry with him as he sits locked in Bobby's panic room, tortured by visions of Dean and Mary, the two people he loves most in the world, telling him what a failure he is. I cringe harder when I remember my own failures, my own loved ones being let down by *my* actions. But once Sam realized that he'd been tricked, that his addiction had taken hold, and that he wanted freedom from it, he fought like hell (pardon the pun) to get clean.

One of the most powerful scenes to me is in the episode "Free to be You and Me," when the hunters force demon blood directly into Sam's mouth . . . and Sam spits it back out. The strength it must have taken to not give in at that moment is overwhelming to me. As I went through many sleepless, shaky nights detoxing, I thought, "If Sam can make it through detox, so can I." When I wanted a drink so badly I could almost feel the burn of whiskey in my throat, I thought, "If Sam can stay clean, so can I." When I wanted to give up, to throw in the towel, to roll over and let my depression and anxiety overtake me, I told myself, "If Sam can keep going, so can I."

Sam Winchester taught me that I don't have to feed the darkest parts of myself. That "it doesn't matter what you are, it only matters what you do. It's your choice." I leaned on Sam heavily in my early months of recovery, looking to him to find the strength I couldn't pull from within myself. While my real-life friends and family were proud of me for getting sober, they didn't understand the "*Supernatural* thing." You know what I've learned? *It is absolutely okay to find hope through a fictional character, and it is absolutely okay to ask for help.* Thankfully, when I reached out through the darkness, I had my *Supernatural* family reaching back just as earnestly. The incredible support that exists within this community is nothing short of mind-blowing. This family, the family I chose, the family that doesn't end with blood, the family that chose me back, gave me a reason to *want* to get better. Literally every single day of the first year of my sobriety, I received at least one message of encouragement and support. I am overwhelmingly blessed to have the friends who became family that I made through this show, and through Tumblr. I owe every one of you my life, and a million thank-yous could never come close to being enough to show the depth of my gratitude.

In September 2014, I attended DallasCon with a purpose. This convention wasn't about me; it was about Jared Padalecki. When I was a couple of months sober, I decided that if I made it to half a year I wanted to give my six-month sobriety chip to Jared, the most meaningful way I felt I could offer my thanks. With that goal in mind, I fought every day to make it to six months. When I reached that milestone, when I held that blue aluminum token in my hands and realized where it would end up if I just kept fighting a little longer, I broke down in tears. I carried it with me every day, praying words of peace and strength over it. September finally arrived, and I don't think I stopped shaking the entire weekend. I knew I would have just a few moments at the autograph table, so I sat down in the hotel room and wrote a letter to Jared, briefly explaining what I was doing and why. Hundreds of messages of support and joyous excitement filled my inbox, and I remember scrolling through all of them and feeling as though the arms of my family were holding me tightly in that moment.

When my time at the table arrived, I stepped forward, introducing myself, and said a few words before handing over the chip and the letter. I remember very little, as I was overwhelmed in the moment, but I do remember him sincerely listening, then looking straight into my eyes and (I immediately wrote this down so I wouldn't lose the memory amidst the adrenaline) saying, "I will never, ever lose this, or forget how much this means. I am so proud of you as a human being; that is amazing. Seriously, I will never, ever lose this," before putting both chip and letter into his shirt pocket. A friend who was behind me in line and a convention volunteer both later told me that Jared got choked up after I'd walked away and had to pause autographs momentarily. I was absolutely floored that my teary mess made any sort of sense, let alone struck a chord with someone I consider a hero.

Since that time, a few incredibly gracious individuals have offered a portion of their time at the autograph table to update Jared on my progress at various other conventions, letting him know I was nearing a year sober, and then passing along the news that I'd made it to a year. As a result of these encounters, I learned that Jared keeps my letter and sobriety chip in a drawer near his bed, and takes them out when he's having a rough day to remind himself that we're all going through battles of our own. That piece of news came when I'd had quite the difficult day. I had just walked out of an AA meeting in a rather upset state, and soon after had to explain to several concerned individuals that, "No, these are *happy* tears now!" Jared draws strength from all of us just as much as we draw strength from him. How affirming is that to know?

To those struggling alongside me with addiction and/or mental illness, please hear this: At one point (well, at several points, but one in particular), I considered relapse, and my sponsor told me something that has really stuck with me—whether I give in or not, the stressful thing will go away. I can either choose a quick fix that will calm me for a moment, but create more problems down the line, or I can be willing to learn ways to cope for the long term. The latter may come slower, and I can attest to the fact that it sometimes sucks, but it gets easier, it gets better, and the desire to use/drink/harm yourself/whatever it may be will get easier to manage. I promise.

When I was active in my disease, every little thing that went wrong seemed like the end of the world, and when big bad things happened, I felt like I was splitting at the seams—like there was absolutely no way I could make it through whatever it was. The longer I've been sober, the more I've realized that things are leveling out. It's not intense highs and lows anymore, it's more of a natural, normal ebb and flow, and the tough stuff is easier to cope with. It's difficult to try to stop harming ourselves in an attempt to escape the overwhelming panic/fear/anger/frustration when stressful and painful situations arise, but I promise you it is worth it. Take it one day at a time, one hour at a time, one minute at a time if you have to. Keep pushing forward, just focusing on today, and do the best you can to keep yourself happy and healthy. Take Jared's campaign to heart, and always keep fighting.

Someone messaged me when I got a year sober and told me they'd heard that once a person in recovery achieves a year, they've pretty much beat it, and, for the most part, it's easy going from there on out. While I deeply appreciated the sentiment of encouragement behind the message, I need to emphasize how untrue that is. A friend of mine who had gained a year and a half sober relapsed last week. Another friend who had five years relapsed recently and nearly overdosed. Another friend can't keep a needle out of her arm long enough to properly nourish the baby she just found out she's carrying. Most recently, a dear friend of mine died of a drug overdose. The last time I saw him alive was when I met up with him at an AA meeting. People in sobriety have relapsed with five, ten, twenty, thirty years of clean time. People in the rooms of Alcoholics Anonymous like to say, "It's good that I'm in this meeting, but my disease is outside in the parking lot doing push-ups." It doesn't end. It's a battle that never stops. It's the disease that tells you that you don't have a disease. How terrifying is that?

Since committing to recovery, I've learned to be honest and vulnerable with what I'm dealing with. I've learned that I can be loved exactly as I am, and that I'm deserving of that love. I've learned that the meaning of true friendship doesn't necessarily include having met in person. I've learned that it's better to feel than to be numb, even if feeling is painful and difficult. In doing so, I've discovered that I am stronger than I believed myself to be, and I am not alone. Countless people have sent me messages of identification, relating their own experience or the experience of a friend or family member to exactly what I was going through at that point in time. A veritable legion of warriors amassed, all of us linking arms and becoming something bigger than ourselves in the midst of our collective battle.

So there it is: I'm sober for Sam. Sober for Sam who thinks he isn't worth a damn. Sober for Sam who thinks he's a monster, a freak. Sober for Sam who doesn't think he deserves love or even the slightest bit of kindness. Sober for Sam who believes he isn't worthy of saving. Sober for Sam who thinks he's unclean and disgusting and vile and untouchable. Sober for Sam who saved my life because I knew exactly what that felt like.

I'll close with some words from Sam that I've clung to over the course of this journey, and will carry with me every day going forward: "You've got this dark pit inside of you. I know, believe me, I know . . . but that doesn't mean you have to fall into it."

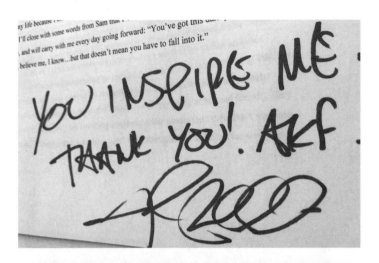

September 2015, following up the year after our initial meeting by giving Jared my one-year and one-and-a-half-year sobriety chips.

STROKE OF LUCK

ROB BENEDICT

I was working my way through a long autograph line. It was the end of the Toronto *Supernatural* convention: October 13, 2013, a Sunday night. My line was especially long as I was signing Louden Swain CDs, which were sold with the promise of an autograph. All the other actors had left, tired after a long convention weekend. I had said to my friend, actor Richard Speight Jr., to let me know when they got to dinner and I'd meet them there.

I never would make it to the restaurant.

"When is your wedding anniversary?"

The question came from a pleasant woman who was waiting in line. She looked a bit uncomfortable, like perhaps she'd overstepped her bounds. But not at all—it's such an easy question to answer, and I'm happy to do it. My wife and I always joke that I'm better at remembering anniversaries. We had just celebrated our eighteenth wedding anniversary; it's something I'm proud of.

I looked up and began to address the woman, but when I started to speak, I couldn't find the words. It was as if I were caught in that state of something being on the tip of your tongue. I stuttered and spat. I made a face like what's wrong with me. I kind of laughed. I remember thinking,

"Well, this is embarrassing." I mean, good timing, right? Now I look like the dumb husband, not knowing his anniversary.

I peered down at the long line, everyone still waiting patiently. In my memory it stretched longer than it probably was, like in a horror movie when a long hallway stretches into an infinite distance. I mimed to the woman that I would talk to her after I finished the line. She stepped to the side and waited.

For the remainder of the session I signed with my head down. Jen Gannon, who volunteered for Creation Entertainment and was assisting me that evening, would later say she thought it was odd because I appeared to be "over it." But that's not me. Anyone who has met me at a convention knows that I will take the time to interact with fans.

Soon, I would finish the line. At this point I had no idea what was going on. I thought I was having a panic attack. I am an anxious person by nature, and I was beat from a weekend of socializing and staying up too late. It only made sense that my system was shutting down.

Jen and fellow Creation volunteer Mandy Creech walked me back to my room. I'd worked with Jen and Mandy before, but this was uncharted

territory. I wasn't sure how to tell them that I thought I needed help. I didn't want to freak them out, and I literally couldn't find the words.

Once in my room, I sat on the bed. I was suddenly very sleepy and lay down.

The phone rang. It was Richard Speight.

"We're at this steak place. Myself, Misha, Jensen, and Jared . . . You'll have to take a cab." I mumbled that I didn't feel well. He said I was probably just hungry. But I mumbled again, and just said, "No, no." Again, not a typical response from me—I don't like to turn down an invitation to the party! And Rich knew this. We'd been doing conventions together for almost four years. We've traveled the world together. Truly no one knew me better in this situation than he did.

"I'm coming back for you."

There was a knock on the door. It was Mandy. People had started to talk. Mandy said she was going to sit with me. I nodded, so happy to have her there. She sat and tidied up the room while I rested. Just having her there gave me a sense of relief.

Soon, Richard got there. In typical Rich form, he took control of the ship. "Let's get you some food. Let's put the game on. What's going on; how do you feel, exactly?"

I ate some food but still found it hard to put words together. I remember he asked me who the quarterback for Washington was. I'm an avid football watcher and that's an easy one: Robert Griffin III! But all I could say was, "Uh . . . oh . . . um . . . ah . . . R-r-r . . . uh . . ."

Richard called Misha, still at the restaurant. He had told the group that he was concerned about me when he left. Misha asked to talk to me; he had a relative who had recently experienced a stroke. I can't remember what I said but it was enough for Misha to tell Rich to get me to the hospital.

I never want to go to the hospital. Hospital is never good. Hospital means *this is serious*. *This is serious* throws me into a state where I'm not quite sure what reality is. I should also mention that at this point, aside from a persistent headache, there were no clear symptoms. Physically there seemed to be nothing wrong with me. To the outside world I looked fine. I even felt okay. I thought, *Do we really need to go to the hospital?*

Rich made it seem like no big deal. "Let's just go, see what's what." If I'd had my words I would have debated, but I didn't. So after some resistance I agreed. Off to the hospital we went: Rich, Jen, Jen Gregory (another Creation volunteer), Mandy, and me. We were like a team on *The Amazing Race*, navigating in a foreign country where no one quite knew where to go. We couldn't find the hospital despite the fact that we were told it was close. We got lost and had to call a cab to lead us.

The waiting room for the ER was surprisingly empty. There was one homeless-looking guy, who I think was drunk. We politely waited, baffled as to where all the people were. We were called up and when I couldn't tell the admitting nurse my name, we were rushed right in.

We happened to be at a hospital that specializes in strokes, St. Michael's. There was a stroke wing, with residents being trained specifically in that field. After a quick initial examination, they noted I was shaking and Rich said, "Oh, no, that's normal. He's a shaky person. Not out of the ordinary." We would later recount this story and laugh our faces off.

No time for that now. I was rushed upstairs where they gave me a CT scan. I was holding on to the idea that it was a virus that had affected my nervous system. Now, of course, that feels like a bit of a reach. But at the time, it was what I hoped for. Some antibiotics and I'd be on my way home. I had a plane to catch the next day!

But before I knew it, I was back in the ER and the reality of the situation came in a sobering message delivered by your run-of-the-mill icy doctor. It was as if they were casting the miniseries and needed to find a *somber doctor with no bedside manner*. Poof: there he is. It was so on the nose that the director would have said, "Nobody is going to buy this. Those doctors don't really exist." Oh, but they do, hypothetical director.

Surrounded by a team of physicians, he spoke to me strictly, as if I were in trouble. I remember the key words: "You're having a stroke . . . fully dissected carotid artery . . . blood clot in the left frontal lobe . . . your window is closing . . ." And then for the grand finale: "We need to give you TPA [a blood-clot buster], but there is a 7 percent chance the shot will kill you."

Whoa, whoa, whoa. Say what?

I tried to process it all. Just four hours earlier I was onstage doing my panel. I was having a beer with Rich and laughing about the fun of the weekend. Now I'm having a stroke? And the 7 percent thing really threw me. I remember trying to do the math quickly. A room of 100 people, seven will die. I mean, in a room of five million, I was the one who had a dissected artery; who's to say I wouldn't be one of the seven, the way my luck was going?

It felt like an eternity but in reality it was five seconds. "I can't administer it without your permission," said Dr. Downer, MD. "I need a yes or a no. And I need it now."

"M-M-Mollie!" I blurted out.

"Who's Mollie?" said the doctor.

Rich, who'd been standing there the entire time, tears forming in his eyes, leaned in. "That's his wife."

"There's no time for Mollie," said Dr. D, right to me. "Mollie can't help you now." Those were his exact words. It was then that I noticed a nurse crouching near my arm, ready to administer the drug.

"I need a yes or a no."

"What happens if he doesn't?" asked Rich, speaking on my behalf.

"He strokes out, and then, who knows?"

Who knows? Well, you, Doc! I can't make this decision. Even if I could, I can't bloody talk. I look to Rich who nervously puts his hands through his hair and gives me a look like, "I don't know, buddy!" I could feel him wanting to answer for me, but this had to be my call. I stared back and kind of laughed, beyond belief. It was a moment I will never forget. I lay there and realized, *This is all on me.* At the end of the day, at the end of your life, *you* are truly all you have.

In retrospect it seemed inevitable that this would happen to me. It's hard to explain, but as terrifying and unknown as the whole event was, there was a part of me that thought, "Oh, of course, and this is the bit where I have a stroke." Like I was destined for this moment.

Finally I looked at the doctor and nodded my head yes. The shot was administered. I closed my eyes not knowing if I'd open them again. The sound of blips and whooshes enveloped me and I went to sleep.

I was awakened an hour later, with tubes and plugs sticking out of me, the ever-present beep reflecting my vitals. My calves were trapped inside compression sleeves that would pulsate in and out, a sort of leg massage that bordered on constriction. I was in ICU and a nurse who wore an expression that said "Don't get used to me" was in front of me holding a piece of paper with basic kindergarten pictures: a hammock, a chair, a key, a feather, a baseball bat.

I quickly realized I had gotten worse. I could not say any of those things. No matter how hard I tried.

"What's this?"

"Gu, gu, gu."

"Chair."

"Gu, gu, gu."

"Chair."

"Chair."

"Right!"

And then when she'd ask me again a few minutes later, I'd already forgotten. This excruciating process went on every hour for the next two days. I'd forgotten how to speak. Language is something we so take for granted. Look at the nearest object to you right now. For the normal person, the name your native tongue has for that object will come to you at first glance. For me, I knew conceptually it was the object that you sit on at a table, but I didn't have a word for it. The neural pathway to my voice was unable to decode the word. I could only make noises that weren't even close to being correct. I was a caveman. A newborn.

After this initial test I felt painfully alone. I needed to be with someone who knew me. I wanted to see Rich. But I wasn't sure if he'd left. I tried to tell the nurse but I didn't know how. I moaned until she handed me a piece of paper. "Wa-wa-wa."

"Can you write it down?"

I sat holding the pencil to paper, but I could only make scribbles. I tried miming it to her. But how do you mime, "I need to see my friend, the guy who brought me in"? I just made faces until, miraculously, she said, "You want me to get your friend?" I nodded. Yes, yes, oh, thank god. It was such a victory.

Moments later, Rich was there.

"Hey, buddy!" What a breath of fresh air. He proceeded to tell me that in the waiting room fellow *Supernatural* actors Misha Collins and Jensen Ackles were making phone calls, working on getting Mollie here. And Mandy, Jen, and Jen, bless their hearts, were still there as well. I would find out later that the waiting room was like HQ: Misha was assigned getting my wife to Canada, not an easy task because Mollie, who had been in Cleveland on business, would be driving up and didn't have her passport. Meanwhile, Jensen was calling Los Angeles and getting my best friend, Bruce, to wake my house sitter (in the middle of the night) to get Mollie's passport just in case, and additionally buying Bruce a ticket to Toronto. And Rich, of course, was at the helm, managing the entire operation. At this point, the gravity of the situation was very high. No one knew what might happen to me.

No more than two visitors could be in the ICU at one time, so that first night—which felt like an eternity—they would come in shifts. I remember Jensen and Richard talking over me as I lay there like a guy in a full-body cast, unable to speak. It was dreamlike. I remember having the urge to offer a thought, finding a window into that familiar banter that we had developed. We all think so fast when we're together and share a quick sense of humor. But that night I could only watch. Later, Misha came in. He hugged me and looked very upset. "I'm just so sorry, man," he kept saying.

And, every hour, the nurse was there to see if I was still alive and to give me "the test." Which I failed time and time again. "What's this?" "G-g-g-g-g-g—" "Feather." "Feather, yeah." "What's this again?" "P-p-p-p-p—" "Feather." "F-f-feather, yeah."

Morning came, and with it Jensen and Misha's departing flights. Richard had his flight pushed back a couple of days so he could stay with me. My wife finally got there, and by that time I could no longer say her name. I looked at her and knew exactly who she was, but the nurse said, "Who's this?" and I opened my mouth but nothing came out. It was soul crushing for both of us. There I was, tubes coming out of me, machines beeping, this constant pulsating coming from the apparatus around my legs, and I had lost all of my words. It was the rock bottom of the entire experience.

Soon my friend Bruce would get there and, as prompted by the doctors, he kept trying to get me to talk. They said the first forty-eight hours were the most crucial for maintaining my speech. Little did I know, my brain was rewiring itself. I spent about an hour answering, "Who is your favorite actor?" Working my miming skills and fishing for words while Bruce and my nurse Pam tried to figure out what I was saying. It was an excruciating game of Charades. After mimicking a bowler (a la

Big Lebowski) and doing "Sounds like *stitches*," they finally guessed: Jeff Bridges.

The next morning, the news was good. An overnight MRI showed that the clotting had stopped, and was possibly smaller. The picture of my brain was pretty terrifying—a cloud of black represented the dead brain on my frontal lobe. But the TPA had done its job and hadn't killed me in the process. I was through the worst of it, but I still had a long road ahead of me.

Mollie was finally able to describe to me exactly what had happened. I had experienced an ischemic stroke due to a complete dissection of my left carotid artery. The dissection formed a clot that lodged itself in the left front cranial lobe. Right where speech is formed. The speaking trouble I was experiencing is called aphasia, a disorder caused by damage to the parts of the brain that control language.

Usually a stroke of this kind is caused by whiplash, which explains why the doctors kept asking me if I'd been in a car accident, played a physical sport, or gone to a chiropractor within the last three days. There was a moment when Misha and Ty Olsson came onstage during my Q&A at the convention and jokingly lifted me upside down. Lasted maybe five seconds. But, truthfully, that did not give me the stroke. I was a healthy man, often doing upside-down pushups in workouts. Of course I could go upside down onstage. It was just a freak event, an anatomical accident.

During my recovery this was something that would haunt me. It would be so much easier if I had a reason to point to. There are a few syndromes that can give younger people strokes, disorders of connective tissue and other genetically determined syndromes. I've even read that something as small as a sneeze or cough can cause a dissection. I've often retraced my day, trying to recall if I'd had a big sneeze that morning. Ultimately, I had to let it go. Sometimes things just happen.

The doctors said my carotid artery would probably never work again. The MRI of my neck showed blood traveling up one carotid artery, while the left side was stopped. No traffic on that freeway. Nothing. I could live on just one, but if anything were to happen to it, my life would be over. A "bridge" called the Circle of Willis in the back of the brain, reserved for this kind of emergency, was carrying the blood over to the other side so my brain could still function. Amazing how resilient the body is, and yet how fragile.

I was moved out of the ICU and into a normal hospital room. Very slowly but surely, the words started coming back. It wasn't like a faucet turning back on; it was more like short bursts from a hose with a leak. One time, the therapist was trying to get me to say *buttercup* and I couldn't say it. She left the room as Rich entered and he asked me what was wrong. "I couldn't say BUTTERCUP!" I blurted out. I had no control of when my brain would work and when it wouldn't.

Another time there was a team of therapists in the room. They gave me a test in which they fed me pairs of words and I was supposed to say which item came first. One pair was "March/July," and I said "July." They said, "Comes first?" I said yeah. I asked, did I get that wrong? They said yeah, and a few others, too.

After about the fourth day, it was time for Rich to leave. That night Mollie and Bruce went back to their hotel and I watched the St. Louis Cardinals playoff game on my personal TV, which swiveled out in front of the bed. My roommate *du jour* was an especially troubled young guy who had suffered several strokes and seizures, and was literally missing a part of his head. He frequently woke up with migraines. That night he made a phone call to a friend asking him to sneak in some illicit drugs.

I was more than a little freaked. I had only my phone to keep me company. I checked it, looking for solace. Much to my surprise, I had dozens of unread texts and emails. People had come out in droves to wish me well. I felt like Jimmy Stewart at the end of *It's a Wonderful Life*. Among all my family and friends, there were notes from the *Supernatural* Family: Misha, Jensen, Jared Padalecki, Matt Cohen, Sebastian Roche, Ty Olsson, Samantha Smith, James Patrick Stuart, Gabe Tigerman, Julie McNiven, Jason Manns, Steve Carlson, and on and on. I had video messages from Sebastian and his wife, Allie, and from Matt and his wife, Mandy. I had food sent to me by *Supernatural* creator Eric Kripke, more food came from writer/producer Robbie Thompson, and a gift basket from the entire *Supernatural* writers' room.

It blew me away. Here is a group of people that five years ago I didn't even know. We have traveled the world together in support of this crazy phenomenon that is *Supernatural*. But it's more than that. We actually like one another. We enjoy hanging out. I have never even worked on the show with many of these people, and I can honestly say they are some of my best friends.

After ten days, I would fly home with a warning that the high altitude might cause another clot. Scariest flight ever, but it did not harm me. I would go into intense speech therapy and work with a team of local doctors at UCLA.

And the emails and support kept coming in. Soon fans learned what had happened and began wishing me well via letters and posts. Donations were made on my behalf to the Heart and Stroke Society. Prayers were said. And miracles started to happen.

The day before Thanksgiving a sonogram revealed that my injured carotid artery was completely functioning again. The doctor at UCLA was thrilled. He took me off of the aggravating blood thinners. But I had been told this was not possible.

"Well," he said, "anything is possible."

My word recall at that point was about 50 percent, and I had developed a bad speech impediment due to nerve damage when the artery tore. That, too, they said, may never heal. In fact, in Canada they said they'd never seen anything like it. I have since found research that says that it happens in approximately one in a million ischemic stroke survivors. So out of one in five million to even have an ischemic stroke, I was one in a million. Oh, the luck!

In February 2014, I had my last speech therapist appointment. I was at about 90 percent. Later that month, I would have my final appointment with the UCLA doctor. He gave me a full checkup and said, "Go live your life." By March of that year, my tongue was fully functioning again. The speech impediment was gone.

I'm not sure which side of the fence I stand on when it comes to organized religion. But I do believe in spirit and the healing power of energy and love. It is no coincidence that I fully healed. The outpouring of support from my family, friends, and the *Supernatural* Family and fan base was nothing less than extraordinary. To have this devoted group of people that *know you even exist* is preposterous, but more than that—to know that they care. They honestly care. It is truly humbling.

I still don't know what the purpose of all of this was and what I am to do with it. I only know it changed my life forever. It will always be with me. The most salient takeaway I feel is the love from everyone who reached out. And especially those who were there, who could have just as easily chosen *not* to help: Mandy and Jen, Jen Gregory, Misha and Jensen, my friend Bruce, and Mollie's brother Don, who also flew out to help. The doctors and nurses at St. Michael's in Canada who were absolutely top-notch. The doctors and therapists here at UCLA and Cedars-Sinai were caring and meticulous. And of course my wife, Mollie, whose unwavering love is my reason for being.

But the man of the hour was Richard Speight Jr. He literally saved my life. It all goes back to that moment when he called my room and knew something was wrong. We laugh now and say it was because he'd never known me to pass up a beer. But it was because he truly *understands* me. We became friends through the *Supernatural* world, but our friendship has surpassed the convention circuit. Now we are connected for life. He is a great person, a kind and generous man (underneath his jokey facade)— and I am fortunate to know him.

This experience could have gone either way. Rich could have not called me and I probably would have stroked out, perhaps fatally. Our hospital just happened to be one of the premier stroke hospitals in Toronto. My wife made it through the border with no passport, simply on the trust of the officer she spoke to. The medicine could have killed me. My artery might never have healed; my tongue might never have worked.

Perhaps I am lucky after all.

One last thing. I have to answer a certain question. It's been on the tip of my tongue since that Toronto convention:

My wedding was in Bloomington, Illinois. It was about 100 degrees and humid in a way that only Midwesterners can appreciate. Tuxes were peeling off like wallpaper, exposing layers underneath. Grandmas were being rushed to the one room with air-conditioning. Bridesmaids were sweating like long-distance runners. We were all young and naïve. The day might have been chaotic and clunky, but it was perfect.

August 12, 1995.

CANCER WATCHES WITH ME

SHERI CHEN

Not too long ago, I would have considered myself an average, middle-aged mother of two. To be sure, you would not mistake the path my life had taken with what I'd consider a "Soccer Mom" (not that I'm knocking that), but in general I thought myself a pretty typical chick: I get up in the morning, brush my teeth, run a comb through my hair, and get the kids ready for school. I bebop around town in my minivan, blasting my favorite tunes, while running the usual errands we mothers tend to run: first the coffee shop (I mean, c'mon, priorities), the grocery store, the post office, etc. Then, of course, there is my non-mom job, the "nine-to-five" (this job happens in between the mommy jobs around the house). Finally, it's back to the school to pick up the kids, cook dinner, and put them to bed, only to start it all over again tomorrow. It's a little Groundhog Day, isn't it?

At least, that was my life until September 2014, when my surgeon called to inform me that I had a rare and deadly form of cancer.

What has any of this to do with *Supernatural* and fandom, you may ask? Please allow me to explain.

I discovered the world of sci-fi and fantasy in my glory days as a Gen-Xer in the '90s. *The X-Files* hit the scene in 1993, and my taste in television programming has swayed little ever since. The Internet was in its infancy back then, when pretty much the only thing it was good for was AOL (which practically *was* the Internet—it was *the* thing, and anybody who was going to be anybody was dialing up, logging on, and making connections). Many an evening you'd find me sitting in front of a giant, blinding CRT screen, modem trilling, chatting away with like-minded "X-philes" miles apart, and yet all connected through this new technology (and by "chatting," I mean staying up until 3 A.M. gushing over Mulder and Scully, their latest adventure, and conspiracy theories: essentially, giving birth to online fandom).

It should come as no surprise that when *Supernatural* premiered in September of 2005, I once again found my eyes glued to the TV set every week. The mid-2000s was the beginning of an era for me: I was in college, wet behind the ears, and eager to learn—much like my beloved Winchester boys, Dean and Sam. Episode by episode, year by year, as the boys grew and changed, so did I. The show was enjoyable, the writing was solid—it didn't hurt that the actors were easy on the eyes—and I found myself soaking it up. As the seasons passed and we changed from year to year (the boys and I), my fervor for the fandom waxed and waned like the moon, but I never felt the pull I have toward it more strongly than in the year after my diagnosis, because when that surgeon called, my world shattered.

It felt like the earth had been pulled out from beneath me, and I honestly could not even tell which way was up. Some really dark thoughts crossed my mind in those first few weeks after the diagnosis—how could they not? I was internalizing my pain, grief, and anger, and found myself in a very dark, very scary, and very ugly place. It was no place for a young mother with a loving husband and two very small children to be. And it sucked.

It was during one of those moments of despair that I turned on my TV and found *Supernatural* staring me in the face. The episode playing was "In My Time of Dying" (season 2, episode 1). I had seen this episode in the past, of course. This time, however, its meaning was transformed. It had become relevant to me in a strikingly new way. It felt so good and so comforting to watch the characters on the screen and let my emotions flow along with them.

Opening scene: From out of nowhere, a speeding semi slams into Dean Winchester's car, totaling the classic Impala with a sickening crunch of metal, along with the men inside it. Due to forces beyond his control, Dean has been in a terrible accident. He is in the hospital, comatose, being watched over by his brother Sam.

Cancer had slammed into my life like a runaway truck. I had my family with me, but there was little they could do, except watch and stand beside me.

Dean wakes up confused, and slips out of bed. He wanders down a long hallway until he reaches the nurses' station. He tries in vain to get their attention, but they cannot see him.

I am screaming inside my head. I am in pain. I am scared, yet no one can see that. Like a ghost, I wear a sheet of pretend emotions to hide myself. Everyone keeps moving on about their lives like nothing is wrong.

Unable to elicit any sort of response from the nurses, Dean runs back to his room, his suspicions confirmed as he looks down at his broken body still lying on the bed: he is a spirit now, a literal ghost of himself.

I am not myself anymore. I am but a shell of the person I once was. I don't understand this sick person I see in the mirror.

Dean learns that his father is in an adjacent room, and goes to his bedside. He is distraught to find his father hurt as well.

To me, my family is more important than I am. I choose to focus on them, to put their needs before my own.

Dean is angry now, and in denial about the situation: this isn't happening; it isn't going to play out this way. He decides to take matters into his own hands and disobey the natural order of things. He shouts to the room, to his brother, "Find some hoodoo priest to lay some mojo on me!"

This can't be happening to me. I don't have cancer; there must be some mistake. Let me talk to the doctor. I want answers, and then we'll fix me up. I don't have cancer . . .

"Dean Winchester," by Sheri Chen.

Dean returns to his father's room. "Aren't you going to do something, Dad? I gave up everything for you!" Dean shouts in desperation.

I beg my oncologist for answers. Tears in my eyes, I plead with him to help me, to give me "The Answer" that will fix me. There are no answers.

Dean comes to the realization that after everything he's given, after giving it all, it is still not enough. It can never be enough. In the end, it doesn't matter. There is nothing he can do.

The realization that I have given my all—my everything—to everyone, and in the end, taken little for myself, stares me in the face.

Dean watches impotently as Sam and his father argue over him. Sam is visibly shaken and accuses their father of caring more about "killing some demon" than he does about saving his own son.

I often wonder if my doctors and even my family are more concerned with killing my cancer, or saving me.

When Dean sees the Reaper for the first time, she is trying to claim someone else. She is ugly as sin, and he is frightened. He grabs hold of her, and pulls her away from the patient's body.

Cancer is very ugly. In plain English, it scared the shit out of me. Every day, I try to push the physical and emotional pain away from me. I want it gone. I just want it to leave me alone.

In desperation, Sam uses a Ouija board in an attempt to make contact with his brother. It works, and Dean—relieved to finally have an impact on his life—tells Sam that a Reaper is after him. Sam poignantly reminds Dean that if it's there naturally, there's nothing they can do. Scared and heartbroken, Dean looks up at his brother. Even though he is unable to see Dean in that moment, Sam rejects the idea of accepting death, and storms out to find a solution.

My cancer occurred naturally. I did not smoke two packs a day to gain it, nor did I poison myself by drinking water from plastic bottles with BPA in them while not using sunblock and talking on my cell phone . . . you get the point. But it still happened. As much as I may wish it hadn't, it did.

Dean is pissed, to say the least, when he confronts the Reaper, Tessa. She has deceived him. He desperately pleads the case for his life: he must stay in the battle, to keep his family safe. His pleas fall on deaf ears, however, for by the end of their conversation, Tessa reveals that no matter how hard he fights, he won't win this one, and that's all right. Life will go on. His family will get along without him. She reminds him he is not the first soldier she's "plucked from the field."

I am not the first soldier to be plucked from the field in the war against cancer, nor will I be the last. It is a sad truth that cancer will go on long after me. We are all unified in our common feelings; we have lives and families we desperately want to hold on to and protect. We are fighting our own battles. That doesn't make any one of us any more special than the others.

Dean counters that his death is not "honorable"; that at the end of the day, his corpse will be in the ground, rotting, and all that he's done up until now to protect his family will have been for nothing, because they will be without him.

It doesn't matter how "honorably" I fight my cancer; the result will eventually be the same.

Dean eventually gives in to acceptance—he doesn't want to be an angry spirit, after all—and questions Tessa about what will happen to him, and where he will go. She jokingly replies that she "can't give away the big punchline."

"Baby," by Sheri Chen.

When I die, I haven't a clue what will happen—and that scares me, just like it does Dean.

Just as Dean turns to Tessa, and you know—just know—that he has decided to accept her offer, he is drawn back and is able to resist again, to wake up and fight another day.

There is a constant battle being raged in my mind between accepting my cancer at its worst, lying down and calling it quits, or choosing to pop back up and fight. I like to think that most days, I choose to fight the good fight, but there are some days when that decision is not so easy to make. There is certainty in death. It's final; unlike life, the greatest of unknowns. Each and every day contains risks, and safety can only be found in the grave. I take comfort in knowing I'm not alone in my struggle, and that I'm not the only one to be tempted by certainty.

Over the next few weeks after my diagnosis, I found myself completely engrossed in the series again, with a fresh set of eyes and brand-new perspective. This fictional television series had transformed me in a very real way. The adventures and misadventures, joys and sorrows broke me down while simultaneously building me back up. This I know for certain: Dean and Sam Winchester's reality made sense to me when my own did not.

This sparked my artistic creativity, and the need to express myself by creating fanart for the show spurred other creative processes, like writing fan fiction. Releasing my emotions through the canvas and printed word was beyond cathartic, and I found myself slowly healing. Crossing the bridge from passive watcher to active participant ultimately led me to find the SPNFamily, my new comfort zone. The fandom encouraged and supported me every step of the way.

In the ensuing weeks, which turned into months, I had the opportunity to get to know some of the other fans—and, to my sheer amazement and delight, some of the actors and staff from *Supernatural* itself (seriously, how cool is that?). Each encounter brought me a smile, bringing me back from the brink and continuing the healing process. The once-dark thoughts that plagued my mind began to recede as I opened the blinds in the window of my mind, letting in more and more light.

You may be asking, how does my real flesh-and-blood family fit into all of this? Make no mistake, they are there, and I wouldn't be where I am right now without them. As the show so famously says, though, and as this book's title and contents affirm: "Family don't end with blood." The SPNFamily delivers a safe and healthy environment for me to express things I wouldn't, and couldn't, burden my "blood" with.

With my fandom family, I can joke about becoming a ghost and haunting the Wi-Fi system or live tweeting from the afterlife. I get it and they get it, but as I found out the hard way, my husband doesn't (and can't) appreciate those types of jokes as much as I thought he would. I can't say I blame him. If the situation were reversed, I don't know that I would appreciate the humor either. My fandom family gives me the freedom and support I need and crave to help me deal with this otherwise impossible situation. They are outside, viewing my life from a safe space, which gives them great power to support me without emotional limits. In a flesh-and-blood family, things can get cloudy when you hold yourself back to protect those you love. There is an odd sort of beauty in the support found in online communities sharing a fandom. The shared purpose forms deep connections, where often you find yourself willing to open up and share more with a "stranger" than you do with your own real-life family.

Is my cancer gone? As I write this in 2016, nearly two years after my diagnosis, sadly, no. But there are enough distractions with the wonderful friendships I've made within the fandom family, the stunning writers who bring us script after script of wit and humor, and the amazing actors who bring them to life each week that it goes a long way toward helping me forget.

NON TIMEBO MALA

BREDA WAITE

I was raised in a Christian cult. The cult had its own private school, day care, and radio station, so it was my entire world. I attended the school from kindergarten to twelfth grade, and spent most evenings and weekends there as well, participating in "service." After two failed attempts to leave the cult by myself during and after college, my entire family finally left when I was twenty-four.

I moved to Seattle and jumped into graduate school at a seminary that meshes theology and psychology, The Seattle School of Theology & Psychology. The Seattle School focused on the belief that, whether we are pastors or therapists, we bring our story into the room with us—so it forced me to pay attention to my story. I was studying to be a therapist, and began to explore my story only to find I was deeply traumatized by my upbringing. I wrestled with the psychological ramifications of the theology I had been taught, especially the belief that I am evil at my core and that because "God has a plan for my life" I had no freedom to choose or pursue what I wanted. In 2014, as I started my final year at the school, after three incredibly hard years of becoming a person and failing a lot of classes in the midst of my PTSD, depression, and dissociation, I found *Supernatural.* I dove in and fell in love.

The show was wrestling with deep, hard topics in beautiful, gut-wrenching ways, and I found I could relate to a lot of it. Whether it was Dean's doubt in the existence of God or any goodness, the fight for free will, Sam's struggle to believe the reality that he had escaped Hell, or them both questioning whether their own natures were good or evil, I could relate. I had fought all these battles, and still fight them almost daily.

Sometime around when I was watching seasons 3 and 4 for the first time, I had a dream that I ran into Sam and Dean in my old cult, and earned their trust and help with fighting demons there because of a tattoo I had. It was on my back, between my shoulders, and was a half sun (from the anti-possession symbol), all in black. To Sam, who was running on demon blood, it looked like a sun setting into darkness, so he trusted my darkness. To Dean, it looked like a sun rising into light, so he trusted my light. In my dream, the boys allowed me to hunt with them and helped me leave when we were done. I woke up from the dream feeling strong, grounded, and empowered by the idea that the Winchesters had my back in my fight to leave behind my cult and what it had taught me. And if the Winchesters have my back, together we're pretty much unstoppable.

By November 2014 I was caught up on the show and a devoted fan, and to celebrate my birthday, I got the tattoo. By then, I had modified the image slightly. The top half of the sun is darker, and the bottom half is its reflection in light, with the phrase "non timebo mala" in the middle as the horizon. This is the Latin phrase on the Colt the Winchesters use to shoot demons, which translates to "I will fear no evil."

It symbolizes my fight, firstly, to own my body for myself, because the cult always told me that my body wasn't mine and that tattoos were evil. Secondly, it's about my fight to hold my darkness and my light in balance, like in "There's No Place Like Home" when Charlie is split into Dark Charlie and Good Charlie before eventually being recombined in one body, in balance. Finally, it reminds me not to live in fear of evil, whether it's in people around me (the cult told me everyone outside the cult was untrustworthy and evil) or in myself. I will no longer live in fear.

The psychologist in me also really likes how the tattoo plays with the Jungian ideas of the Shadow Self. Carl Jung conceptualized the Shadow Self as either the negative aspects of a person's character that they repress, or anything in the unconscious that they are unaware of, whether positive or negative. I choose the second definition: to look at it simply as parts of myself I am unfamiliar with. My cult told me not to trust myself because my true nature was evil. But as I begin to explore who I am and who I want to be, it turns out that sometimes what I thought was evil is not. For example, my cult would have said anger was a sin. I have had to learn that, in the face of abuse, anger is a justified response that tells me I am worth better treatment. Thus, my Shadow Self that is often angry about the trauma I experienced is brought into the light and shown to be love for myself, a belief that I am worth more than they told me. Likewise, depression and anxiety often tip me off to old, harmful ways of thinking, or clue me in to grief that I still need to address, and thus my Shadow begins to inform my healing. It's not something to be feared. (Eventually, I want to add a line around my tattoo from the *Doctor Who* episode "A Christmas Carol" that will say, "Let in the light of your bright shadow.")

The deeper I fell into the *Supernatural* fandom, the more astounded I was by everyone's kindness. I had found kind people, where my cult had told me they didn't exist. I had found a safe community that was supportive and believed in me. The celebrities/actors who had so much power in this fandom were consciously using it for kindness. Watching con videos and gag reels helped me laugh on dark days when I had forgotten how to do so without fear. Misha's silliness taught me to not take life so seriously, even if my past was dark. Then Jared started his Always Keep Fighting campaign. I had gotten my sister hooked on the show as well, and when I shared Jared's campaign with her, it opened the door for both of us to talk about our struggles with depression, anxiety, and suicidal ideation since leaving the cult. We started ending our conversations asking each other, "Will you keep fighting?" "Yeah, I'm gonna keep fighting." We both bought AKF shirts.

Then SeaCon 2015 came around and I prepared to meet the boys, trying to figure out how to communicate how much they've meant to me. I ended up getting the chance to meet Jared at his sister's table on the Saturday before my J2 photo op. I told him a truncated version of this story and thanked him for his work on this show and for the AKF campaign. The next day, I managed to be at the end of the photo-op line, so I got a few extra seconds with J2. Jared remembered me from the day before (GAAAHHH!!!! :D), so I briefly explained to Jensen. Jensen put his arm around me and wrapped me in the strongest hug for our picture, as they held the signs I had prepared that tell a little bit of my story using lines from the show. After Chris took the photo, Jensen leaned his head down on mine and said, "Thanks, babe." I left the room shaking with gratitude and happiness. I feel like they are now a little (read: big) part of my family and like they have my back in spirit as I continue to fight for myself.

Sometimes, when I'm having a rough day, or I've woken up from a dream about the cult, I'll look at this picture and tell myself, "You got away. We got you out." And I'll start to breathe more freely. I'll study the boys' faces, with their fierce pride and protection of me, and I'll grow a little braver. And I'll look at my own grin of pure happiness and remember that good things still happen.

When Jared announced his second AKF campaign, with the Moose & Squirrel shirt, I was broke due to grad school and heartbroken I couldn't get one. I reached out to a friend I had met at SeaCon who was organizing donors who had offered to purchase shirts for those who couldn't afford one and asked to be put on the list. She instantly offered to buy a shirt for me, knowing some of my story and why it was important to me. I realized during this experience that as a kid I'd had a school uniform and church clothes, and any other clothes were hand-me-downs because the majority of my family's money went to the cult. On top of that, for certain events kids were made to wear shirts that said we were future members of the cult's adult programs. I had never had clothes of my own that expressed me and my personality, and certainly none that communicated that I belonged to myself and my body is no one's but my own. Being given a shirt that both expressed what I love and encouraged me to fight for myself and to own my body was a deep, rich gift. A shirt seems like such a small thing, but it felt like a lifeline. Each time I put on one of my AKF shirts, I breathe a full-body sigh of relief. I own me, I can love what I love, and I can keep fighting for myself.

On Jared's birthday this past summer, five years after my family left the cult, my dad called me up out of the blue and apologized for raising me in it. He asked for my forgiveness, and as I sat there weeping on the floor, I was able to give it. It seemed so fitting that it happened on Jared's birthday, like he was part of it all somehow. Almost as if, as I have been learning to fight for myself, my family has begun to fight for themselves and for me, too. And the SPNFamily is now part of that fight as well.

At SeaCon 2016, I got to speak with Jared again while getting his autograph on my J2 picture from the year before. As soon as I cued his memory, he remembered me, even though it had been a year! He reached for my hands and asked how I was. I was able to tell him about my dad's apology on his birthday, and thank him for being with us, even if it was in spirit, encouraging me to fight for myself and the health of my family. As he held my hands and listened, we both teared up at the rich goodness that has come about in just the two years I've been a part of this fandom. When I turned to go, I told him I was proud of him, and he said a simple "Ditto!" with a small smile. Isn't it funny how you can sometimes feel the need to weep for joy, not sadness?

I have so many stories of other moments along the way, and friendships forged at conventions and through GISHWHES, but this is what I'll share here: this show has saved and changed my life in so many ways. It has given me stories and characters that have helped me fight on dark days to believe that I am good and that I am worth fighting for, because if the boys can keep fighting, so can I. The fandom has shown me community that can be kind and generous, and full of laughter. The actors have shown me how to play and how to fight for myself. It's like that line in the episode "Fan Fiction": "*Supernatural* has everything! Life, death, resurrection, redemption. But above all, family." I have found them all by being a part of this family.

The phrase in my tattoo, "non timebo mala," or "I will fear no evil," is from Psalm 23 in the Bible. What is not included in my tattoo, but is implied in every inch of my story, is the second part of the phrase: "For you are with me." I will fear no evil, for you are with me. I will not fear, because I am not alone. I have a family that doesn't end with blood.

CHOOSING LIFE

BURNER CADE

March 12, 2013:

How are you feeling? read the message in the AIM chat window.

Could be better was my diplomatic response. *Could be a lot worse, though.*

Did you get any sleep last night? Sheena, my best friend, stationed at Fort Gordon, Georgia, responded. I didn't need to hear her voice to read the concern in her words.

A little bit. Again with diplomacy, because I knew how worried she got. But the truth was I had been in so much pain the night before that sleep had been impossible. As it was, I only felt marginally better after sleeping until 2 P.M. The only reason I was awake was because I had set my alarm. I lived in Arizona at the time, and a three-hour time difference (with Sheena ahead) made it hard for us to "hang out" on days I worked. I had called in sick that day, too tired, nauseated, and broken to climb out of bed, much less sling 100-pound bales of hay, clean twenty horse stalls, and scrub eighty-four horse hooves, all in 90+ degree temps.

And there's nothing they can do for you. That's so shitty, Sheena responded, and I couldn't help but smile a little. *I'm so sorry this happened.*

Yeah, me too, and just as I could hear her, I knew she heard the defeat, the sigh, the tears in my voice. *I just want it to stop hurting.*

I didn't just mean the symptoms of toxic hepatitis, the illness that had kept me in bed that day; I also meant my heart. I had contracted the hepatitis from a rare side effect of a medication I had been taking for a false-positive tuberculosis skin test because, when testing false positive, even with a clear chest X-ray, the United States Armed Forces requires treatment for TB as a precaution before you can enlist.

I had always been a military dreamer. I wanted to be a pilot, or a mechanic for the Blue Angels, since I was five years old, but as I grew up and became a short, chubby kid, I didn't believe I could handle the military. My mother wanted me to be an artist. She was a loving woman, but suffered from both chronic depression and cancer. My father left us when I was fifteen, when she started chemo treatments. To help my mother and me survive, my sister, older than me by twenty-five years, moved in with us.

I was able to get a job and help pay the bills, and kept that job as my sister lost hers on a bi-yearly basis. I went to college, a college my mother picked out, for art as she wanted (I wanted to be a dentist; I'm a regular misfit elf). But the school was a "for profit" college, and I realized I needed to obtain a degree from a "reputable" school so that I could make a living. I racked up $100,000 worth of student loan debt and spent three years of my life, only to find out when I went to enroll into a nursing program at my local community college that none of my credits were transferable. The very expensive "education" I received was as good as useless. My job (which I had held on to) had for a while been enough to pay for my sister's shortcomings—but now we had a mortgage.

I had foolishly trusted my sister when she asked me to go in on a mortgage with her (I had better credit) so our mother would "always have a home." This also allowed me to rescue a small horse in dire need of a better situation. I didn't like the house we bought, nor was it horse property, and I ended up rehoming the horse because I was unable to keep his small feed bill paid; my funds always had to go elsewhere. My sister's inability to keep a job kept me scrambling for income; we were always behind on the mortgage. At one point I worked two jobs, with no days off, but this only made her angry.

Sheena, whom I met back in 2009 in a *Star Trek* LiveJournal community, discussing the JJ Abrams reboot, had inspired me to follow my dreams. The Navy would give me credit for my college degree, my debt would be much easier to pay off, and I could take care of my family and the house. So I worked out three hours every day, ate right, lost thirty pounds in three months, spoke with recruiters, and signed up to take the Armed Services Vocational Aptitude Battery, or ASVAB. A positive TB test on my latest physical just meant I needed to be treated before shipping out. "It's completely safe," my doctor assured me. "Only one in a million people have an adverse side effect. You're young and healthy. You'll be fine."

He was wrong.

Because my diagnosis was "borderline"—my liver enzymes were elevated and I was obviously sick, but not sick "enough" to be considered as having full-on hepatitis—my primary-care physician and specialist could not come to an agreement on whether or not the drugs were in fact the cause. After discontinuing the original medication, the only thing that could be done was to offer me painkillers that would not adversely affect my liver, which I had to have tested every two weeks to ensure its function, and monitor my symptoms in case they became worse rather than better. They also agreed that I did not need to go on antivirals, and that we should let the toxic hepatitis run its course. My specialist did, however, give me a letter stating my blood tests indicated I did *not* have TB, so alternative treatments would not be needed.

But when it came time to sign the papers, my credit history was run, and my recruiter informed me that despite having gone through and suffered an agonizing treatment for a disease I didn't have, the amount of student loan and mortgage debt I had would prevent me from enlisting in the United States Navy, or any other branch of the Armed Forces. Though I had never missed a payment on my loans and they were in good standing, the military will not accept recruits whose total outstanding debt exceeds more than double their estimated yearly income while enlisted. A portion of my government-funded loans would have been forgiven with active duty service, but the majority of my student loans are private, and that plus having half a mortgage to my name meant I had $135,000 of "nonforgivable" debt.

I remember trying to explain to them that if they would let me enlist, I could have it paid down, if not completely off, in less than three years, but unfortunately, recruiters are bound by their rules. He thanked me, said I was very inspiring, and wished me the best.

My broken heart hurt far worse than my body. That had been my only chance to escape—to make good on my obligations to my family, to the bank, to myself as a human being—and it had been shut out. I had worked so hard, had begun to believe I could do something, that I could be proud of myself. And now I had destroyed my body for nothing.

I'm watching this new show. Sheena's AIM box blinked again. *It's called* Supernatural. *It's been on a while, but it's really cool. I'd really like to watch it with you. Can I come visit?*

Of course, was my response. *When?*

Friday, her reply flashed back.

Uh . . . this Friday? I was perplexed. *Can you get your leave approved that quick?*

I . . . may have already put in for it, she confessed after a long moment. *Trust me, I think you'll really like this.*

That Friday I picked her up in the evening, around 6 P.M. The airport was only twenty minutes from my job, so it was easy to just grab her on the way home. I was pleasant, but she could tell that the work and heat of the day had left me tired. I parked my truck and we went inside. We exchanged a few pleasantries with my mother and made our way to my room, in the back of the house, to hide before my sister got home.

"You feeling up to watching an episode or two?" Sheena asked, a kind smile on her face. "I understand if you're too tired."

"No way," I said. "Just let me shower and change first. You didn't fly out here so I could sleep the whole time."

By the time I returned she already had the menu screen up. She looked mischievous as she hit the play button, and immediately I found myself getting sucked into the pilot, the story of these two brothers who were "saving people, hunting things—the family business." One or two episodes became six, my eyes hardly leaving the screen. I was becoming more and more interested in the evolving story of these Winchester brothers.

It was Sam whom I felt a particularly deep resonance with: the constant obligation of family always overshadowing his personal choices, how making any decision for his own benefit only seemed to lead to others' disappointment and loathing in himself. His life was not his own, and while it was obvious he cared for Dean and their father, he was expected to live his whole life for them. It was a struggle I faced every day. My monsters were not wendigos or yellow-eyed demons, but they were real nonetheless.

We got through four and a half seasons in eight days, and once Sheena returned to Georgia we would meet up on AIM and watch three or four episodes nightly on Netflix until we were caught up.

OMG there's a Supernatural *convention!!* she messaged excitedly some weeks later. *In Burbank! Do you want to go?*

I can't afford it, I lamented. *But say hi to Sam for me!*

That's not what I asked, she shot back. *You can tell him yourself. Happy birthday!*

At first I didn't want to accept such a generous gift, but the more I thought about it, the more I wanted to go. Every day was getting more and more difficult to handle. The pain medication I was taking wasn't doing me much good, and my home environment was deteriorating further (my sister had lost another job). I decided it would be good to get away.

That was in June. When November rolled around, I found myself quietly resigned: it was going to be a life of pain, of this constant chain of house payments, student loans, a much-older sister who used me and abused me emotionally, and a job I wouldn't be able to get out of . . . or the bottle of painkillers I had in my carry-on. By this time, I was taking the highest recommended amount. It was the only way I could sleep, or try to work, but even then I was taking a lot of partial days off because I was simply unable to stand up. I hadn't been able to get FMLA (Family Medical Leave Act); my specialist and primary-care physician were too busy arguing about the diagnosis to sign the paper I needed.

I'll enjoy the convention, spend time with Sheena, and after I get my picture with Jared—it's over. I can't handle this anymore.

I hadn't been able to afford much in terms of photo opportunities, but that was fine. While I liked the other actors and their characters, none of them meant as much to me as Sam did. Sheena was kind enough to share some of her photos with me, all of which were fun. Karaoke and the cocktail party were trials on my body, and I found myself having to sit more than I wanted, because I was too nauseated and hurting to stand.

I met many wonderful people throughout the con, all of whom I keep in contact with, two years and several cons later. The girl who sat in front of me, named Jennifer, I consider one of my best friends.

She dubbed herself a "Castiel girl," and I said, "Well, I must be a Sam girl!"

"You must be so excited," Jennifer said that Sunday morning. "Are you nervous?"

"Not really," I said with what at the time was honesty. "I'm ready." And I was, for so much. I was ready for it all to be over. Once I had my picture taken with Jared, I planned on going back to the hotel room and swallowing all of my pain medication. This was going to be my final hurrah.

I hadn't seen Sheena much during the convention, as she had a VIP pass. That was fine. I didn't like her seeing me this sick and weak. But much to my surprise, Sheena had also bought a Jared photo ticket, and her VIP pass allowed us to go to the front of the line. When we were called up, Jared turned to look at us. He was wearing a blue plaid shirt, a hat, and the biggest smile I had ever seen. "I like your shirt!" he told me exuberantly. I had bought a shirt that said, "I heart Sam," with an anatomically correct heart.

It was then he looked up at me and noticed the tears in my eyes. There were a lot of people crying at the opportunity to meet him, but he saw something that my family, my coworkers, and my closest friends did not: I was hurting. Badly.

His smile faded and he furrowed his brows; his hat tipped forward just a bit as he took a step toward me. "Are you okay?" he asked.

No one had asked me that. In all the months, the heartbreak, the turmoil, and the drama, I had been given condolences and pep talks, but I had been expected to pick up my shattered dreams, my hopes of living my own life, of freedom, and just move on.

It took everything I had not to start sobbing. My throat was almost too tight to speak and my posture went rigid. I'm not sure what Sheena's expression was, because I was too busy trying not to make a fool of myself.

Despite the long line of people behind us, Jared waited patiently until I managed to answer with a shaky, "No."

"Hey." His voice became softer as he moved forward to give me one of the biggest, tightest hugs I have ever had. "I don't know what's bothering you, but I promise it's going to get better, and I'm glad that you're here. Go wash your face, and come back to the front of the line."

I scurried to the bathroom, hid for a few moments with Sheena standing awkwardly behind me, and when I returned to the photo room, I was again greeted with another huge smile. "Hey!" Jared said. "What can I do to make you feel better?"

"Can you make her jealous?" I managed, regarding my friend Sheena.

"I sure can." Jared laughed, and scooped me up into another hug. I held on to him for my own picture. "Hey," he said before I left the photo area, "I promise you it's gonna get better."

His words stuck with me. They were heavy and warm in my chest: things would get better, somehow.

I knew then that I had to start living my own life; my current situation was destroying me. When I returned to Arizona, I sought help from a coworker whose in-law worked with crisis management, and spoke with my mother and sister at length about how I wanted to move to Georgia to live with Sheena. I said I would pay what I was able to on the house, but didn't know what kind of job I would be able to get, and thus couldn't promise a specific amount.

By March 4, 2014, I had moved across the country with only a few of my possessions, clothes, and the hope that, yes, things would get better. I kept in contact with my mother, who supported my decision wholeheartedly, but my sister kept badgering me for money I didn't have. I paid her nearly a third of my income for a house I wanted to sell (she refused), a house she should have been more than able to afford on her own with her salary at the time. But it was my name on the house, too. My family, my responsibility.

Just like Sam.

It was at the *Supernatural* Burbank convention in 2014 (which Sheena generously took me to) that I informed my mother and sister I would no longer be giving them money because I just didn't have it, and that the only reason I was able to go to the convention was because someone (Sheena) was kind enough to bring me along. Just minutes before I was scheduled to leave for my Jared photo, my sister called to tell me what an awful person I was. I sobbed in my seat, my phone discarded.

After composing myself, I did go to the photo room to collect my two pictures of Jared (I had splurged) and again he looked at my shirt and smiled. "Hey, I like that shirt! It's cool; it's a real heart."

"You said that last year," I informed him with a weak smile, but it was no use; I could feel the tears forming in my eyes.

"I hope those are tears of joy." His smile was a little faded, and just like before, his brow furrowed. "Are you okay?"

"Yes," I said. "Will you wear these antlers for me?"

"Duh!" He laughed, and we posed with our moose antlers on, as well as in another basic hug photo. "Feel better, sweetheart," he called after me.

Thankfully, it was after the picture was taken that I discovered my sister had been calling and texting Sheena, cursing us both, saying how dare I think I could have my own life and abandon her.

As I stood in the autograph line, the weight of everything got to me, and old wounds felt new. My muscles ached more than they had been; I felt sick. Maybe I was selfish for having bought two photos with Jared (my only real purchase for myself for the year). Maybe I was a terrible person for having fun while my family struggled. Maybe wanting my own life after having lived for other people was wrong.

When it was my turn, I set my custom Sam plush and a large pile of packaged candy down for Jared.

Jared's eyes widened and he gasped. "Is this for me?" He didn't wait for my answer to start eating the Sour Patch Kids.

"I'm so sorry. I'm going to be 'that' fan," I informed him with a quivering bottom lip. I could see his expression becoming curious and cautious. "Last year at BurCon, I was going to kill myself," I said quietly, my tears heavy and consistent on my cheeks. "But I didn't, because you promised it would get better. I'm trying, I'm trying so hard, and I just wanted you to know that."

I was so embarrassed, especially when I managed to look up and see the horrified look on both his and his handler's face. I felt horrible, like

I had overstepped some boundary, and all I wanted to do was go hide. I didn't care if I got my autograph or not. When I went to move away from the table, Jared reached both hands across it to quickly grab my hands and give them a gentle squeeze.

"Don't you fucking apologize!" he said with surprising sternness. "Hey, hey," he repeated until I could bring myself to look back at him. "You've got nothing to apologize for. We're a family, we're supposed to help each other, and I'm glad I could do that for you. You're stronger than you think, just keep fighting and keep your head up. You need to smile more; it's too pretty for you to hide it all the time."

He signed the leg of the Sam plush I had brought, with a small customization, before reaching out to hold my hand one more time. "I want to see you again, okay?" he said with a slow nod.

"I'll try," was all I could promise.

Fortunately, I was able to attend three more conventions. Sheena was set to deploy in July for a three-year tour, so she acquired us tickets to the 2015 San Francisco, Phoenix, and Las Vegas conventions. Every Sunday when Jared was there, I wore the same "I heart Sam" shirt with the anatomically correct heart.

In San Francisco when I shyly approached Jared for my photo—a duo with Tahmoh Penikett—Jared smiled widely. "Hey, you!" He hugged me. "How are you feeling? Tahmoh, did you see her shirt?"

"Not enough angel for me," Tahmoh replied with a laugh.

"What do you want us to do, sweetheart?" Jared asked me.

"Can you try to make each other jealous?" I asked, still shy, but not crying this time.

"Of course!" Jared grinned and tugged me in for a hug, making some face at Tahmoh when the other man took my arm in an attempt to be in on the picture.

"What should we do in *our* picture?" Jared asked when I returned for his solo picture, which I also got two of.

"Can we hug, and then just look happy?" I requested.

"We won't just look happy—we'll *be* happy!" Jared declared before wrapping an arm around me, and the pair of us struck a funny pose.

Every time I saw him after that—his autograph in San Francisco, our photos and autographs in Phoenix—Jared made a point to ask me how I was feeling. He'd say he loved my shirt, that he was glad I was there, how I "always brightened his day," and that he loved the candy, because I always made it a point to bring him something sour. No longer did I have tears in my eyes during our brief meetings, guilt no longer heavy.

"This is going to be our last photo for a while," I told him in Vegas. "I'm not gonna be at any more cons for a bit."

"Then let's make this one count!" Jared said, pulling me in for another one of his big bear hugs—but this time? I wasn't crying; I was smiling, so happily. "I just want you to know that I believe in you, and I'm rooting for you," he said, and even though our photo was over, he offered me another tight hug. "Take care, sweetheart. We'll see each other again. Keep smiling."

It is because of Jared Padalecki that I am alive today, that I am still fighting. No, things are not perfect, and there is still progress to be made. I am finding happiness; I am slowly finding confidence again. It is because of this fandom, this "family," that I have such a strong support group and I no longer feel like I have to suffer alone or in silence. I have the love and support of my mother, whom I still help out but on more feasible terms. I have the most wonderful friend and partner (in crime!) in the world, Sheena, and my best friend, Jennifer, whom I met through this show.

And, as it turns out, the Army Reserves do not have such tight financial restrictions, and as of November 2016, I am speaking with a recruiter. I had filed bankruptcy, and hadn't given it much thought, but having eliminated the mortgage from my name, it left a potential door open to follow my dreams. It's not a sure thing, and I have some hurdles to leap and hoops to jump through, but it's more a chance than I would have had if I were no longer here. To have the opportunity to try means everything.

Thank you, Jared. Thank you for showing me that I wasn't ready to throw all of that away. Thank you for showing me that my life, despite its hurdles, is worth fighting for.

WHAT DOES THE FANDOM MEAN TO ME?

JARED PADALECKI

What does the fandom mean to me?

A daunting question, made no less difficult by the fact that my answer would simply be my opinion, incapable (by definition) of being incorrect.

Though it would be easy to answer this arguably rhetorical question with "So much," or "I could never even begin to explain it," those answers would be cop-outs. They would be simple plaudits, and they would be doing the fandom a huge disservice.

So I'm going to attempt to put into words what "fandom" (and, more specifically, the *Supernatural* fandom) means to me.

It's going to take a little backstory, so bear with me. :)

My first brush with fandom wasn't an adoring gaggle of young ladies rushing me with posters to sign, or adolescents with smartphones asking for selfies. No, my first brush with fandom was a young boy, couldn't have been more than three or four years old, and he was HEAD OVER HEELS in love with *Star Wars* (the originals, obviously, because no one could possibly enjoy Jar Jar Binks). He had all of the toys and figures his family could afford, he watched the movies incessantly (via the prehistoric VHS medium), and his favorite character was the bounty hunter known as Boba Fett.

That young boy was none other than yours truly.

Even as a young child, I found comfort and escape in the archetype-laden *Star Wars* saga—the reluctant hero (Luke Skywalker), the swash-buckling rogue (Han Solo), the intimidating-yet-benevolent beast (Chew-bacca)—and in the impossible task, the seemingly unachievable mission. Oh, yeah, and I thought lightsabers and spaceships were cool (because they are!). It may go without saying, but I thought (hoped?) that maybe I, too, had The Force. I tested that theory on more than one occasion, and later on in life than I care to admit—and I know y'all did, too, so don't try and act cool!

Furthermore, I was fascinated with the idea that someone could be born with a blessing that was simultaneously a curse: it spoke to me in a way that even my young, still-forming mind could somehow comprehend and appreciate. I was intrigued by the enormous responsibility that the protagonists bore: that they, and they alone, could save the world. The idea that they had a call to action that couldn't be ignored, and that their contribution was imperative to the success of the mission.

Little did I know that I would one day have the opportunity to tell that same story.

Now, Boba Fett was my boy. I don't quite know why. To this day, I can't identify any specific reasons why he was my favorite. Maybe the helmet? Maybe his trusty spacecraft, *Slave 1*? Maybe because everybody (namely, Han Solo) seemed to be scared of him? All I know is that, to this day, my Boba Fett "collectibles" (the word I use to help me justify adult ownership of toys) still sit in the bedroom I grew up in, patiently waiting to be played with by my two sons.

Left: My Star Wars "collectibles."
Right: With another childhood "collectible," this one He-Man.

As further evidence, my first-ever email account password (via the ubiquitous AOL "free trial" CDs that came in the mail, as all you other children of the '80s will remember) was "Slave1."

Yes. I was a superfan. Of *Star Wars*. Of Boba Fett. Of the very same Joseph Campbell–identified archetypes that I now get to portray for a living. Even after having seen the movies hundreds of times, even after I had spent hundreds (thousands?) of hours of my life watching them, even after I could recite them from beginning to end, even after I knew the outcome (poor Boba: Sarlacc Pit Monsters are the worst), I *still* found my escape in those films. I would watch them regularly. I would think about them. I would act them out. I would play with the toys with my older brother (funnily enough, he was always Han Solo and I was always Luke Skywalker).

Subconsciously, I think I felt better about my own struggles knowing that there was someone out there who had to deal with worse, and who still fought through.

That was my first brush with fandom.

(Slightly) later in life, I found the Teenage Mutant Ninja Turtles.

Now, I didn't just watch Ninja Turtles cartoons because they were the only option on television while my parents made breakfast. No, I *loved* the Ninja Turtles. I *lived* them. I *understood* them, and they seemed to understand me back. This time around, Michelangelo was my boy. I had all the figures (that we could afford), all the video games (that we could afford), all the VHS tapes (that we could afford), all the apparel that would fit me (and, yes, that we could afford). I even had a Ninja Turtle–themed birthday cake.

I was *such* a fan that I even dragged my mother (who didn't seem to be kicking and screaming at the time) to a small theater in San Antonio to watch a bunch of people in Ninja Turtle costumes lip-synch to random songs (in hindsight, I'm not certain their costume mouths even moved).

I was a superfan. A one-man fandom. In fact, I would bet a pretty penny that I could still sing the Ninja Turtles theme, word for precious word, if I needed to. In my head, I imagine it would be a fun way to win free drinks at the bar, though I doubt anyone would care enough (and/or know the words well enough themselves to verify whether or not my rendition was or wasn't verbatim). So, alas, it'll have to remain a pipe dream for a different life.

Side note: My first paying gig as an actor was on a never-to-be-picked-up pilot called *Silent Witness*. I played a character named Sam. At the time, I was a senior at James Madison High School in San Antonio, in my second semester, so my teachers offered to let me do my schoolwork from afar (thanks, teachers!). It was based on a female medical examiner and we filmed it in Chicago, in February of 2000. *Silent Witness* didn't get picked up for network television, but I was told that the pilot got retooled a little bit and became the very successful *Crossing Jordan*. I've never verified that (nor do I think NBC ever *would* verify that). Anyway, I played the nephew of the lead actress, and we had a couple of scenes together. That actress was none other than the lovely and talented Paige Turco, aka April O'Neil from the second and third *Teenage Mutant Ninja Turtles* movies! I gotta admit, I nerded out a little bit. I mean, this was April O'Neil, the strong-willed reporter who covered all the heroic antics of my favorite turtline (is there a word like "feline" or "porcine" for "turtle-hood"?) four-some!! I was in superfan heaven. I'm not sure if I ever told her or not. I don't think I did. I was probably too busy trying to act tough and play it cool (as one does when he's about to graduate high school and just *knows* he's going to conquer the world).

But back to my TMNT fandom. Again, I had found a story where the protagonists had a blessing that was also a curse. Though, in this case, maybe the curse (being a freakin' turtle!) was a little more apparent than the blessing (having cool ninja moves, friends to rely on, and getting to help people). I had found another outlet for channeling my imagination and inner thoughts, and in which to spend time with my new friends (of the turtle persuasion).

Then I found James Bond.

My papa (my mom's dad) was, and still is, a big James Bond fan, and I would rifle through his old VHS tapes to find where he had recorded them off the TV (the original form of pirating . . . sorry, entertainment industry). I can vividly remember, on several occasions, fast-forwarding through *Rio Bravo* so I could watch *For Your Eyes Only*.

As before, I had found an escape. I discovered a character who, against insurmountable odds, found a way to make it out alive. A guy who was blessed with charm and wits and skills and grit to keep on fighting. A guy with cool clothes and cool cars. This time around, the protagonist was cursed with a bevy of assorted dastardly villains and was always watching

his back (and his front, I suppose, when it came to his conquests!), never sure whom he could trust and whom he couldn't.

I would immerse myself in the films. I would pretend I was in them. I would memorize the lines and the scenes and watch them over and over and over again. As a senior in high school, I remember driving around San Antonio to all the different Blockbusters to see if they had any of the original James Bond films on VHS so I could have the entire collection.

I never did finish that collection. But the search provided me some form of solace. It felt good to "earn" my superfan status, and to make sacrifices for "them" (those involved in the creation of the franchise) as a thank-you for their sacrifices to me. Rest assured, I have all the films on DVD now.

Side note: My favorite Bond was Roger Moore. Possibly because he was my papa's favorite, possibly because I always found that the Connery films had bad action sequences (cutting frames to make fight scenes seem faster; punches and kicks that *clearly* missed their targets, even to an eight-year-old's eyes) and a lot of sexual innuendos that weren't clear to me until later in life (I'm fairly certain that ten-year-old Jared had *no idea* "Pussy Galore" or "Plenty O'Toole" were anything more than just names). George Lazenby felt a little greasy, and Timothy Dalton seemed a little smug (though I have watched *The Living Daylights* more times than I can count). The Pierce Brosnan films didn't start getting released until I was thirteen.

What's most interesting about my passion for the James Bond franchise is that it led me to my very first fan convention experience. While filming *Gilmore Girls* in Burbank and living in North Hollywood (near Vineland and Moorpark, for all you Angelenos), my buddy Dane and I went to a multi-fandom convention where I met the one and only Richard Kiel, aka Jaws. I never got to meet Boba Fett or Michelangelo (neither the talking Teenage Turtle nor the amazing ancient artist, obviously . . .), so meeting Richard Kiel was my first experience coming face-to-face with one of my idols.

I had considered myself a fairly large human at 6 feet, 4 inches. Then I met Richard, who towered over me at a supplementary-oxygen-needing 7 feet, 2 inches tall. We took a picture and he signed my freshly purchased copy of his autobiography, *Making It Big in the Movies*. I told him how I loved his performances in *Moonraker* and *The Spy Who Loved Me*, and how I owned (and still own) an original theater advertisement poster from *The Spy Who Loved Me* (which I had bought via eBay years earlier when I first started earning a paycheck).

Left: A picture of my The Spy Who Loved Me poster in my old apartment. Original pic circa 2000.
Right: Where the poster now lives: in my home theater in Austin, Texas. :)

I also mentioned that I originally used his character "Jaws" when I played the Nintendo 64 version of *GoldenEye*, but that I had moved on to a different character because his character was larger than the other options, ergo easier to kill. He grinned and said that he, too, had chosen a different character to play with during his gaming sessions. (I kind of doubt he really played Nintendo, but his gesture was clear to me; he didn't want me to feel like a nerd.) He was a kind man. The way he spoke to me and looked me in the eyes and smiled, and the way his giant hands shook mine, made me feel special. Unique. Appreciated. I was struck by his warmth. May he rest in peace.

My other fandoms, in no particular order, have been: the San Antonio Spurs, the Dallas Cowboys, baseball cards, coins, Pearl Jam, Wade Boggs (I once tried to trade my entire baseball card collection for my brother's five Wade Boggs cards; luckily, my father stepped in), dinosaurs, wine, mechanical watches, yada, yada, yada.

Long story short (er, well . . . a little less long), I am a fan. I am passionate about that which brings me happiness, and committed in my support of it. I have been (and still am) dedicated to the things that bring me (and others) joy and excitement, laughter and tears, escape and adventure, understanding and forgiveness.

Now, to the subject at hand . . .

Supernatural.

When *Supernatural* began, *Gilmore Girls* was entering its sixth season (I had been an actor on the first five seasons), and it really seemed to be hitting its stride. As a result, most of the fans who would approach me during that first year were more familiar with my work on *Gilmore Girls* than *Supernatural*. However, late during the filming of season 1, in March 2006, I attended a multi-show convention in Pasadena, California. I was there as the lone representative of *Supernatural*. Jensen had other obligations that weekend, and we didn't yet really have any recurring guest stars who would have been invited. (Funnily enough, the actor who played Jango Fett, the father of my fave, Boba Fett [for all you non–*Star Wars* nerds, curse the lot of you], was there as well . . . life is full of coincidences.)

I can still remember my experience at that convention. I was extremely nervous, and I was certain that nobody there would know who I was and/or

be interested in what I had to say. I wasn't too far off. There were a couple of *Supernatural* fans there, and they are, wonderfully, still with the fandom today. But, by and large, I wasn't a big attraction. I think I was there so the con-goers could take a potty break in between the cast of the new hit show *Lost* and the other science-fiction-genre favorites. I remember sweating profusely onstage, scrambling to figure out what to talk about in the lull between questions (I developed a newfound respect for improv artists and stand-up comedians), and not really knowing what to make of the whole thing. Oh, yeah, and I had filmed until the wee hours of the morning in Vancouver only to go STRAIGHT to the Vancouver International Airport and fly STRAIGHT to Los Angeles to go STRAIGHT to the convention to take pictures with people I had never met. I remember thinking I probably smelled bad. I think my deodorant had been taken away at airport security. Either that or I had outright forgotten it.

That was my first-ever experience as a convention attraction. And it was almost my last.

It wasn't a fault of the organizers, or of the fans, or of my busy schedule. But I had long dealt with anxiety, and being in front of hundreds of people without a prepared script was almost unbearable. It was then that I truly realized I hadn't gotten into the industry to become famous (nothing against those who desire it), and that I didn't enjoy being stared at by people I didn't know. I could fake it, and I suppose I could fake it fairly well. But I felt excessively nervous. I felt judged. I felt like an animal in a cage in a zoo.

Thankfully, I have a short memory. A year and a half later, in November 2007, I was a guest at my second convention. This time it was based around *Supernatural*, so I suppose I felt comforted knowing that at least the attendees would be familiar with my work. It was a small convention, with only Jensen, Fred Lehne, Samantha Ferris, and me as the "guests of honor" (I had to look that up to remember. Thanks, SuperWiki!). By that time, we were about thirteen episodes into the filming of season 3, so the first two seasons of *Supernatural* had already aired, as had the first couple episodes of season 3. Now there was *plenty* for us to talk about! I don't remember too many specifics, seeing as it was almost nine years ago, but I do remember that I had a damn good time. I vaguely remember fielding questions about the show: about the way we filmed it, and what the casting process was like for Jensen and me. Though I don't remember exact questions or exact answers, I *do* remember what it felt like to have a conversation (of sorts) with someone who was passionate about my work, and the story I was a part of telling. I loved it. It's as if the fans were saying,

Still a fan! In my Pearl Jam scarf and "Love Yourself First" shirt, with Jensen.

"Hey, if you ever question whether or not it was a good idea to set out to be a storyteller, don't! And not because you're on the cover of magazines, and/or have famous friends. We appreciate it." It was a great feeling.

Up to that point, Jensen and I had been so busy with life and work that we hadn't really taken the opportunity to hear from the people who were watching what we were making. We had both received fan mail and fan letters, but it is *so* incredibly different and more meaningful to have a one-on-one connection (albeit briefly) in person.

There was one experience I vividly remember from that day as if it were yesterday: Jensen and I were informed that a Green Beret wanted to present us with Special Forces coins and a letter from the head of the Army, Gen. David Petraeus, as a thank-you for providing our overseas troops with so many great hours of entertainment. We were told that the first two seasons were the most requested TV seasons of all with our overseas troops, and that the story of two guys taking the hard road to help others and do what is right really hit home with our troops. Jensen and I, being huge supporters of our vets and our military, were floored. We let the powers that be know that we were so proud and honored to be able to give even just a little bit of distraction and enjoyment to the wonderful women and men who were abroad risking their lives so we could live in a safer world. I mean, I wear makeup for a living and have a stunt man standing by in case I break a nail; I can't imagine the stresses our wonderful troops (and their families) have to endure. So, in a short, impromptu ceremony, Jensen and I were presented with the coins (one for each of us) and the letter from Gen. Petraeus. I had never been so proud to do what I do. I couldn't believe that, through the fandom, we were making such a difference.

Well . . . some of you know where this is going. It was all fake. The scumbag who presented us with "Special Forces coins and a hand-signed letter" was a fake. A con man. Guilty of stolen valor and fraud, among other things.

Yet again, I questioned whether or not conventions were something I wanted to remain a part of. Between recurring anxiety and this total fraud, I was twice bitten/thrice shy. But I had already agreed to do a couple more conventions, and I didn't want to renege on my obligations, fear be damned.

More importantly, I had been met with such support and love from the fans as a whole that I felt this was going to be a special thing. I saw that there was genuine interest in the show, and I had the opportunity to field questions that truly made me think about the show, and my part in it, in a deeper way. Our fandom was (and is) bright, passionate, and inquisitive. I viewed our time together as more of a dialogue than a speech. I reminded myself that I, too, had experienced fandom from that end.

I started to wonder if maybe I could be somebody's Richard Kiel. :)

So, I carried on, as did *Supernatural* (obviously).

In the immediate years following ChiCon 2007 I had a front-row seat to watch what a wonderful force the *Supernatural* fandom could be. As I attended more conventions and met more fans face-to-face, it became increasingly evident that not only did the *Supernatural* fandom exist because of the television show *Supernatural*, but also the television show *Supernatural* existed because of the *Supernatural* fandom. It was a perfect symbiosis.

And we needed that relationship, because in the first few seasons, *Supernatural* went through a lot of hardships that can end most young shows: writers coming and going, producers getting hired and fired, guest stars getting hired and fired, even the dissolution of the WB channel (which we originally aired on in the United States) when it merged with UPN to become the CW. That was the most concerned I have ever been about the continued life of the show. I was wracked with thoughts like, *Why would the new bosses keep us around if they can't take full credit for our possible success?* and *Are we gonna get lost in the fray with all the new shows?* etc. Then, as if to accentuate my fears, a new show began to air on our network. It was going to be a sci-fi show (just like us!). It was going to be filmed in Vancouver (yay, friends!). It was about a ghost hunter (waitasecond) . . . named Sam (uhhhhhhh) . . . I thought *I* was their ghost hunter named Sam!!! I'd be lying if I said it wasn't a bit hurtful. I genuinely wondered (and kind of still do) whether our new network president had ever seen *Supernatural*. But, suck it. I never had to ask. We survived. :) And in the years that followed, I got to see why.

As I met innumerable new fans face-to-face, I was fortunate to be able to see, firsthand, just *how many* members of our *Supernatural* family had been brought to us by other fans of the show: *not* through commercials, *not* through posters in Times Square, *not* through our faces plastered all over magazines and buses . . . but through the fandom.

The *Supernatural* fandom was spreading the word, and an entire community of one-man and one-woman fandoms was expanding worldwide. As far as I could tell, they weren't going to be stopped. In those years, the questions and comments and conversations were largely about the show. They were about the enjoyment of the characters, of the writing, of the fact that we would make fun of ourselves and break the fourth wall. There were lots of personal connections, and it was always awesome to reconnect with the fandom on a regular basis, in all of the corners of the world, in person. Even as social media proliferated into the ubiquitous Goliath it now is, and as it became possible to connect with millions of fans through the screen of my cell phone, nothing replaced the experience of a face-to-face meeting.

There was always tremendous support, both on the part of the fans and (hopefully!) on the part of us thespians. The sacrifice of traveling to a city on our precious and few days off, without family, to take photos and sign autographs was always balanced by the payoff of the experiences we would have: the smiles we would see, the stories we would hear, and the letters we would receive.

I always loved (and still love, so *tell me* if this is true for you!) hearing about new friendships formed through *Supernatural*. I am in the same boat. If it weren't for this little show, I would not have had the chance to meet my wife or one of my best friends (not to mention all of my other dear friends I have met because of the show). In the ten-plus years that *Supernatural* has been a part of my world, my life has changed in more ways than I could elaborate (shy of hundreds of pages). I've had friends come and go. I've seen births, deaths, marriages, and divorces. I'm sure y'all have as well. Those who have stuck by and stuck around in my life through thick and thin will always have a special place in my heart, and I will always be grateful and humbled by the SPNFamily.

But . . .

Just exactly what the fandom *could* mean to me didn't *truly* hit me until March 2015, with the launch of the first Always Keep Fighting T-shirt campaign.

In the months leading up to the launch, my friend and fellow actor Stephen Amell had done a charity T-shirt campaign to raise awareness and funds toward treating and, hopefully one day, curing cancer. We were hanging out (probably watching football) and he told me all about it. He told me it was a cause dear to his heart, and how he was absolutely flabbergasted when he saw the outpouring of support from his fans. He suggested that I think of something I cared about, something that was near and dear to me, and do a campaign to raise awareness and funds to fight it. It wasn't immediately clear to me which direction I wanted to go in. Gen and I had had a history of donating to assorted causes, such as St. Jude's, the Down Syndrome Connection, the Wounded Warrior Project, and more, but I didn't know yet where I felt I should direct my energy and message.

But as the days progressed, I began to realize exactly what I wanted to do . . . and it was scaring the shit out of me.

I've had an ongoing struggle with anxiety and depression most of my adult life. I won't go into boring detail (because that's not what this essay is about), but suffice it to say, it was always there in the background, lurking, waiting for an opportunity to pounce. By and large, I had a pretty good handle on it and it has remained under control. That's largely due to the fact that I'm blessed to often be surrounded by friends and family, doing what I love, and I've been able to keep my head up.

But it did win a few battles along the way (though I am proud to say, I am winning the WAR!). One of those battles was in season 3, during the filming of "A Very *Supernatural* Christmas." It was a day like any other: I woke up, worked out, memorized my lines, and headed to the set. But something I couldn't identify (or, maybe, that I was choosing to ignore) was eating at me. Beating me down. Convincing me that it was going to win, and that I didn't have a chance to stop it. I made it through my daily hair and makeup and was taken to set for a rehearsal and blocking of our day's first scene. I got in the car and rode to set, and then I was sent back to my trailer to finish changing into wardrobe and to wait while the crew set up the lighting. I walked into my trailer, sat down on the couch, and I couldn't get up. I could no longer, on my own, muster the will to carry on. I heard the knocks on my door and I knew my crew was ready for me on set, but I couldn't make it out of my trailer. After a bit of time, Jensen came into my trailer to see what was going on, and he knew I was not okay. He had the assistant director call for a doctor, and he sat with me to talk. The doctor showed up a bit later and sat with me in my trailer to ask me a few questions. After some time, the doctor told me that his professional opinion was that I was clinically depressed, and I should take some time off from filming.

That's when it hit me.

I *couldn't* stop filming.

I *couldn't* put my crew out of work for a day, a week, a month.

I also couldn't face, or admit, what was going on in my head.

I met the doctor in the middle. I went home, and we pushed that day's scenes to another time. After a long sleep and a long jog and a long bath, I was ready to show back up for work the next day.

Supernatural has continued for many years after that. And then, seven years later, we went back to film at *the very same house* we were using the day I sat in my trailer and couldn't make it to set.

That day was the day I also launched the first Always Keep Fighting campaign. In over 200 episodes, over 1,600 filming days, and hundreds of locations, what are the odds?

The inaugural AKF campaign was met with an outrageous amount of love and support. We set out to sell 1,000 shirts and ended up selling over thirty times that! The money that was raised toward great causes (To Write Love on Her Arms, Attitudes In Reverse, Wounded Warrior Project, and more) and the awareness and acceptance that flowed through everybody who was involved were things I could never have expected, never even dreamed of . . . but they happened.

Throughout the campaign, I still knew I wasn't yet okay. I was able to function at a high level: I finished the filming of season 10, fulfilled my day-to-day duties as a husband and father, even did another AKF campaign with Jensen, but I still didn't feel 100 percent. Something was still eating at me and beating on me. I could sense that, though my head was above water, I was sinking.

But, as I had done in the past (and as I assumed everybody expected of me), I shut my mouth and kept moving forward.

Season 10 finished. I had done some work I was proud of, and I was excited about the writing and the direction of the story line. Now it was time to go overseas and talk face-to-face with our overseas fans about the show, about life, and about anything and everything that crossed our minds.

Truth be told (and hindsight can be 20/20), I should have just stayed in Austin and taken the time to reconnect with my family, my friends, and myself. But I had committed to traveling around the world to have some face-to-face time with the very people who make me excited and proud to do what I do. I told myself I would see family and friends some other time, and that I would take my personal time when it didn't burden somebody else. I had always been led to believe that taking personal time was a sign of weakness, and that "you can sleep when you're dead." I am a perfectionist by nature *and* nurture. I had never really learned to love myself first.

So, shortly after season 10 finished filming, I hopped on a plane with my wife, Genevieve, leaving the kids at home with family, and headed to Europe to see some of Gen's extended family before the *Supernatural* conventions began. Her mother's side of the family is from Belgium and she grew up spending summers with her extended European family. We went to Leuven so she could catch up with them and I could get to meet them and experience a big part of her childhood.

Everything seemed, and felt, fine, at least on the surface. But there was something malevolent boiling inside me.

I didn't tell Gen this at the time, but the entire time we were traveling, I felt a deep desire to be home in Austin, a deep longing to wake up with nothing on my schedule for the day, a need to just be with my wife and my sons and reconnect.

It's not always easy being number one on the call sheet of a network TV show. Don't get me wrong; it's fun, and exciting, and I love what I do. I love my fellow cast, my crew, my dear friend Sam Winchester. I love the stories I get to tell and the message I get to be a part of. I am, and forever will be, grateful that I get to do what I love for a living. But, every hour of every day, I feel an intense awareness that if I mess up and don't perform properly, 150 people will lose their jobs . . . 150 families will be out of their primary source of income. It can sometimes be overwhelming.

Those of us who have encountered bouts of depression and anxiety know that the demons can remain at a lull for months (or years) on end, and then reach a boiling point inside of a day.

That is what happened to me.

I had spent my entire adult life (in fact, I went off to Los Angeles to do *Gilmore Girls* when I was only seventeen) in a crazy business . . . a business that values looks and charm and charisma and wit and a facade of unbridled optimism . . . a business that doesn't always have a lot of patience for, "Hey, I'm human, too. Sometimes I hurt." A business where you're relied on to do the intangible, and even when you try your best, sometimes you fail. And, in your failure, you let down hundreds of people to the tune of millions of dollars (I was a major part of a few pilots that didn't go anywhere and to this day I still beat myself up over their failure).

I had never learned the skills and techniques to be able to balance all the disparate parts of my existence. Some people reach their boiling points at an earlier stage in life. When the fight starts, some fold quicker than others. I have been lucky enough to be surrounded by people I love, who have supported me and accepted me (even though I still sometimes can't support and accept myself). So, I was able to make it thirty-two years and change before I reached my personal boiling point.

But, when it hit, it didn't let up.

After a few days with Gen's family in Belgium, she headed back to Austin to be with our sons as I was slated to be in Rome, then Dubai, then Australia, before finally going back home. My portion of the trip was gonna put me back in Austin roughly fourteen days after her . . . roughly twenty-one total days of being away from my home and my kids . . . during which time I would, literally, be traveling around the world.

I had a few days off before I needed to be in Rome for JIBCon 6, and, being a *huge* fan of mechanical Swiss watches (still one of my personal "fandoms"), I decided to stop in Geneva on my way.

I couldn't *wait* to go to the watch museums and see the original mechanical movements. I couldn't *wait* to see the one-of-a-kind pieces that are entombed behind bulletproof glass in the houses of Rolex, Patek Philippe, Audemars Piguet, Vacheron Constantin, and others. I couldn't *wait* to feel the history and the tradition and the craftsmanship and try to gain watchmaking knowledge through osmosis from being in the mecca of the watch world (remember, I used to think I had The Force, so forgive me).

So, on one of my very rare days off, after bidding farewell to Gen as she headed home from London, I headed to my gate at Heathrow Airport to board a flight to the watchmaking capital of the world. When I landed in Geneva, I hopped in a taxi and asked to head *straight* to the watch museums.

Then I was informed that I had landed, in my mecca, on a national holiday. Everything was closed.

Wow.

This must be some sort of joke.

Is the joke on me? Or, worse yet, is this not a joke at all? Is this a sign? Is this a message? Have I lived life in such a way that this is my fate, on the one day of the year when I had no other obligations?

I don't like to talk about signs—what I do or don't think of them, or their place (or lack thereof) in my life. Everybody has a personal feeling about signs, or coincidences, or fate. Some even go so far as to make it part of their religion. I'm not going to go into what I do or don't think about signs and coincidences. But, suffice to say, this was the proverbial final straw that broke my back.

In hindsight, it seems laughable. "Yeah, Padalecki, the watch museums in Geneva happened to be closed when you were there, but at least you can afford to go back!" Or, "Well, things happen. Geneva is certainly not a terrible place to be 'stuck' for twenty-four hours en route from London to Rome!" Or, "Why didn't you just sit in the park and read a great book? You're always whining about how you don't get the chance to read anymore!" I could go on ad infinitum.

But, at the time (and those who have dealt with anxiety/depression can understand this), I was overwhelmed beyond all measure.

Something as simple as landing in Geneva on a national holiday had become an insurmountable obstacle. A sign. An omen. An albatross. A portent of what was to come.

On top of the weeks, and months, and years of feeling the need to break down, but not feeling that I had permission to.

I broke.

Plain and simple.

I. Broke.

I sat in a park in Geneva, surrounded by thousands of people, young and old, celebrating their beautiful day off, and I felt more alone than I ever had my life. All my pain, all my self-doubt, all my insecurities, came to a head. I hated myself. I hated that I hadn't taken the time to look on a calendar or call ahead, or at least make a plan in some way that could have solved this issue. I hated myself for assuming that *of course* the museums would be open when I was there! I hated that my friends were eastbound to Rome and my wife was westbound to home and I was in a foreign place with no one to be there for, and no one to be there for me. Though my rational brain was telling me everything was fine and everything *would* be fine, I couldn't get past the feeling that I wanted to be anywhere but where I was, that I wanted to be anybody but me.

It took hours. And tears. The kind of tears that don't stop until your stomach hurts from convulsing. Until your face no longer moves because every ounce of water in your body has freed itself from the burden of being part of you. The kind of tears that don't care if the passersby stare (or maybe the tears realize they couldn't stay hidden anyway). My lips chapped, but I couldn't force myself to drink water. I felt like anything that went down would swiftly work its way back up. I literally had to hold my eyes open with two fingers so I could see the outside world.

I *knew* I wouldn't get out of Switzerland alive.

Then, I was hit by another "sign" (if you want to call it that). I got a call from a friend. A friend who had been through some severely emotional and difficult times with me. A friend who had lost somebody special by their own hand . . .

The friend I needed.

"Hey, Brian, what's up?"

"J-Pad . . . how you doin', brother?"

" . . . "

Phone calls . . . more tears . . . more phone calls . . . Steps back toward my hotel . . . more tears . . . sideways glances from folks who didn't speak my language, but understood the universal language of human anguish. Help up off the grass . . . phone calls.

"I have to get on the plane to Rome tomorrow, people are counting on me!"

Falling down to the grass yet again.

"You're not okay. Put the oxygen mask on yourself first."

Arguments. "They'd be better off without me . . . "

Silence.

I had been away from a charger for a while, and apparently iPhones lose battery very quickly when they're roaming in foreign lands . . . my phone had died.

I had a decision to make.

In a moment of clarity (and with help from people I love), I realized that I didn't want to burden my friend, or my wife, with having been the last person to talk to me. I didn't want somebody else to think that whatever was wrong with me was somehow their fault. So I gathered all the courage I had left and I headed back to my hotel. I went upstairs, charged my phone, and booked a Geneva-to-Austin flight for nine hours later.

I was gonna go home. I was going to go and *finally*, after fifteen years in the real, adult working world, make the necessary time to take a long and hard look at myself in the mirror.

There would be hell to pay: I was about to cancel (for the second time!) a convention in Rome *and* one in Australia . . . I was going to let (literally) thousands of people down: people who had spent their hard-earned money and valuable time off to get that chance to meet and talk about *Supernatural*. I hated myself for leaving.

But I knew I only had two options: go to Austin, or go away forever.

Not a lot of sleep was had between Geneva and London, London and Chicago, and Chicago and Austin (my last-minute ticket required some interesting routing). It seemed that, now that I had decided to live, I had become uncomfortably aware of my mortality. I laughed to myself at how ironic it would be if, now that I had made the commitment to live, something out of my control happened to make that not possible.

I had always been a good flier. For me, sitting in an airplane seat was one of the few times where I felt able to turn off, where I didn't feel like I had obligations that I *had* to take care of or phone calls or emails that I *had* to make (until they introduced in-flight Wi-Fi—damn you, technology!). Also, it was (and still is) one of the few situations where I truly feel a connection to the people around me: No matter where they're from, or the language they speak, or the religion they follow, it seems like we are all "in it together" (whatever "it" may be) until we land safely at our destination.

But these flights were different. I had god-awful anxiety the entire time, and no one to turn to for help. I found myself LITERALLY mumbling "Always Keep Fighting" to myself and even grabbed a pen from my bag and did something I hadn't done since high school: I wrote on my arm. "AKF" up and down my left arm, over and over and over again. It seemed to calm me down better than listening to music or reading, so I did it, and I didn't stop until I ran out of space.

When I landed in Chicago for the last layover of my journey, I got a phone call from my friend Paul. I had met Paul when he worked as a stuntman and actor on *Supernatural* many years before, and I found him to be a great guy. He's big and strong and has fought MMA professionally. He looks like the kind of guy you wouldn't want to piss off in a back alley, but he has a heart of gold. He talked to me for an hour, and he helped me feel better about myself. He helped me understand that it's not weakness to need help sometimes. I will be forever grateful to him for that. (Side note: It was great to have him back in season 11 as Hellrazor in the episode "Beyond the Mat" . . . even though his character made fun of my hair. Ha.)

So, Paul got me through my final layover and I boarded my flight to Austin: the final leg of my journey home.

When I finally arrived, I could see in Gen's eyes how worried she was. We had, obviously, been in contact, and she knew I wasn't in a good place. It probably didn't help that I hadn't been sleeping well for days and looked like I had gotten a full-sleeve tattoo on my left arm. She was waiting for me at the airport with my friend and manager, Dan, who had flown out from LA to spend some time with me, and my friend Danneel, who wanted to be there to offer me support and love. I will never be able to tell the three of them exactly how much that meant to me.

Finally, I was home. I wasn't healed yet; there was a lot of work to be done. But I was at least in a place where the only thing people expected of me was to figure out who I am, and take care of that person.

A couple weeks (and a LOT of work) after I arrived back home in Austin, there was something I had really been looking forward to: being a part of the Austin Television Festival to celebrate the fifteen-year reunion of my first job, *Gilmore Girls*. I had gone off the radar for a bit. I wasn't using social media, I wasn't returning texts or answering my phone, I wasn't going out in public, I was just taking care of me and my emotional and mental health. I had actually considered backing out of the festival. I still had some healing to do and I wasn't certain I was ready for the scrutiny (even though it was likely going to be positive) that being at a public appearance would bring. But I bit the bullet and did it . . . and I'm *so* happy I did. It was a wonderfully positive experience. The irony, to me, was particularly special: in 2000, I had left Austin (where I was enrolled as an engineering student at the University of Texas) to do a brand-new show that would be called *Gilmore Girls*, and now *Gilmore Girls* was doing its fifteen-year reunion in the city where I lived. Not Los Angeles. Not New York. Not Chicago or San Francisco or any of the other larger US cities, but Austin. I usually seem to ignore the good signs in my life and focus instead on the bad signs, but I allowed myself to accept this festival, and my involvement in it, as a good sign.

Anyway, Gen and I went to the festival. For the first time in several weeks, I was going to be in a place where people I didn't know would be expecting me, and, I assumed, expecting something *from* me. That is always a source of great anxiety for me (even now), but I figured "the juice was worth the squeeze" (to borrow a quote from my friend Richard the Speight).

For those who are not familiar with Texas weather, let me tell you: Texas gets HOT! Especially in the summer in the afternoon sun. The festival started late in the day and our red-carpet line was in full view of the setting sun, which seemed to have particular vigor that day. When I get nervous, I can break a sweat in the snow, so for someone who deals with anxiety *and* is dressed up in a tucked-in button-down shirt *and* is looking directly into the sun *and* hasn't been in public in several weeks and is now doing on-camera interviews, it would be safe to say I lost a lot of body weight during my thirty-minute red-carpet session. So much that they had to give me a T-shirt to wear during the panel, since I had sweated through the shirt I showed up in. Fun times . . . (I still have the shirt and wear it proudly. It says "I [state of Texas graphic] TV," so it kinda looks like "I LOVE TV," but with my home state.)

The panel went off without a hitch. It was really special to me to be sitting onstage with people who were responsible for not only giving me my first real job in the industry but also for keeping me around and supporting both me personally and my career. It was also really nice to not be the center of attention, and to be able to celebrate the other actors and writers on the stage with me. I think I would rather be bathed in the overflow of somebody else's spotlight than to be the one staring into it (and not just because that makes me sweat!).

Symbolically, that experience seemed like a new beginning. A chance to start over. Originally, I did *Gilmore Girls* as a seventeen-year-old kid, fresh out of Texas, and I had no idea how to take care of myself or be true to what I really needed. But now, I had spent some intensive time working on being comfortable with me, and I was able to be a part of *Gilmore Girls* again, but with a more prepared mind. It's as if I were given the chance to restart my adulthood from its beginning.

Another good sign. :)

After the festival ended, I still had quite a bit more time before I would start filming season 11. We were scheduled to shoot our first day in Vancouver on July 7, so I had exactly one more month to buckle down and rest. As I had done in the weeks prior to the festival, I used that time to focus on me. On my family. On my physical and mental health. I knew I wouldn't have a lot of time during the filming of season 11 to do intense reflective work, so I was committed to using that time to grow as a man, husband, and father. It became like a school assignment to me. I treated it very seriously. I knew I would have to take a proactive approach. Mental health and well-being are still very much taboo (unfortunately), so people can feel embarrassed or ashamed to admit or acknowledge that they could use some help to understand why their brain sometimes does things that somebody else's might not. I reminded myself that if I wanted to learn how to eat properly, I would consult a nutritionist; if I wanted to get in peak physical shape, I would employ a personal trainer. Well, I wanted to get in peak mental shape, so I talked to friends and family and professionals. I read books and watched videos. Every single day (no exaggeration) I made a conscious effort to do something to bolster my mental health. And I'm glad I did. I was shocked by how much I actually enjoyed it. I learned so much about human nature, and about myself. It can be difficult at times, trying to take a long, hard look at yourself. But the things I learned and figured out (with help) have had an immeasurably positive impact on my life and my relationships, including my relationship with myself.

The month flew by (as time always does when you're having fun!), and it was back up to Vancouver for the start of season 11. As I mentioned earlier, we started principal photography for season 11 on July 7, which was a Tuesday, and we were slated to be working in San Diego the following Saturday and Sunday for Comic-Con! I remember thinking how lucky I was to have had the month in Austin to spend with my family, because this is largely what the nine months of the filming season are like for me: filming in Vancouver on weekdays, and flying away on weekends to talk about the show. Sometimes (temporarily) I don't even want to *hear* the word *Supernatural!*

So, there I was, sitting in an airplane after filming for four days, en route to San Diego. I read my script and looked through my interview schedule for the weekend. I wanted to make sure I was prepared for everything that would be required of me. And that's when I was hit with a wave of anxiety. It occurred to me that I had learned to handle my nerves and doubts really well while in my little microcosm in Austin, surrounded by family and friends, and I had even been able to go back to work in Vancouver and be at ease with my fellow cast and crew, whom I've spent so many years with on *Supernatural.* But this was different. Now, I was going to a city where I had no home base, where I had no quiet corner to excuse myself to in case of a panic attack. I was going to a city that gets an influx of 200,000+ visitors during the week of Comic-Con. I was going to a place where I would be looked at by thousands of people. Would they judge me? Did they think less of me after my not-so-private struggles? Would there be people in the audience who'd worked long and hard to see me (and others) in Rome and Australia, whose money and time I'd wasted? How would I apologize? How could I even *begin* to apologize? Was I supposed to just get up there onstage in Hall H and smile and pretend I hadn't let thousands of fans down? Hell, I would hate me, too. What do I do???

As I mentioned before, an airplane is a terrible place to have a panic attack.

But I got through it. I employed some of the breathing techniques I had learned and practiced, and I was able to read a few things I have that are special and private to me, and that help a lot when I start to panic or feel helpless. And I made it to San Diego. Saturday night, I spent some time with friends and work partners I hadn't yet had the chance to see in person, and I tried to get to bed at a reasonable hour to be in top form for Sunday's activities. My Sunday experience at Comic-Con is always a whirlwind: round-table interviews and red carpets, photo shoots and meetings, Nerd HQ, and, of course, Hall H.

Now, for those of you who haven't had the good fortune and opportunity to experience Hall H in person, lemme tell you, it is a sight to see. It is a room that seems large enough for an airplane to take off, fly around inside, and land. It's enormous. And terrifying. I've been told that it holds 6,000+ people, not counting standing room. I don't find that difficult to believe.

Suffice it to say, I was pretty nervous. My anxieties and self-doubts from my flight down were starting to surface again. Here it was: I was about to confront 6,000+ people whom I had let down. And I didn't know how to apologize. Furthermore, I didn't want to commandeer the mic and start talking about my personal issues. It was sort of a no-win situation.

But then it happened. As I sat onstage, a sea of lights appeared before me. Were they cell phone cameras? Lighters? It wasn't immediately clear to me. But then someone behind me (I still don't know if it was Richard Speight or Rob Benedict—our moderators—or someone else entirely) tapped me on the shoulder and handed me a note. A fan had made thousands of tea lights with a reminder to "Always Keep Fighting" and handed them out to the people in Hall H. The giant hall was lit up in support of me and that message. Since memory is faulty, I'm going to copy my Facebook post from that day, since that will be the best snapshot of how hard it hit me:

A thank you.
To anybody and everybody that had ANY part whatsoever in the Always Keep Fighting Hall H tea light event.

As I travel back to Vancouver from San Diego Comic-Con, with my partners in crime Jensen Ackles and Mark Sheppard, the enormity of what happened is finally starting to sink in . . .

I am beyond moved.

I feel so blessed, and grateful, and honored to be a part of the magical *Supernatural* family.

Sitting on that stage in Hall H, I initially mistook all of the lights for cell phone cameras. It's difficult to discern specific shapes and faces with all of those stage lights shining on you (and it's quite intimidating up there, sitting in front of 6,500 people!!). Then, when I had a light given to me with an explanation of what it was and what it stood for, I was (and am still) gobsmacked.

Thank you.

From the very bottom of my heart and my soul, thank you so much.

I will never forget this day. I will never forget the love that I felt, and still feel. And, to everybody who held a light for me, please know that I hold my light for you.

Though I happened to be the one sitting onstage, I am but one small light in a sea of thousands. TOGETHER, we can and will make a difference!

Keep letting your light shine. I will do the same. And, keep fighting.

Always Keep Fighting.

The light that was given to me that day still sits in my office (as does the note that was handed to me on the stage explaining what was going on). It always will. It is more valuable to me than any award or accolade ever will be. It helps put to rest one of my greatest fears: that I've let the fans down. Sometimes, when I still feel like I've failed somebody, or let somebody down, I'll walk into my office, and see it, and remember that

I have an entire family out there that wants me to know that "just" me is "just" fine.

That little light reminds me of all the things this show and this fandom have given me.

The *Supernatural* fandom has taught me acceptance.

From the outside, it may seem like being part of a show that has millions of viewers worldwide should, in itself, have taught me that. But for me the inverse was true. I have the tendency to ignore the good and magnify the bad. *Supernatural*'s continued success actually made me doubt myself more. I began to convince myself that it was a fraud, that I was a fraud. For a long time, I couldn't escape the feeling of, *If they only knew . . .*

The fandom has taught me trust.

Not "Hey, y'all, here's the key to my house and the code to my safe" trust (that's useless anyway. Possessions come and go, and don't, for me at least, hold great importance). No, the fandom has taught me that it's okay to open the door a little further. And know that, though there may be some bad that sneaks its way in, that bad will be outnumbered and outpowered by the good.

The fandom has taught me that it's okay to fall.

Those are not just the words on the page, but the feeling in my heart and in my soul. The fandom has taught me that being a role model, or a public figure, doesn't mean you have to be flawless. Role models aren't perfect. And that's okay. It's not about being perfect. It's about doing the best you can, and understanding that you *will* falter. That's human.

The fandom has taught me strength.

Not "Whaddaya bench-press?" strength, but the strength to *choose* to fight to keep going. The fandom helped me understand that strength is not a birthright. It's a choice. A lot of times, it's an incredibly difficult choice. The fandom has taught me that it's okay to ask for help in making that choice and sticking to it.

The fandom has taught me forgiveness.

The belief that everybody is doing the best they can under the circumstances they are in is a big part of forgiveness. The fandom helped me understand that I first must forgive myself. My friend Jason once said, "Always be kind. Every soul is engaged in a great battle." The fandom taught me that that includes ME.

The fandom has taught me to Always Keep Fighting.

More often than not, the fight sucks. But I guess that's why it's a fight. The fandom has helped me realize that there will be a brighter day on the horizon. It may be further off than you'd hope, but it's there, and if you believe that and commit to fighting through hardships, you will find that peace.

The fandom has taught me to Love Myself First.

Even if all seven-billion-plus people on this earth think you're the bee's knees, there's truly only one opinion that matters, that sticks with you twenty-four hours a day, and that opinion is your own. I spent a lot of time creating different Jareds. I was convinced that there must be some version of me I would accept. So I tried and tried to find him. To paraphrase Thom Yorke, I kept breaking mirrors, and turning myself into something I was not. The fandom insisted that "me" is okay, "me" is enough, and that "those who mind don't matter, and those who matter don't mind." Eventually, the fandom made me believe it.

That's what the fandom means to me.

So, thank you, fandom.

ALWAYS KEEP FIGHTING

In the spring of 2015, *Supernatural* actor Jared Padalecki launched a campaign to raise funds and awareness about depression, mental health issues, and suicide. Inspired in part by friend Stephen Amell's successful "Fuck Cancer" fund-raiser, Padalecki partnered with Represent.com to sell T-shirts and sweatshirts with the slogan "Always Keep Fighting."

On March 3, Jared tweeted "Launching my 1st ever t-shirt for a cause that's super close to my heart." The campaign was prompted by the loss of a close friend, who had committed suicide on New Year's Eve. Jared stressed that "there is no shame in needing support" and said that he hoped the campaign would help people be vocal about their own struggles or in their support of someone who might need it. In less than twenty-four hours, the campaign had sold more than 6,000 shirts, setting a record for Represent.com. By the end of the first weekend, 20,000 had been sold. Proceeds went to the nonprofit To Write Love on Her Arms (TWLOHA), which helps people battling addiction, depression, self-injury, and suicidal thoughts.

There have been multiple charity campaigns since, many of them joint endeavors by Jared and costars Jensen Ackles and Misha Collins. In addition to the "Always Keep Fighting" mantra, the T-shirts have reminded fans that "You Are Not Alone," "I Am Enough," and "Family Always Has Your Back." In late 2016, the trio launched the "SPN Family Love" campaign with CreationStands, the charitable branch of Creation Entertainment, to help needy families over the holidays. Previous campaigns benefited various charities that support the fight against depression, suicide, and self-harm; a portion of the "I Am Enough" campaign proceeds helped support victims of the Orlando Pulse Nightclub shooting.

Just as the Winchesters' mantra is saving people, the Always Keep Fighting campaign aims to save lives, too. Jared says that he hopes the campaigns are helping to destigmatize these issues, which are all around us and yet people hide them. He wants the campaigns to be a proactive approach, to take these issues head-on and treat it like a fight, because they're not just going to go away. Challenging the self-doubt that often goes along with facing mental health issues, Jared reminds fans that people who are dealing with depression, addiction, suicidal thoughts, or mental illness are not weak—they're strong. They are in this fight for their lives, and every day they wake up thinking, "I'm going to beat it again today."

Supernatural deals with these kinds of issues, too—people feeling like they've been beaten down and yet knowing that they need to fight through. The Winchesters, too, "always keep fighting." Fans often recognize one another by their T-shirts, and at conventions, many fans wear their Always Keep Fighting shirts proudly to spread the word and combat stigma.

Jared summed up his hope for the message he wants to convey with these campaigns: "Most of all, when life seems to want to beat you down, I hope you'll Always Keep Fighting."

BONUS FOR
FAMILY DON'T
END WITH BLOOD
READERS!

GET A FREE DIGITAL DOWNLOAD OF
"SLIGHTEST THING"
BY **THE STATION BREAKS**, FEATURING
JASON MANNS, ROB BENEDICT, AND BILLY
MORAN, AT:

https://jasonmanns.bandcamp.com
/track/slightest-thing

ACKNOWLEDGMENTS

Thank you to all of the contributors, who shared their personal stories with courage and genuineness in the hope of inspiring others and in celebration of the one-of-a-kind little television show that brought us all together. Thanks to Amy Tipton for taking me and this project on and being instrumental in finding the perfect match for us in BenBella and Smart Pop Books; to Sarah Dombrowsky for making the cover of *FDEWB* look beautiful; and to talented artist and fellow fangirl Christine Griffin for making Sam and Dean look like . . . well, Sam and Dean! Thanks also to Glenn Yeffeth, Heather Butterfield, Monica Lowry, and everyone else at BenBella, who were immediately on board with donating a portion of the proceeds of this book to charity so we could all help make a difference. Special thanks to kick-ass editors Alicia Ramos and Leah Wilson, who sometimes told me what I didn't want to hear, but ultimately made every chapter better.

I'm grateful to my family for being endlessly patient every time I say "I'm taking some time off" and change my mind; to my friends for the always-available supportive shoulders and cheerleading; and to my university colleagues for never questioning the legitimacy of my research even when they weren't sure what "fandom" actually was. I'm also grateful to the gang at Creation Entertainment who bring cast and fans together (Adam, Gary, Steph, Chris, Max, Liz, Jen, Connie, Monica, and everyone else who makes those weekends happen) and to Mark Pedowitz and the CW for having the wisdom to keep *Supernatural* on the air, thirteen seasons and counting!

Thank you to my fellow fans, for sharing such powerful stories and for building the community that has supported, inspired, and nourished me for over a decade. Thank you to the cast and crew of *Supernatural* for sharing equally powerful stories about how being on the show has also changed you, and to Jensen Ackles, Misha Collins, and Mark Sheppard for adding your personal messages. And finally, a heartfelt thank-you to Jared Padalecki, without whose courage and perseverance this book would not have happened. This has been a journey we've taken together, and one that was not always easy, but you consistently embodied the mantra that so many of us live by—Always Keep Fighting. Sam Winchester has nothing on you when it comes to bravery and we're all the better for it.

PHOTOGRAPHY CREDITS

INTERIOR

Pages 58, 87, 109, 124, 137, 160, 168 (bottom), 171, 179 (bottom), 205, 227, and 246 by Chris Schmelke

Pages 11, 63, 77, 79, 81, 82, 83, 88, 117, 151, 153, 155, 181, 186, and 192 by Kim Prior

Pages 97, 100, 104, 115, 116, 147, and 148 by Stardust and Melancholy

Page 65 by Travis Hodges

Pages 19, 21, 22, and 30 by Karen Cooke

Pages 39 and 72 by Lynn Zubernis

Page 143 by Kelli Anne

Page 52 by Lauren Aker

Art on pages 196 and 198 by Sheri Chen

INSERT

Pages 1, 6–7, 12, 19, 21 (top left), by Chris Schmelke

Pages 2 (top left and right), 3 (bottom), 4, 5 (top, bottom right), 8–11, 13, 14 (top left), 16 (bottom right), 17, 20 (top left and right, bottom left), 21 (top right, bottom left and right), 23 (top), and 24 by Kim Prior

Page 16 (bottom left) by Karen Cooke

ABOUT THE EDITOR

Lynn Zubernis is a clinical psychologist and professor at West Chester University, and a passionate fangirl. She has researched and written about fandom for the past decade, after falling head over heels in love with *Supernatural* shortly after its debut. With fellow fangirl/professor Katherine Larsen, Lynn has also written *Fangasm: Supernatural Fangirls* and *Fandom at the Crossroads*, as well as edited *Fan Phenomena: Supernatural* and *Fan Culture: Theory/Practice*. Lynn has also written for Slate, *Supernatural Magazine*, The Conversation, and Movie TV Tech Geeks, and blogs at fangasmthebook.wordpress.com about fandom and, of course, *Supernatural*.

Follow her on social media:

Twitter: @FangasmSPN
Facebook: facebook.com/FangasmSPN
Instagram: @FangasmSPN
Tumblr: fangasmSPN.tumblr.com

The author and publisher will donate 20% of the royalties from sales of *Family Don't End with Blood* to Attitudes in Reverse and Random Acts.

We hope that the messages in *Family Don't End with Blood*, from both cast and fans, will encourage us all to be unafraid to ask for help and to be ourselves, to carry out random acts of kindness globally and locally, and to Always Keep Fighting—and that these donations will help AIR and RA carry on their important work toward these goals.

ATTITUDES IN REVERSE is a 100% volunteer driven organization which offers multiple programs to educate youth about good mental health and eliminate stigma. **More information at attitudesinreverse.org.**

RANDOM ACTS is a registered nonprofit whose mission is to conquer the world one random act of kindness at a time. **More information at randomacts.org.**

WANT MORE *SUPERNATURAL*?

IN THE HUNT

Unauthorized
Essays on
Supernatural

Edited by
Supernatural.TV